PUBLIC SPEAKING FOR SUCCESS - 3 in 1

Effective Public Speaking +

Dark Psychology and Manipulation with Hypnosis +

Brain Training and Memory Improvement

By

TED ROBBINS

EFFECTIVE PUBLIC SPEAKING

COMMUNICATION SKILLS TRAINING FOR A SELF CONFIDENCE, NO FEAR & NO NERVOUS SPEAKER—PERSUASION, MIND PROGRAMMING, MENTAL CONTROL & NLP TO INFLUENCE PEOPLE BEHAVIOURS

By

TED ROBBINS

Contents

INTRODUCTION

Communication is a necessary step to enter into a relationship with others. I've always compared the art of public speaking to painting - for which, by the way, I don't have much talent.

But I am convinced that if I take the time to understand and learn to master the drawing, to combine the colors and to use the brush, I will perhaps be able, by dint of practice, to forget the tech to create exciting tables.

It's exactly the same for public speaking. Everyone "knows" how to speak in public, as everyone "knows" how to draw. There are, tips and tricks that you need to know and master if you want to take full advantage of each of your performances in public.

The best speakers will tell you how exhilarating it is to see the effect you can have on crowds of people when you talk to them. This is what makes the difference between a bad and a good politician, whose art is to convince others of the correctness of his point of view.

This is what distinguishes a talented actor who succeeds in convincing us of the realism of his character by the accuracy of his interpretation.

Opening Credit

The art of public speaking does not belong only to politicians, comedians, or certain bosses of big companies.

Even if, as the wise old man said, it is not always those who knows how to speak best in public have the most interesting things to say, we all have an obligation to become better communicators and that, in our own interest.

Indeed, some philosophers who have looked into the matter estimate that 85% of our success in life depends on our ability to communicate with others.

When you think about it, you can easily agree that clumsily formulating your opinion, not expressing it clearly, is a bit like being unable to think. It's almost not to exist.

I do not pretend here to lead you to believe that a Cicero, a famous Roman orator, is dormant in each of you. Even with a lot of practice, some will still find it difficult to communicate brilliantly.

However, I am convinced that you, like others before you, can become more effective communicators by rigorously applying certain basic techniques. This is the goal that I pursue in this book.

It is usually the preparation, or rather the lack of preparation, that is the most important problem for those who want to speak in public, whatever the situation.

We take it for granted that we are ready to make such a presentation or such an interview with a journalist, that we know his subject, that we know who we are talking to, that we master his environment, and this is precisely where the trap closes.

Prepare his presentation, be it! But also, prepare yourself well. You have to practice becoming a better communicator. You can never be too prepared to give a good presentation in public.

I myself once received this wise advice from an old public relations pro: in communication, you should never take anything for granted. You have to practice, prepare for everything, check everything, and double-check again.

Of course, others before me have written on this important subject. I don't pretend to rewrite history.

However, after more than 30 years in this profession and tens of thousands of hours spent as a professional communicator, in particular helping hundreds of people to express themselves better in public, I wanted to add my stone to the building.

I wrote this book **EFFECTIVE PUBLIC SPEAKING** *Self Confidence And No Fear, Persuasion, Nlp, Mind Programming, And Mental Control To Influence Behaviors;* the same way I teach them to people who trust me.

I wrote it the way I say it. I have voluntarily adopted a clear style, easy to read and use, in the tone of practical advice, intentionally ignoring academic surges and scholarly references.

I designed this book as a practical guide, like a cookbook, a reference to consult when you have to speak in public.

The advice it contains is useful in all circumstances, whether you're talking to one person or hundreds, whether you're in front of an audience or in the media, whether you're dealing with a dissatisfied employee or customer.

The tools offered in this book will help you deliver your messages effectively and project a better image of yourself, whatever your sector of activity, your occupation, the country, or the region you live in.

In closing, please take this little advise: never refuse the opportunities that present themselves to you to speak in public. Even provoke them. Over time and with practice, it will become easier and even more enjoyable than you might think.

The more you express yourself in front of an audience, the more you will learn to use a tool that will become irreplaceable and essential.

I hope I have convinced you of the importance of learning to prepare for better communication. The art of communicating your thinking effectively will become a major asset for you, as it has always been for those whose names have been remembered in history. Are you ready? Let's go!

COPYRIGHT BY TED ROBBINS 2020

The information provided here is correct and reliable, as any lack of attention or other means resulting from the misuse or use of the procedures, procedures, or instructions contained therein is the total and absolute obligation of the user addressed.

The author is not obliged, directly or indirectly, to assume civil or civil liability for any restoration, damage, or loss resulting from the data collected here. The respective authors retain all copyrights not kept by the publisher.

The information contained herein is solely and universally available for information purposes. The data is presented without a warranty or promise of any kind.

The trademarks used are without approval, and the patent is issued without the trademark owner's permission or protection.

The logos and labels in this book are the property of the owners themselves and are not associated with this text.

PREPARE TO SPEAK IN PUBLIC

This work is divided into two parts. In the first, we will see the basic rules that govern public speaking and, above all, how to prepare for the desired effect.

Are you one-on-one with your spouse? Are you attending a meeting with your boss, and are you about to ask him for a salary increase? Are you presenting a new program to your work colleagues or a group of customers?

Are you in the spotlight to answer questions from journalists? Are you on a stage delivering the talk of your life before the general meeting of shareholders of your firm? Whatever the occasion, the tips and advice that we will cover in the first chapter apply at all times.

In the following pages, you will discover the main principles that govern the communication between human beings, the three main basic rules of any communication situation, rules that you must know if you want to succeed in your process.

You will then see how to prepare and also how to be more efficient, whatever the public communication exercise you are engaged in.

THE FOUNDATIONS OF COMMUNICATION

One of the reasons you keep reading this book is most certainly to find practical advice that will help you become better when you speak publicly.

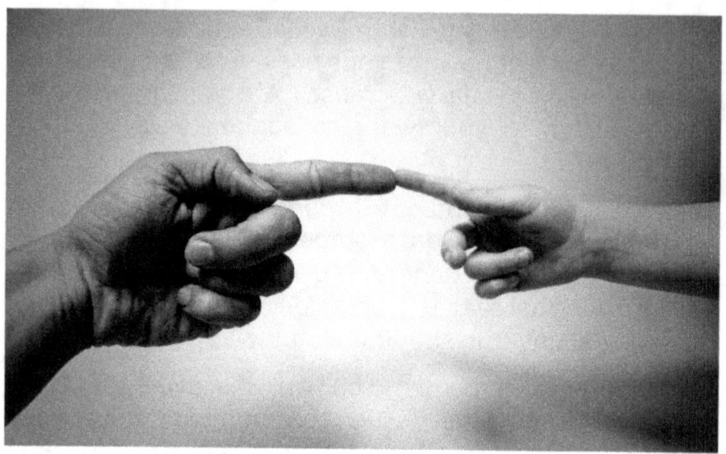

Let's all agree that in order to reach any objective, we must first agree on a starting point from which we will establish its trajectory.

Eventually, along the way, we will make all the necessary corrections to arrive at our destination. Public speaking is no exception rule. So in order not to skip this important step in establishing the starting point, let's start with an easy practical exercise.

Take stock of your difficulties as a communicator, both as a receiver and as a sender of a message. Armed with this introspection, then come back here to continue reading.

"Know yourself," said Socrates. If you did the exercise with an application, you now have an interesting list of your weaknesses, both as a receiver and as a transmitter. Check this list regularly and see how the tips on the following pages help you mitigate them.

It is also from this analysis that you should plan your continuous improvement program, starting with your most glaring shortcoming. When you are sure that you have eliminated it, or at least have better control over it, tackle the second most important fault, and so on until the end.

On the strength of these initial observations, I immediately approach the most theoretical part of my guide, which is the cornerstone of the art of communication.

Whoever you talk to or who your audience is, the principles stated here are essential and everything else flows from them.

It would be so simple when we communicate and people understood exactly what we just said, as we just said. Alas, that's not how it works!

When we try to understand a theory or a technique, there is always someone to try to explain it by a model. Communications is no exception, and one of the most famous models is used for this purpose.

In the middle of the last century, Claude Shannon published a mathematical theory of communication, inspired by telegraph transmission and the work of Taylor, an engineer from Bell Canada. For Shannon, communication is the product of a chain of elements that interact with each other.

For the purposes of my demonstration, let's simplify and establish that the communication chain has three main elements: the sender, the message, and the receiver, as illustrated in the following figure:

In other words, the message starts from point A and goes directly to point B. Is this really the case, in your opinion? Think about it! The answer is not as simple as it sounds.

If you answered "no" to the previous question, you are already on the right track. But before I explain why, let me illustrate my point with a somewhat sad story that takes place at the beginning of the last century.

It is that of a beautiful lady, badly married, whom her husband neglects and even beats. Taking advantage of his prolonged absence, the beautify finds herself at her lover's place to spend the night.

The next morning, she told him that she absolutely had to return home as soon as possible, before her husband returned and noticed his infidelity.

So she hurriedly leaves her lover's house and goes to the bridge spanning an extremely fast-flowing river, which she must cross to get to her house.

But now, to her amazement, a bear is on the bridge, blocking her way. She must therefore turn back, She then remembers that a little further upstream there is a smuggler who could take her across.

So she goes to meet him and telling him about her misfortune, asks him to take her on board. The smuggler is happy to welcome him on board but claims the amount of his passage, amount which the lady does not have.

Despite her pleas, the man remains intractable and refuses to do her this service without what he considers to be his just retribution.

The beautify has no other choice but to return to her lover to borrow the amount claimed, but the latter refuses to lend her the money.

Very disappointed but always eager to return home, before the arrival of her jealous and violent husband, she remembers an old flame who does not live very far from there and decides to go there.

Apologizing for not having been able to maintain more assiduous relationships with him in the past, the lady tells this old acquaintance how she is badly married, she told him about recent events and especially tells him about her haste to return to the matrimonial home.

She concluded by asking him too, the amount claimed by the smuggler to make her cross the river.

Her former lover replies that at another time, he would have given her a gift of his own life but that today since nothing is binding them anymore, he does not feel obligated towards her.

He therefore rejects her request, and the beautiful girl turns around dead in her soul to find that the bear is still on deck.

As she absolutely must go back and time is running out, she finally decides to jump into the water to cross the river at the swims, despite the extremely fast flow. Inevitably, she drowns. This is a sad story!

However, it leads me to ask you a question, for which there is no right or wrong answer: who do you think is responsible for her death? You probably have an answer in mind. Is it about herself, who was foolish about her gesture?

From her lover, who refused to give her the money to give to the smuggler? The smuggler himself, who refused her access to his boat despite the circumstances?

Or her old flame who obviously didn't love her anymore? From her husband, who is ultimately the source of all her ills? Is it finally the fault of the bear, or the river, or the money as I already heard?

Your answer is not necessarily that of everyone else who has been told this story. Believe me, and I've experienced it hundreds of times! Why does each of us have our own answer to this question?

It's simple though. Because we understand, we interpret, we decode this story from what we are, from our values, from the importance that we give to love, friendship and loyalty.

We have been shaped by our own lives, our experiences, our home group, our education, and many other factors. We understand things from this distinct baggage that characterizes us and which is necessarily different from that of the neighbor.

In the same way, our message is understood, interpreted, decoded through a whole series of prisms filters which ultimately alter their understanding. Thus, the trajectory of our communication begins to resemble the following:

Because of our education, our values, our vocabulary, our experience, our knowledge, and our prejudices, there are indeed parasites that come to modify our message. Our tics, our involuntary gestures (caused by nervousness or others), and our nonverbal language is also a barrier.

In other words, everyone perceives the situation differently because everyone assesses it from their own point of view, from their tip of the lens, from their own experience and identity.

You have to understand that perception is the key to communication and to perceive is to evaluate and to interpret.

Indeed, perception is influenced by need, memory and experience, prejudices, affectivity, association and senses etc.

To reduce distortions and consequently improve our communication skills, we must develop better antennas, learn to master feedback, and above all become a follower of dynamic listening.

I define this as being a very attentive listener to the words of others, in which we will draw to relaunch, continue and build the conversation.

Very quickly, we manage to develop dynamic listening. We learn to decode the "waves" transmitted by our interlocutor (s) as we speak and to draw inspiration from them to better prepare for our next intervention.

Eventually, we will even be able to read the face of our interlocutors, the result of our effort if our communication has been effective, so much the better! Otherwise, we have to start the explanation again or clarify.

In fact, this brings me to share with you two important communications secrets:

1. When speaking to someone or a group of people, 100% of the responsibility for communication rests on the shoulders of the transmitter and therefore on ours.

When I speak in public, whether it's a conference, a meeting, or just one-on-one with someone, it's up to me to make sure people understand what I say and that the communication link remains open.

When I speak in front of a group, although I seem to be doing a monologue, that is not the case. By their attitude, their reactions to my words, their nods, the occasional note-taking, I can see that each member of the audience follows my demonstration.

If I lose the contact, it's up to me to restore it. In this regard, one of my good friends has developed an infallible trick: if he realizes that his audience is starting to fall asleep, he will generally ask a gentleman or a lady in the front row what he or she thinks of his words.

Obviously, the person wakes up. In fact, everyone in the audience wakes up for fear of being the subject of the next question.

2. When talking to a person or a group of people, it is because you want to cause a change in attitude or behavior. It is not to please yourself that you speak in public.

Because, if that's the case, send yourself emails, sing in the shower or leave messages in your voicemail!

If we make contact with other people, it is to provoke a change either in behavior or in attitude. We want to convince people to do or not to do such and such, to think or not to think such and such.

We want to let them know or know something that they didn't already know. That's why we communicate.

Which leads me to show you, if you haven't already done so, that the most important element between the sender, the message and the receiver, is the last of the three which is the receiver.

Indeed, since all the responsibility for communication rests on our shoulders, we must articulate our message according to the audience. We can say exactly the same thing to a class of 8-year-olds, a congregation of engineers, and a group of seniors.

We simply will not say it in the same way or with the same words. You don't talk to your spouse the same way you talk to your boss! At least, I hope so.

Therefore, although we generally give ourselves some importance in communication, although we are often obsessed with what we mean, it is even more important to code our message according to our current audience.

This is why, of the three elements of communication mentioned above, the sender, the message, and the receiver the latter takes precedence.

This rule requires us to know our audience well before we even open our mouths. In fact, this rule is so important that the first question to ask yourself before speaking to a person or group is not, "What should I tell them?

Which worries most people, but rather, "How should I tell them what I have to say to make sure they understand what I want them to understand?"

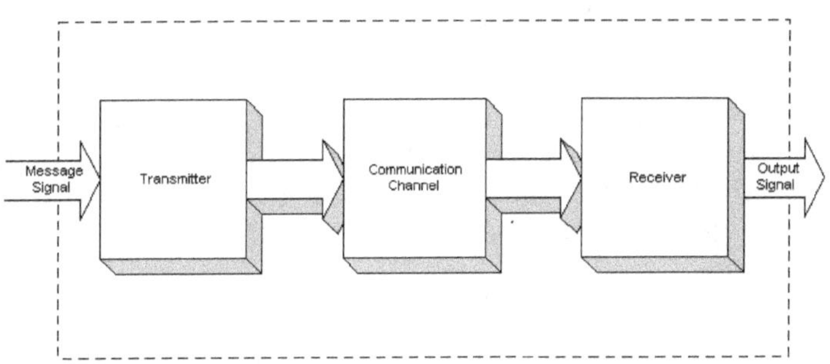

The above illustration helps us to understand better that communication is not a linear process, which goes from the transmitter to the receiver, but rather a circular process in which the transmitted message must come back to us if we want to make sure people understand it.

Otherwise, we have to repeat the exercise until we are sure that our interlocutor is following us well. What do we do with the kids to make sure they understand us? Do You understand? we repeat.

It already seems complicated, but we are not yet at the end of our pain. See why: imagine that we are meeting as a group at the dinner of the local Chamber of Commerce.

Today's speaker is known and respected in our community, and we look forward to hearing his talk.

So we're sitting at the table, chatting about other things with our table neighbors when the presenter comes to interrupt the flow of conversations.

As soon as our speaker goes up on the stage, we applaud him warmly to indicate his pleasure to receive him. The first moments are crucial since it is the first eye contact, from which we already form an opinion on the speaker.

Very attentive during the first minutes, we suddenly get distracted by the thought of making a phone call when we get back to the office. We take note of this effect and return to the topic of the day.

After a while, hypnotized by the tone of his voice, we allow ourselves to be overcome by a pleasant thought that suddenly arises. A long weekend is coming, for which we have put together a whole program.

A burst of laughter in the room brings us back to the conference, from which we will regularly move away in successive waves to come back to it later. Finally, our speaker announces his conclusion.

Everyone wakes up on time to hear his last words and applaud him all the time for his brilliant flight.

This is usually when your neighbor at the table asks you what you understand from the presentation and what do you think about it.

The latter has just finished, and what you have left is only a vague, confused memory of the elements of his presentation. And yet, you were so anxious to hear it.

Do you know why? A statistic in this regard is quite revealing. It pretty well demonstrates that it's not just the content that matters when we speak in public.

In fact, studies on the issue have shown that when we speak, content accounts for 7% of communication. The container, i.e., voice, diction, flow, rhythm, visuals, clothing, decor, environment, etc., accounts for 38% of the communication.

The rest, 55%, consists of the non-verbal. In other words, globally, 93% of communication is based on something other than the words spoken.

If the content only counts for 7%, that does not mean that it is not important, on the contrary.

This statistic makes us realize how essential it is to choose the right words carefully to effectively say what we want to say to a particular person or group.

However, it is important to understand that our audience is influenced and sometimes distracted by our general attitude, by the way we are dressed, by our expressions, our look, and our gestures.

You have no doubt lived the experience and know that after a conference or a public intervention of any kind, what you retain from communication however recent it is, This is an indistinct general impression that you briefly share with the other guests before quickly move on.

Soon, you will vaguely remember having experienced a pleasant or unpleasant moment, as the case may be.

On 30 minutes of presentation, you will only remember two or three salient points of the content, while you will answer with ease questions such as: "Did you like the speaker?"; "Did you believe it?"; "Would you trust him?"; "Did you find him in good shape? And other similar questions.

Do not feel guilty! It is even mathematically and physiologically easy to explain why our mind wanders while we try to listen to the speaker. We will see later that a normal rate is 140 to 160 words per minute.

However, the human brain is so made that we could understand someone speaking to us with a rate of up to 700 words per minute.

As there is a large gap between these two numbers, it is not surprising that in addition to listening to the person speaking to us, our brain has all the latitude necessary for us to linger on anything except the content of the presentation.

Either we will get lost on a thousand questions directly related to the present situation (clothing, appearance, decor, tie, skirt length, jewelry, hairstyle, people in the room, etc.) or we will be distracted by personal concerns that is strange to the present situation (forgotten telephone, race to be made, upcoming meeting, etc.).

Keep in mind that as a sender, we have the full responsibility for ensuring that communication goes through. We must repeat our message as long as we are not sure that people have understood it.

At the end of this chapter, reflect for a moment on the virtues of repetition, the cornerstone of teaching. In advertising, we say this:

The first time a person watches an advertisement, they do not see it.

The second time, she doesn't notice it.

The third time, she is aware of its existence.

The 4th time, she vaguely remembers having seen it before.

The 5th time, she reads it.

The 6th time, she looks up at her sight.

The 7th time, she reads it completely and says to herself: "Damn it!"

The 8th time, she says: "Again, this sacred announcement!"

The 9th time, she wonders if what you offer gives something.

The 10th time, she asks her neighbor if he has tried this product.

The 11th time, she wonders how her advertiser pays for it.

The 12th time, she believes it must be a good product.

The 13th time, she thinks it might be worth something.

The 14th time, she remembers wanting such a product long ago.

The 15th time, she torments herself because she cannot afford to buy this product.

The 16th time, she believes that she will buy this product one day.

The 17th time, she writes a note to remember to buy this product.

The 18th time, she complained about her lack of money.

The 19th time, she still complains about her lack of money.

The 20th time she sees the ad, she buys the product.

If you believe this list is the work of a modern marketing and advertising theorist, think again. This list was written by a certain Thomas Smith in London in 1885 and is still true today.

THREE RULES OF THREE

If it is not done yet, I foresee that with the pages yet to come, we will become friends. It is with this in mind that I wrote this practical guide to public speaking because it is with a friend that one comes back to seek support.

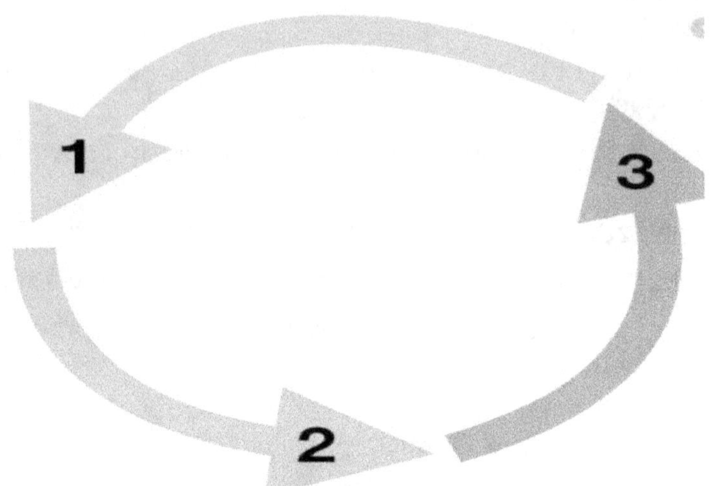

So let me start with confidence. If I chose to study law one day, it was because I had difficulties in mathematics. Undoubtedly, I'm not the only one to have chosen the legal profession for this reason - although several disciples of Themis also know how to cheerfully handle several columns of figures at a time, in particular their fees.

Anyway, even if my math skills are lacking, I have always tried to summarize the theoretical approach to public speaking from three main rules of three. The first is that when we communicate, we are seen and heard.

The second states that the sequence in which we should express ourselves is this: "you, I and we."

And according to the third rule, we must never lose sight of the fact that our objective is to inform, to convince, but also to move our interlocutor. Let's take it all in detail.

The First Rule Of Three: We Are Seen, Seen And Heard

Whether in front of a single person or a crowd, in an interview, conference, or media interview, when we speak we are seen and heard.

It is first of all from this reality that our audience perceives our message. Several studies show that it takes very little time to get an idea about a person: seven or eight seconds would be sufficient! The rest of the time is used to confirm or deny this first impression.

We are seen

In the previous chapter, we talked about perception and unsaid. I invite you to read it again if gray areas persist in your understanding of this phenomenon.

It is essential to be well prepared to improve your performance as a communicator.

I would also like to add this saying: "Why are you shouting so loudly that I cannot hear what you are saying.

Several books deal with nonverbal language, and I refer to it because I do not intend to make it the central theme of my remarks.

However, because of its importance, the subject deserves a little more attention. We can define the unsaid as what our physiognomy, our gestures, our gaze, our posture and our attitude reveal about us often even without our knowledge.

In other words, it is all the information transmitted to our interlocutor (s) without saying it and often without even wanting to.

In fact, after your intervention in public, the people who saw and heard you would keep over time an increasingly vague memory of what you said but will keep alive a positive or negative impression of your performance.

Whether it's our movements, the inflection of our voice, the position of our body, the height of our gaze, our attitude, our smile, or even our touch, everything in our body can betray our thoughts, even secret ones.

For example, a raised chin gives the impression of a person who is or believes himself to be superior to others. The arms crossed read as a good indication of distrust or closure.

The recessed bust suggests distrust or disapproval. Smiling clenched teeth indicates aggressiveness.

On the contrary, an open smile reveals a person who is happy or eager to help improve our level of confidence. Blinking frequently is sometimes indicative of lies and duplicity.

The way we move also says a lot. Abrupt, nervous, unnecessary, repetitive gestures should be avoided. It is best to make slow, calm gestures for a message of power and confidence.

Experience watching your favorite news on television while muting the sound. I assure you that, even without hearing the reader's words you will be able to understand a good deal of what he simply says with the images, the reaction of the presenter, journalists and interviewees.

The unspoken offer important clues at both ends of the communication process. As a sender, if our actions are not in line with our words the message will simply not get through.

The unspoken indeed makes it possible to decode the impressions and feelings of the person speaking. On the other hand, the unsaid is very eloquent for a speaker to be able to read the reactions of his audience.

It is an essential tool for adjusting speech according to the reactions of the audience. In fact, it is necessary to reconcile gestures and words to make the message more convincing.

Here are two tips to improve your perception of you.

Firstly, make your body reflect what you are expressing. Like it or not public communication is a bit theatrical. We cannot defend a position when our body language says otherwise.

I will always remember the president of a major insurance company who came to speak to us for the upcoming shareholders' meeting of his firm. An amazing speech, filled with promise that would make a big difference in the course of the company's business.

Alas, he was delivered soulless, almost speechless in an almost motionless position. Move my faith! I understand that there is a margin between gesticulating without stopping and staying still like Lot's wife, but it is necessary to know how to highlight an important passage of speech using an appropriate gesture made at the right time.

On the other hand, give off an impression of energy. We are naturally inclined towards self-confident people who express themselves easily and energetically. This attitude in front of a group will help you to be perceived as a leader.

Remember that we communicate to provoke a change in attitude or behavior. So we have the desire to convince people of the correctness of our words and of our position.

So how do we persuade if we don't give the impression of being convinced ourselves? It is impossible, and our audience will quickly realize the deception. Speak sincerely, energetically, enthusiastically, and be expressive. Your message will only be better conveyed and consequently better understood.

We are seen

With the exception of a telephone conversation or an interview on the radio or in the newspapers, our first step towards an interlocutor constitutes our first contact.

Practicing this profession for several years, I could give you hundreds of examples of people whose attitude expresses exactly the opposite of their words. You yourself probably have several in mind. Here is one.

One day or the other, we all experienced the following scene: sitting in a room, you see the speaker appear and sit at a table at the front to deliver his presentation.

We've told you a lot of good things about it, and you're looking forward to hearing about it. But already, you are a little annoyed by the fact that in front of you participants partially mask the speaker who did not find it useful to stand up.

The presentation begins, delivered in a monotone voice the speaker reading his text, the sentences are long, complex, filled with incomprehensible words. The speaker dwells on what seems to you to be irrelevant details.

Five minutes before the end of his performance, he admits having to skip important portions of his presentation due to lack of time.

Frantically delving into his notes, he delivers a conclusion that is completely disconnected from the presentation.

How do people manage to give such a soporific and disjointed presentation? There are several explanations — first cultural.

For example, most baby boomers were told being young that they shouldn't talk, but listen to "the grown-ups."

No wonder they appear a little awkward when the time comes to express themselves in public. But let's avoid caricatures because each generation has its problems!

Second, we lack self-confidence and prefer to trust a text prepared in advance. In this way, our words will have been thoroughly matured, weighed, and measured, and there will be no room for possible slippages like when we have to improvise.

However, when we speak publicly, our job is to speak with people.

Besides, the most important reason for our amorphous behavior as a speaker undoubtedly comes from the fact that when we were students, the type of soporific presentation mentioned above was exactly the model used by most of our teachers.

However, among the latter - I like to think that things have changed since many did not necessarily consider the art of oral expression as part of their career plan.

Speaking in public means putting forward our ideas and arguments, convincing the audience of the soundness of our claims, convincing them that this is the truth while being interesting and entertaining.

Many speakers easily forget the last item on this list. However, it is impossible to communicate and persuade without also being a bit of a distraction.

This "show" element is, whether we like it or not the only way to capture and maintain attention. In addition, our audience is knowledgeable and demanding.

We are heard

Everyone has the memory of that school teacher who spoke in a dull, monotonous voice. Let's agree that this is not the perfect recipe for capturing the attention of an audience.

This is why vocal technique i.e voice, rhythm, speed, volume, etc., is so important in communication.

Have you chosen to speak in public? So do it in a firm, strong and clear voice, and with conviction.

Your voice must convey the meaning of your words. So you have to find the right intonation. For example, if you say:

"I am very happy to have arrived safely," the words "very happy" must be supported. You should feel the joy in your voice, a feeling that you will accentuate with the appropriate inflection. You can't say that in a boring voice.

In vocal technique, it is important to focus on the lower level of our register from the first words of our speech. In other words, start your presentation in a lower tone.

This tone is generally the one with which you will manage to speak the loudest and with the most authority. This advice is particularly useful for women.

Poor humans that we are, when we have to speak in public our tone generally rises with our level of stress.

Since women usually speak louder than men, the voice often becomes nasal and shrill in some, which is not pleasant to the ear.

Breathing deeply is essential for controlling the volume of the voice. Without yelling, always speak as if you are speaking to the person in the back row of the room and make sure they can hear you well.

"When we are heard, we always speak well! Said Moliere. And if you use graphics or tables to illustrate your point, remember always to face the room during your demonstration.

You may have a very nice back, but you can convince them by looking at your audience from the front.

The second rule of three: you, I, we

From the very first minutes of our speech, it is important to capture the attention of our audience and position ourselves favorably in the opinion of our audience. How to do it? It's easy!

Imagine that your name is Jenny or Michael and that you come across me on the street. I reach out to you and say to you:

"Hello! I am doing very well ! "How do you react? Surprised, no doubt, you would have expected me to ask you how you were. By saying, "I'm fine," I disrupted the normal order of things.

What is most important to you? For all of us, in fact! Happiness? The balance? A pleasant family life? Realize our dreams? To have money? All of these are good answers, but it's not the one I'm looking for.

The most important thing for each of us, believe me, is ourselves! Let me prove it to you. If I tell you about you, your talents, your beautiful personality, the bright future that awaits you, and as long as I speak, you will listen to me very carefully.

If I tell you about your neighbors, although they may be charming, you are already less interested in them. But if I start talking to you again about you, here you are again paying maximum attention to my words.

Moral: If we talk to people about themselves, or about things that affect them directly and closely, they will listen to us very carefully and maintain this level of focus as long as we talk to them about themselves.

Here's the secret! Each member of your audience must feel personally concerned by your words and be convinced that they will personally benefit from them. It is on this condition that he or she will give you full attention.

Yet, as we have all heard, the overwhelming majority of speakers and presenters begin their remarks by saying, "I am very pleased to be here today! "We hope so! We went to hear it and maybe even paid an entrance fee for it. It's the least that this person is happy to be there.

Here is another proof. Imagine being a member of a selection board, responsible for choosing a new person to take care of the sales management of our business.

The first candidate arrived and said to us: "Hello! My name is Mark Jones, and I have been a sales director for 10 years". Why does this introduction leave us with an appetite?

And what would have been our reaction if he had said to us: "Hello! My name is Mark Jones, and for 10 years, I have worked with companies to improve the performance of sales personnel so that they can do more business and improve the sales volume of the company"?

This is what you have to understand here.

As a member of a selection board, we want to know how the candidate interviewed can help us achieve our goals. Do the same when speaking to an audience.

Offer a solution to one of their problems. Suggest a new way of thinking or acting that will benefit them. Give them a chance to learn something new.

This is why, when we speak to an audience, regardless of this audience and the number of people who compose it, the sequence of intervention should be as follows: you - I - us.

This is what I was explaining to a deputy who confessed sheepishly his difficulties in improvising and the mad fright he felt if he had to speak without the text in front of a group and without having been able to prepare.

It is obvious that any public figure who attends a meeting or assembly will invariably be asked:

"Sir, are you going to tell us a few words?" Here is the secret that I revealed to this deputy.

From the outset, speak specifically and directly to your audience the one in front of you. Too often, we make the same presentation, regardless of the audience.

I have always been amazed to find that some speakers appear before their audience and have absolutely no idea who they are talking to.

Maybe they think their message is so important that everyone wants to hear it?.

We couldn't be more wrong! Your audience should feel that your presentation has been specially prepared for them. People will then feel more concerned with your words and follow you much more easily.

Let's go back to my MP and see how this board can apply to him. Imagine he has to speak to a group of retirees.

It must first be remembered that of the three elements of our communication model, the receiver is the most important. He will therefore wonder who he should speak to.

In this case, these are older people who live in his electoral district and who presumably voted for him; otherwise, they would not be in this assembly.

These are the fathers and mothers of current developers in the region, people involved in their community who have children who go to school, play on the streets and need security, etc.

Armed with this information, my MP rushed to them saying:

"You who are the builders of this corner of the country, you who helped make us who we are today, you who have children and perhaps grandchildren who aspire to a better future, thank you for inviting me to speak before you..."

The public's attention is caught instantly by the words of our speaker because the participants really feel that he is addressing them.

Then make your presentation and develop it. You speak either on your own behalf or on behalf of your organization.

Now is a good time to get your message across or deliver the key elements of your presentation, taking care to modify passages according to the audience you are addressing.

It is here that my MP recalls his main achievements in the riding and thanks to people for supporting him.

Thanks to you, he told them, I was able to achieve this or that other project, win this or that other fight.

We saw it above; if we communicate, it is to provoke a change in attitude in behavior. So you want your presentation to be meaningful, lead to action, get your audience on board with your message.

You must therefore, conclude by proposing the involvement of both parties. "The elections are fast approaching," said my MP, "and that's why I always need your support.

Together, we have achieved great things, and I want to be able to count on your votes to continue to defend your interests..." Imitate it by proposing to your audience a concrete action that follows naturally from the presentation you have just made.

The third rule of three: inform, convince, move

Inform

I will not need to dwell long on the first element of this third equation. It is certain that by communicating, we deliver a wealth of information to our interlocutors, often even without our knowledge, as we have seen.

We tell them lots of things, give them lots of information, knowingly or not, willingly or not.

To convince

Do you really believe that your speech is worth the time you use, multiplied by the number of people in the room?

If you take all this time, otherwise so precious to these people, don't you think it would be a good idea to use it to enrich them with your presentation?

Inform, so be it! But, be as communicative. Be animated by your subject. Let it be your passion, a passion that you intend to transmit to the members of your audience.

The more you are convinced that you can convince people of the merits of your proposals, the more you will be able to convince them. "True eloquence makes fun of eloquence".

This famous phrase from Pascal simply means that knowing all the rules of the art of speaking in public is useless without the intimate and passionate conviction of the legitimacy of the usefulness of your words.

Through your passion and deep conviction, give your audience a taste for action. Make him want to get involved. Communicate to him the desire to apply the advice you give him by offering him winning solutions.

Make them want to learn more before they make a move or use your services and products rather than those of the competitor.

You and your audience will come out enriched by the experience. But again, to convince your audience, you must first be convinced.

Why communicate? We said it: to cause a change in habit or behavior. It is that, from now on, we want our interlocutor to think this something that he did not think before. Do this he didn't do before.

Know this that he did not know before, in order to change attitude or behavior. In other words, we want to convince. To achieve this, let's explore four possible avenues.

The authority

We can first impose it, as long as we have this latitude. If a law, a regulation, or our superior hierarchical position compared to our interlocutors give us this advantage, our work of conviction will be facilitated all the more.

Seduction

On the other hand, we can seduce our interlocutors, but there it is a talent which is not given to everyone, let's agree.

But, for those in possession of this talent, which proceeds from several qualities, it is astonishing to see how easily they manage to make others roughly what they want.

The persuasion

Third, we can argue in such a way that we can persuade our interlocutor (s) to adopt such an attitude or such behavior.

Those who have studied the issue of persuasion agree that there are five different ways of convincing.

First, we can work to bring out the decisive argument in our interlocutor. He may be balancing between two or more avenues that will guide his choice.

Our mission is to present him with a decisive argument, which he probably carries within him, and to which we will owe his final decision.

We can also help our contact to discover all the consequences of their choice. Perhaps the trend that is taking its direction is provisional and based on a summary analysis of the situation? Could a closer look change his decision?

Another way to persuade is to force the choice. Often, even if he is convinced of the soundness of our arguments, external elements lead him to procrastinate. We must, therefore, find and assert what will force his choice, ideally in the sense that we propose.

In addition, specialists argue that forcing our interlocutor to admit reality is another great way to get them to decide and persuade them to act.

Last but not least, the last possibility to convince, let us admit that adding significant information to the scales (perhaps hitherto hidden, for all kinds of reasons) risks tilting the decision in the direction of our claims.

Manipulation

The fourth way to convince our interlocutors to change their attitude or behavior is in fact an action that we immediately tend to want to dismiss because it does not look very chic, but that we have been practicing for our most tender childhood.

I am talking about manipulation here. That's it; the bad word is dropped. I can already see some who are taking a step back.

Do not play the Pharisees and recognize that we all happen to manipulate people. We all do it or undergo its days. To manipulate people is to make them believe that the decision to act one way or the other came from themselves and that it has freely consented.

Once the decision is made, people adhere to it no matter what, even if they admit that they may have been foiled by a ploy.

Manipulation takes place through various methods. The first is called an escalation of engagement. Once we agree to an uninviting action, the argumenter can take us to another step that is more.

For example, we'll probably react coldly to someone who approaches us on the street and asks us for money. It's a whole different story if you're approached by someone who starts by asking for the time which we will give easily, and then ask for money.

It has been proven that the success rate of our applicant is far higher in the second approach.

The second technique is presented as that of wasted spending. We tend to keep our old car even longer, for which we have paid so many for repairs, knowing fully well that we should have changed it a long time ago.

But as we have invested so much. The dark trap, another manipulation technique, is also inspired by this reality.

The Vietnam War was a good example when the United States refused to throw in the towel because it had invested so much in this war, even if it knew that victory was eluding them.

The labeling technique is another very effective approach to manipulation when we are asking for our adhesion to a certain product or such action because we belong to such or such other group which just chooses the option that you must choose.

Another very effective form of manipulation is the "And that's not all ..." technique, commonly used in infomercials. By purchasing this, you also get this or that item absolutely free.

But it's not all. Let's be aware: how many other manipulative tricks do we still undergo or practice every day in order to convince?

In closing, remember the string theory that US President Eisenhower used to talk about the art of persuasion. This man was recognized as an outstanding conciliator, who knew how to bring the opposing personalities together light-years away.

He said bluntly that if you gently pull on it, the string comes without resistance. And if you push it, it will settle and pile up.

Move

Finally, let's talk about emotion. If we were all computers, we would talk to each other with "1" and "0". Computers speak in binary mode and understand each other very well.

But now, we are not computers. We are human beings, and we must vibrate the human fiber in each of the members of our audience if we really want to join them.

Emotion is the best tool we know of to get people to take action.

We probably all have in mind this speaker, this politician, this engineer who delivers his message to us in a cerebral and disembodied manner.

Such a speech is of course, an interesting intellectual exercise. But it is rare that at the end of such a presentation, we feel excited and favorably disposed to action.

Repeated use of the same old shots no longer raises crowds. You have to learn to use emotionally stimulating words if you want to improve the impact of your message.

To convince and provoke a change in attitude or behavior, there are several emotions that you can arouse in your audience, simply by choosing the words you use.

Joy, anger, sadness, commitment, and nostalgia are just some of the themes that arouse emotion in us by their mere mention.

It will be easier for you to choose the appropriate words to encourage the desired emotions that you will have taken care to know your audience well and to learn what makes them vibrate.

If, for example, as president of a large insurance company, you tell us that yours is the best in the world, we have a choice whether to believe you or not.

But if to convince us, you tell us about the dedication of your employees and tell us the story of this agent who, one day, helped one of your insured in real need, then you will provoke with us the feeling that your company is unique.

Another way of moving is to ask questions that arouse the feelings of the people who make up your audience.

Comments and questions like: "When you were young and your mother ...?" Or: "How did you react when you realized that you were in love for the first time ...?" Or: "Among you, who are those who have already practiced a team sport?"

I am convinced by that already, by their simple reading, one or the other of these sentences invite you to daydream and brings back the emotions that these memories evoke.

Don't try to inspire your audience; be inspired yourself. Don't try to convince your audience; be convinced yourself. Show sincere interest.

Finally, do not struggle to demonstrate how exciting what you say is. Be passionate about what you say yourself; the rest will follow.

MATERIAL PREPARATION

Purring can be a painful experience. You can choose to read your text, learn it by heart, or use cards or visual aids as a memory aid that will make you feel like you are improvising. To make your life easier, you will have to learn to work with all these tools, each of which meets specific rules.

Deliver a written speech

This method is generally used for important speeches in which each word has been weighed and is so important that it cannot be replaced by another.

 In addition to providing some confidence, the reading text offers the advantage of accuracy. The speaker says exactly what he plans to say and nothing else.

However, you should know that a well-read speech is not the guarantee of a well-heard speech. In addition, the texts we write often reflect those that we are used to reading or that we find in our homegroup. An engineer will write like an engineer.

A businesswoman or a businessman will use the vocabulary of businesspeople. This makes such texts difficult to read, even more difficult for ordinary people to listen to.

In fact, you have to understand that a speaker who reads a text usually loses flexibility in the voice because he loses contact with the ideas behind the words.

In addition, he considerably reduces his effectiveness by failing to keep despite being himself eye contact with his audience. The speaker is often frightened by public speaking and has written his text to reassure himself: it becomes obvious when he delivers his speech.

By "speaking" instead of "reading," you will be much easier to understand while maintaining much closer eye contact with your audience.

In addition, speaking instead of reading the text will help you be clearer by forcing yourself to deliver your message in everyday language.

You will have nothing of a public speaking virtuoso using the perfect grammar, complicated sentences, and sophisticated vocabulary of written texts, if your audience cannot follow you.

However, if you must read a speech that you have written yourself, here is something that will always serve you: you must learn to work with your written speech, and it begins from the moment you begin to write your text.

First, state the idea you want to formulate out loud, and then try to write down what you just heard yourself saying.

This tip will help you produce text that is easier to read and listen to.

When writing your text on the copy, you will read, USE A COMBINATION OF SMALL CAPS AND CAPITAL LETTERS OF THE SAME TYPE, WHICH YOU WILL VOLUNTARILY INCREASE.

Contrary to what many people think, a text written only in capital letters makes it more difficult to read. To make your life easier, type double-spaced text, using an easy-to-read, bold, 20-point font, covering only two-thirds of the page.

This will make it easier for you to scan your text while keeping your head up. This will also leave you some room to record your notes.

This recipe will allow you to count about a minute for each page of your speech, which should be limited to about twenty pages.

Do not make your paragraphs too long; otherwise, you may find it difficult to navigate if you take your eyes off the text to watch your audience.

Start a new paragraph after every sentence or two. Do not cut a paragraph in half to go from one page to another. End each page with a full sentence and paragraph.

When reading it, make sure your text is not broached. This will make it easier to drag each sheet read under the others as you go. Avoid turning the pages with a big gesture, as we sometimes see.

You could touch the microphone, which produces an extremely unpleasant, amplified noise. Your gesture may also distract. As a precaution, you will understand, be sure to page each sheet well.

If you were to drop your speech on the floor, this little precaution would come in handy and would allow you to quickly and easily put your papers in order.

I have already seen speakers who were astonished at the little logical link between the pages of their text- only to realize later, too late, that a loustic had fun mixing up the pages - unnumbered - of their text.

Place markers in your text to indicate the places where you will have to take breaks: a bar for a simple break, two bars for a longer break, for example, after a period.

Indicate the places where you will have to change your tone, your rhythm. You have to learn to use these notes in your text and practice until you master them well.

At least try to seem to improvise in the first moments of your speech as well as in conclusion. As you begin your presentation, make eye contact with your audience right away.

It is very important to create a better link and better arrange those who listen to you. In conclusion, when you deliver your most important message, be sure to look at your audience and take advantage of one of the most valuable communication tools, your gaze.

If you must read, do so with your head held high, not your nose deep in your text. Take care of yourself, make frequent stops to get out of your text, for example, to provide an explanation, illustrate your point with an example or tell an anecdote, all of which need not be written.

Keep open and direct contact with your audience. To do this, practice reading your text until you can recall one or more lines at a glance.

Memorize a few key passages, not forgetting to note landmarks in the text so that you can easily read them again if you have to raise your head completely to look at your audience.

Pay attention to the inflection of your voice while reading. To acquire a natural air, read and reread your text aloud and take breaks.

Bring life and enthusiasm to your reading. Avoid monotony by varying intonation and flow. Ask yourself if the timbre of your voice is natural if it sounds like the one you have when you speak.

Finally, forgetting to move is one of the biggest problems that people who read a text face. And it is understandable. We are so busy reading that we forget to communicate effectively with our whole body.

You have to learn to move a little! Remember that speaking in public must provide more pleasure than suffering . With practice and rigorous preparation, you will be able to deliver an interesting speech, even if you have to read it.

Some of the most important speeches in the history of mankind have been read. But their authors were certainly not at the first reading of their text when they delivered it.

Memorize your text

Tell me why someone who is also an excellent storyteller at the table during a friendly meal, suddenly becomes the bad reader of a text that we find boring?

For a very simple reason: apart from stage fright, which contributes to the explanation of the mystery, written language, and spoken language are not inspired by the same rules.

You don't usually write the way you speak. To repeat a text learned by heart will never be anything other than to declaim a written text. Your audience will quickly realize this.

Memorizing your text is probably the worst way to go. There are so many things that can distract you, cause a devastating memory loss, and make you lose all your means.

Besides, the effort is much more about the need to remember words than about the quality of the presentation. Your audience may not know exactly why, but they will find that you are unnatural.

For these reasons, and the others we have seen previously, this avenue is, therefore, to be avoided at all costs.

Boxes or cards

Certain public services must be based on the transmission of written texts, that is! But here is another technique that has been used successfully by many speakers.

This is the one I prefer. It consists of speaking not with words, but with ideas.

Instead of compelling yourself to read a text and becoming a slave to it to the point of losing all your means if you get lost in words, express yourself with ideas.

Have in front of you an aide-memoire on which you will have noted all the themes or all the ideas to be discussed and, when the time comes, deliver them one by one to your audience.

You are freed from the written text, while, no matter the words, it is the ideas that take over. If your idea is understood by the audience, words suddenly become less important.

This practice will bring you more and more benefits as you learn to master it. Among other things, you will find it easier to focus on your message than on words.

By using this technique, you will no longer have to worry about the rest as a note on your card will tell you.

The use of small boxes or cards on which you will record your notes is one of the characteristic of this method. But you will have to learn to use this tool. Use these little boxes to write down the quotes, statistics, and lists you will need.

Write words, not complete sentences or paragraphs. This is not a text you need, but a checklist. Do not put too much information on each of these cards;

otherwise, you will become a slave to it as if it were a written speech.

It would then be, in fact, just another support for the same technique. The use of index cards is completely different from that of a written speech and follows very specific rules.

As a rule of thumb, to find the measure, write your notes in large letters, at most 5 keywords per file, or even one new idea per file, taking care to underline or accentuate the important words.

If, when you practice delivering your presentation, you find that you are reading your cards, it is because you have put too much information in them.

When you have gone around the question and have a series of cards, do not fold them; do not stitch them up, but number them. This is very important.

I will always remember this speaker who, standing behind his lectern, in a memorable contortion to grab his glass of water, accidentally dropped his stack of unnumbered cards that he had placed on the corner of the lectern in a balance precarious.

Imagine his air as he tried to collect his ideas to launch his talk, while frantically trying to put away a series of boxes that obstinately refused to order logically.

Expressing yourself with ideas and using cards also allows you to leave the table or lectern on occasion to add movement to your presentation.

Don't be afraid to move around a bit and get away from your "comfort zone." Too many speakers hide behind their lecterns and thus deprive themselves of a great tool, called body language, to support their presentation and give it more depth.

Not to mention that this technique promotes maximum visual contact with your audience.

Visual aids as a reminder

Several speakers used visual aids during the presentation as a memory aid, generally electronic acetates, because of their convenience.

Today, this technique is facilitated by increasingly sophisticated projectors and their remote controls. No text to read, no files to manage, only markers projected on the screen to exploit each of the ideas put forward.

As we have seen, the words used are of little importance, and the audience will not know that you have forgotten this or that element if you do not tell them.

Using this type of checklist will force you to have more knowledge of your subject, but will give you the flexibility to adapt to any unforeseen event. The visual support allows you not to worry about the rest, each new slide resulting in its series of keywords.

These act as triggers of ideas that gradually lead you, from one idea to the next, to deliver your entire message. All you have to do is plan transitions that gradually lead you to your conclusion. The words that follow each other, from one table to another, allow you much more freedom and ease to move around the room.

You can come and go without worrying about your notes. Being active helps you release stress and gives you more energy for your presentation.

This will make it easier for participants to focus on you and your message.

A word of advice, however: your movements must have been carefully planned and even repeated in the empty room before your presentation, which is another good reason to arrive before everyone else.

Take two or three steps in one direction, stop for a moment, then take another step with two or three more steps, and so on. Do this slowly; your audience members shouldn't leave feeling like they've been watching a tennis match watching you move from side to side.

Finally, this technique maximizes eye contact with your audience. Except when you stare at the screen or the board to find the word that will allow you to follow, you will have all the freedom of action possible to look at people.

The audience will likely follow your gaze at the board and will not only hear what you say but also read it.

Finally, this approach is reassuring for the audience who will see, thanks to your visual supports, that you have a precise plan indeed and that you made an effort of reflection before coming to meet them.

A word in closing: the visual aids used as a memory aid can be something other than words. These can be diagrams, illustrations, graphics, or photographs.

Amongst the best talks, I've heard in my life was supported only by six photographs projected at the appropriate time of the presentation, one after the other on a screen.

Think about your transitions before you make your presentation and practice. Finally, whatever means you choose to deliver your message, nothing beats preparation.

The Teleprompter

The teleprompter is a projector that scrolls your text on two Plexiglas plates placed on each side of your lectern.

Politicians are often seen using it to give the impression that they are speaking directly to the crowd when, in reality, they are reading their text. As the Plexiglas is transparent, the audience sees nothing but fire.

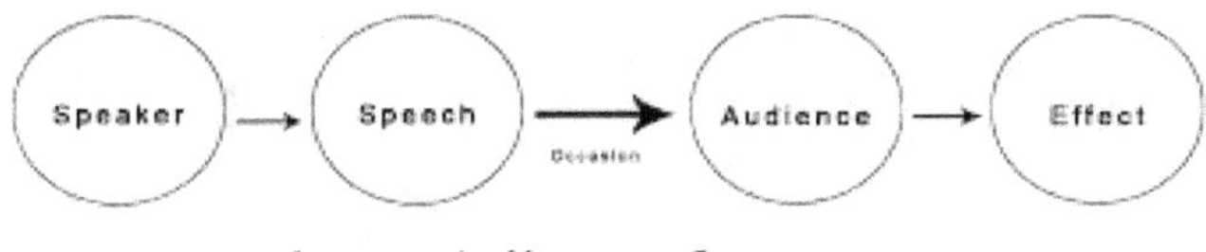

ARISTOTLE'S MODEL OF COMMUNICATION

I cannot stress this enough to deter you from using this device unless you have a large enough bank of hours to practice.

Every year, I see dozens of inexperienced speakers who persist in using such a device because others do so and completely miss their presentation.

A technical problem may arise, ending the projection of the text on the plexiglass, or the technician who operates it can become stuck on one line while you try to continue your presentation.

To be strongly advised against anyone who has not taken the time to learn how to use this tool properly.

Help Yourself

Breathing, projection, and pose of the voice

My purpose here is not to replace a good diction teacher who would greatly help you improve, if necessary. There are some great ones out there, and don't hesitate to check them out.

However, I want to share with you some considerations that will allow you to use better this important communication tool i.e the voice.

Our dictionaries define voice as the set of sounds produced by the larynx when the exhaled air vibrates the vocal cords.

The latter is composed of two groups of muscles of the larynx, which fixed at each end, are stretched like violin strings and form a narrowed space.

This space opens and closes under the effect of the air, which passes there coming from the lungs.

The characteristics of the voice

It is therefore, by vibrating that the vocal cords produce sounds. The more space is closed, the louder the sound. It's the volume.

It is determined by the breath, the force of projection. The intensity of the sounds is controlled by the strength of the vibrations, which depends on the volume of exhaled air.

The pitch or the register of the voice, during a conversation, varies according to the people.

Primarily determined by the length, thickness, and position of the vocal cords, the height can be voluntarily changed, within certain limits, through the respiratory muscles and those of the larynx, by varying the pressured air as well as the tension of the vocal cords (which can move away or approach one from the other).

The association of these elements determines the frequency of the vibration: the higher the vibration, the higher the voice.

The timbre that is to say, the set of characteristics which make it possible to distinguish a voice, results in particular from the resonance in the chest, the throat, the oral cavity, and the nose.

Articulation is the pronunciation of sounds that are differentiated to form words. Speech is articulated by interrupting and modulating the airflow using the lips, tongue, teeth, jaw, and palate.

Voice disorders

Specific books are devoted to voice disorders. Dysphonia (partial voice impairment, hoarse voice, etc.) and aphonia (inability to speak) are called voice disorders caused by a disease or by a functional abnormality affecting the larynx.

The usual cause of dysphonia is vocal overwork, which can ultimately lead to a growth in the vocal cords or edema.

When you use your voice badly, when you "force your voice" some say, or when you "break" your voice say others, you cause mechanical problems that have nothing to do with infections.

We can then develop nodules or polyps of the vocal cords, which we will have to get rid of by surgery in some cases. This particular problem is the obsession of many singers.

Other possible causes of voice disturbances include paralysis of the larynx muscles, and malformations of the vocal cords (incomplete development, for example). Finally, in a smoker, hoarseness that lasts more than three weeks could be caused by chronic laryngitis.

Other difficulties can come from air pollution, pulmonary and respiratory disorders, and viral or bacterial infections, the flu, for example. Poor physical condition, fatigue, and anemia are also causes of voice problems.

Preventing Voice Disorders

Here as elsewhere, it is better to prevent than to cure. To avoid forcing his voice, it must be placed correctly in his middle register.

Like an athlete, you have to practice it. Céline Dion, for example, has never made a secret of the quasi-Olympian training she gives to her voice. It is precisely this unique voice that made her fame and success.

To learn how to make your voice work well while remaining in your register, you must do vocalizations every day, which can be defined as melodies structured in a series of vowels rather than according to the words of a text.

Your voice is also part of your image. It should indicate what you are, and never what you are not. This is a good reason to learn to master it well.

How to work your voice well

The mechanics of the voice pose are broken down into three stages:

1. Breathe through the base of the lungs, through the diaphragm, not from the chest, shrugging the shoulders. You have to breathe deeply and silently: breath in through your nose, with your mouth, closed, and breathe out through your mouth. This way of breathing is very useful to control the stage fright, which we will talk about soon.

2. Speak immediately when inspiration is over.

3. Speak while exhaling only, but without ever going out of breath.

Read the preceding paragraphs while practicing this technique. We realize it here; it is absolutely necessary to take breaks from time to time.

Understand that if you don't take breaks, you will quickly become crimson. We absolutely have to find a way to get some air at some point and therefore take a break. Why not use such breaks for strategic ends, to intensify the impact of our interventions?

The projection of the voice

You have to use the right breath power to project the voice; otherwise, you speak too weakly or too loudly. With stage fright, many people find it difficult to project their voices well.

How to speak louder? It's easy! You have to start by breathing deeply again! On expulsion the air push will give more strength to your voice.

This is not about raising the pitch of the voice, which would result in screams, but rather about increasing the volume. The latter is extremely useful for enriching and highlighting particular points in your presentation.

The pose of voice

You have to find your own register and place your voice at the right pitch, a point that is just between the head voice (high) and the chest voice (low).

To achieve this, place yourself in a small room, 15 cm from the wall. Take a deep breath and project the vowels A E I O U from high to low (from head to chest).

Between these two extremes, listen carefully and find your balance, the level at which you feel most comfortable. When you find it, practice vocalizing and reading aloud every day, exactly where you put your voice.

Tips for keeping your voice

These are a few easy tips to help you keep your voice:

If you have to talk for a whole day, go out at mealtime and rest your voice.

When speaking in public, make sure you have warm (not cold) water on hand. The vocal cords are muscles that need to be treated with great care and, let's face it; lukewarm water is just as refreshing as cold water.

Drink plenty of water the day before your presentation to keep yourself hydrated.

Try to avoid alcohol, coffee, or tea, which tend to dehydrate the vocal cords.

Avoid carbonated drinks, which can cause unsightly bumps during your presentation.

Avoid as much as possible, clearing your back of the throat, speaking very loudly or shouting. It's a great way to "break your voice."

If it is very cold or you need to speak outside in low temperatures, warm your throat before speaking and wear a scarf or turtleneck.

Be careful not to wear clothes that tighten you too much at the waist (pants that are too tight) or your throat (tie that suffocates).

When you start your speech, place your voice in the lower pane of your voice register, and then go upstairs to use voice effects in your presentations. If you speak too loudly or too loud at first and then want to create effects, you will force your voice and maybe even scream.

Stage Fright

It is said that the fear of death comes second in the list of our greatest fears, second only to that of speaking in public. Then comes, but only further, the fear of losing your job or a loved one.

That says it all. When we were young, many of us were told to keep quiet and "listen to the grown-ups." And then, suddenly, our functions or our responsibilities lead us to express ourselves in public without having really been trained in them.

First, at school, where we had to give a presentation to the class one day or the other. For many, this is often where the drama began.

Some feel that stage fright is caused by excessive self-awareness.

Instead of forgetting and engaging with passion in his talk and in his relationship with others, the person who suffers from stage fright focuses too much on himself.

This approach makes us understand why stage fright is not the exclusive preserve of people who speak in public.

It is also true of the salesperson that one surprises were pacing outside the door of a potential customer before finding the courage to enter.

It is often the fear of failure or the fear of not looking good that causes stage fright. Suddenly there is doubt of his abilities, of being up to the task and of succeeding in impressing the speakers favorably. "What if I lose all my means and find myself speechless, remembering nothing of my text?"

And if I was so bad that people started to hit nails, to leave the room in the middle of my presentation or, worse still, tossing me tomatoes?"

What if they waited for me at the end of my presentation to ask me difficult questions or make derogatory comments about my performance?" Faced with danger, the normal reaction of every human being is flight.

Imagine the effect produced on your audience, if in the middle of your presentation, you had to give in to your instincts and run away like a rabbit without asking for your rest!

The stage fright is however, a dragon that must be tamed if one wants to improve his performance as a communicator and become more efficient during his public performances.

Out of control, stage fright can become a major handicap since it prevents concentration. It causes dry mouth, tight throat, sweaty, cold, shaky hands, nausea, fast heart rate, shortness of breath, limp legs, and trembling lips. Some even experience chest pain.

It is not there to be at its best, and it is certainly not in this state that one can deliver a performance worthy of mention. Since doing public speaking training and coaching, I've seen all kinds of stage fright.

I have met people ready to do anything to get rid of this calamity. I even knew someone who asked his doctor to prescribe nitroglycerin pills to help him get nervous when he really didn't have any medical needs for it with no known heart condition. We really don't have to go that far.

The first step towards treating this discomfort is to recognize that stage fright is a normal physical and physiological reaction that everyone is experiencing it and that it as never killed anyone.

On the other hand, I have good news for you: our audience is to a large extent unaware of our nervousness. It is left to us to behave in such a way as not to arouse suspicion.

I have a piece of second good news: stage fright is a normal phenomenon that manifests itself before the triggering event, and which fades as time goes by.

Once the presentation has started, the stage fright gradually dissipates as your concentration increases.

That's why a lot of nervousness tricks find their application before the exercise that causes them begins. Finally, also know that stage fright is an ally, a positive element that it will encourage you to perform, that it will keep you alert. Without worry, your performance may be much less brilliant.

The physiological aspect

The first tool to combat stage fright is to learn to breathe well. However, long breaths alone are not enough to get rid of stage fright, but it is definitely a first step in the right direction.

There is a scholarly explanation for the physiological reactions caused by stress. Suffice it to say that when we are nervous, we involuntarily contract our diaphragm, putting pressure on our lungs, which cannot inflate to capacity.

Deprived of the maximum supply of new oxygen that our brain needs, we experience the unwanted physical reactions that we all experienced one day or another in "Suffering" from stage fright.

When the brain assesses a situation as dangerous, it pours a tremendous amount of adrenaline into the blood.

You must try to take deep breaths, so the full intake oxygen in the brain has a beneficial effect. Indeed, this mechanism helps to release endorphins in the body.

A biochemical compound naturally secreted by the body, endorphin is used to modulate the manifestations of stress and reduce its perverse effects. Endorphin naturally calms down without the need for medication.

Immediately before speaking, take a short 30-60 minute walk outside to get some fresh air. Walk slowly, breathing deeply.

This is not a violent or quick exercise that I offer you here. It is a calm, serene walk, with moderate steps, without sweating or shortness of breath.

And most importantly, keep an eye on your watch to make sure you don't arrive late.

If this is not possible, withdraw to an isolated corner, ideally in the dark. Find a comfortable chair and sit with your back straight, letting your arms hang alongside your body. Shake hands slowly to restore blood circulation.

Make faces and move your jaw to untie your facial muscles. Move your toes but gently, so as not to cause cramps. Yawn. Close your eyes and breathe slowly.

Take a deep breath, take a deep breath, then hold your breath for three seconds, and then slowly release the air. After about 15 minutes of these exercises, you should feel much better.

Finally, immediately before being presented, avoid sitting cross-legged to prevent numbness. If possible, get up well before being introduced to the audience and walk around a bit to stretch your legs well.

The mental aspect

Do you know what is called positive visualization? Some studies show that the more successful you see yourself making your presentation, the more you will know.

The mental image that one makes of oneself in the process of succeeding an exercise is a powerful success factor. Athletes use this technique.

Before setting off on the track, a professional alpine skier sees himself rushing at full speed on the track, threading the doors one after the other.

He thus visualizes his entire career and sees the success he will achieve through his performance.

So imagine yourself making your presentation and see your audience passionate about your words, applauding everything as soon as you finish. Think of the success you will reap by your presentation.

Focus on your main messages. Tell yourself that people want to see you succeed. Stay yourself. Don't try to give yourself a style or genre, or imitate someone else.

It was you that people came to hear. They came to listen to what you have to say.

If you make a phone call or participate in an intimidating interview and the nervousness consumes you, imagine yourself speaking with ease to your interlocutor, using the arguments prepared in advance, and which you adapt as the conversation progresses.

Imagine the person on the other end of the phone or in front of you gradually being convinced or even enthusiastic about listening to your message.

That being said, it should be understood that you do not have to control the behavior of your audience. Your role is to deliver your communication to the best of your science and knowledge, not to play the police.

For example, if you are a speaker at an annual social club dinner, and otherwise well-watered dinner, the state of your audience is not your responsibility.

We come back again! To be ready, you have to prepare! The more ready we are, the more effectively we will be able to combat stage fright.

On the other hand, you have to repeat but not too much. Not to the point of learning your text by heart. As we have seen, you would lack in spontaneity.

But repeat aloud, seven or eight times, in order to master the content enough to then work on the effects, in a sense theatrical term: voice effects, gestures.

At this stage of your preparation, you will feel ready, and it will give you confidence.

Over time, you will gain experience. I do not guarantee the disappearance of stage fright; it would be lying to you and doing you a disservice.

A small dose of stage fright is essential if you want to offer better performance. All the comedians will tell you that their worst performance on stage took place in the evening when they did not feel the jitters.

With experience, you will learn to control stage fright and gradually use it as an ally rather than as an enemy.

SPEAKING IN PUBLIC

COMMUNICATE WITH AN AUDITORIUM

No one has ever died from speaking in public. When you go to the place determined for your presentation review, and repeat the introductory sentence of your presentation several times. Remember what we have already seen about the visualization.

Also, if you change the words along the way, it doesn't really matter because your audience won't know it. And if things don't turn out exactly as you expected, don't take it apart.

We will see together how to establish a "Plan B," an alternative solution, or even a different strategy to make sure that your message carries.

Finally, let's say it; there are not thirty-six ways to present and thank a speaker. There are only two: the bad and the good. We'll say a few words about it, as we'll also see how to accept a prize or reward publicly.

Speak with your audience, not yourself. Think conversation and not presentation. Do not try to look at everyone at the same time, but one person at a time.

Just take your time, relax and enjoy the whole experience; also, above all, have fun doing your presentation in public and show it off.

During your performance, focus on audience responses to your message, not how you look or how you feel. You should have worked out these details before speaking.

Dress according to the circumstances and your contacts

The dress code is constantly evolving and has different meanings depending on the era and the environment.

We value the way we dress and the fashion we marry. Some even tend to say to themselves, "This is my style, and others get used to it."

However, in a communication context, this is the first signal transmitted to our interlocutors who will find comfort or discomfort in our clothing.

If they accept it, they will quickly identify with us and be immediately ready to hear us. Otherwise, they will be less receptive at first.

In fact, they will only listen to us carefully once they have managed to get over their initial perception and focus on what we are saying.

This delay is therefore, harmful to the quality of the communication since, while they get used to us, the spectators do not really listen to us.

The rule of thumb, if there is one, is to dress a notch above the dress code adopted by our audience.

If you are to speak at a business congress, do not hesitate to wear the suit. If on the contrary, we present ourselves before an audience gathered for a leisure activity, we wear tasteful but more relaxed clothes.

In any case, make sure your skill doesn't distract your audience at your expense. So no funny patterns, flashy jewelry, or quirky clothing accessories.

Take the time to arrive

You certainly all have in mind the memory of this speaker who barely show up and not yet really installed behind his lectern, has already started his presentation without even thanking his presenter.

This is a sure way to miss his first contact. When you have been introduced to the room, take the time to sit down and smile to your audience, which will give you capacity and confidence.

People will still applaud you and swap a few final comments with each other before you start. This moment of silence that you will provoke, you will use it to establish first visual contact with the audience.

It will allow you to impose yourself and take the measure and control of the assembly from the start.

Then thank the person who introduced you by name please. Take the time to write his name on your text or on your fact sheets.

The audience often identifies with the presenter because he too comes from the room and returns to sit there to hear from you. Ignoring it at the start of your presentation may be interpreted as a lack of good manners, a sign of rejection, or at the very least, indifference.

When you are really in all your means and contact with the room is established, only then can you start your presentation.

Sitting or standing?

If you are in a conference room and are asked to give a demonstration or present your point of view, it will be easier for you to get up for four reasons.

First, people will see you better because you will become the center of interest. Second, you will occupy a dominant position over your assistance. Your audience needs you to help them stay focused on what you have to say.

So they wants you to take control. When you stand up, you accept this invitation. Third, since you are always a little nervous in this type of situation, getting up will help you breathe better, project your voice better, and better control your stage fright.

There is finally a fourth reason why it is better to speak standing up. The latter may interest you more than the first three.

A study at the University of Minnesota found that if you give your clients a standing presentation, using visual aids, they will be willing to spend 26% more money on your product or service than if you had your demonstration seated at a table, using the same presentation elements.

Another study showed that, in the case of a seated presentation, 58% of potential customers assembled around the table were ready to invest in a product or service offered in this way.

Not so bad, is it? But this rate climbs to 79% if the presenter is standing. And that applies to ideas as well as to the products and services we have to sell.

Establish and maintain eye contact with your listeners

Here's another secret: the eyes are one of the most powerful communication tools we have. "The eyes are the mirror of the soul," it is said.

This means that the eyes carry the conviction that lives in us and by that, we have to convince people with our eyes as much as with our words to express our sincerity.

If I speak in public by looking everywhere around me, above, below, and on my text, I will probably manage to get part of my message. But if I look around the room and look into yours and that of each member of the audience, I get an even bigger impact.

Start by choosing a person and speak to them personally, as if they were alone in the room. Maintain eye contact long enough to connect with this person. We are talking about five to ten seconds here, the time of a sentence, for example.

Then move on to another person, sitting somewhere else, in the center or maybe on the other side of the room. This is relatively easy with a small group. But if you are addressing a crowd make such eye contact with one or two people per room section. Everyone in the audience will soon feel like you are speaking to them personally.

Eye contact with your audience can also help you better control your nervousness . You will indeed be able to better "read the room" and adapt your message to the reactions it returns to you; let's remember our notions of dynamic listening.

The exchange then becomes a two-way process allowing you to become an even more effective communicator.

If looking directly at your audience members intimidates or makes you uncomfortable, look at the people's foreheads or just above their heads, at the roots of their hair, wandering around the room. Several speakers forget this last detail and look only from one side of the room, or only the first rows, or only back and not forward.

Be on time and stick to the schedule

"Punctuality is the politeness of kings," says the maxim. It is essential that you arrive on time for your presentation unless there is a situation or problem that is completely beyond your control.

Arriving late is undoubtedly a blatant disrespect for your audience. Not only will you not be mentally ready to deliver your communication, but the audience will hardly be anymore.

Also, be sure to finish your presentation within the allotted time, at the scheduled time. To do otherwise is also disrespectful to your audience or to the next speaker, if applicable.

The only way to make sure you stay on schedule and on time is to rehearse well. With experience, you will manage to keep a good idea of the time elapsed while speaking.

But it takes practice. Nothing will be more disturbing to you and your audience than a reminder of the length of your presentation or the time that has elapsed while you are at the heart of your presentation

Think before you speak

It seems obvious, but it is often easier said than done. With stage fright, it can happen that you are so preoccupied with your text or your ideas that you cannot anticipate the coming passages.

Yet, while staying focused on what you are saying, "seeing it coming" will help you choose in advance the most appropriate words, phrases, or examples to support your point. Your reading of the room's non-verbal language will help you a lot in this regard.

Reveal the plan

We have seen that when we speak before a group, we must say in the introduction what we are going to talk about, demonstrate it in the body of our presentation and come back to it in general terms in our conclusion.

As we have seen above, the best communicators use the introduction to precisely reveal the plan of their presentation. This approach gives the audience a sort of "road map," allowing them to orient themselves during the presentation.

Not only does it improve his level of understanding, but this plan provides him with benchmarks to help him grasp the whole presentation.

Look at your text, then look at the group and talk

If you have to use cards or notes, or visual aids as a memory aid, you should not read your text while you are speaking. When we use our notes, it is to refresh our memories, to see better where we are in our presentation. We don't need to do this exercise "publicly."

When you have exposed an idea and want to follow up with another one, take the time to take a break, in silence, to find yourself in your notes, then reconnecting with your room, continue with the next argument.

Either way, the break will allow your audience to digest the idea and make room for the next one.

Pretend you are having a conversation with your audience.

As we've said before, don't speak to yourself, but to your audience. Speak with passion, based on your preparation. Speak with ideas rather than words.

Look people in the eye. Watch them react and react accordingly. Take pleasure in what you do. Don't be a slave to your presentation. Those who listen to you are not and only ask to be charmed by you and by what you have to say to them.

Repeat your main messages

Teaching is based on repetition. The more you repeat a message, the more your audience will remember it.

This is also proven in advertising, where the repetition of the message is the cornerstone of product or brand ownership.

Even if it is improper to repeat yourself over and over again, or worse to quote yourself in a conversation, the use of repetition in speech is not only polite but desirable in that it helps the audience to fix the message in their memory.

Perhaps you remember this memorable speech by Pastor Martin Luther King Jr., which was titled "I had a dream."

In this speech, Pastor King kept repeating this phrase over and over and over and over and over with the audience. The crowd was on the same wavelength as him and never tired of hearing him repeat these few words: "I had a dream."

This technique can help make a speech much more powerful and memorable. The repetition of the same expression will fix it in the imagination of your audience, who if you repeat it often enough, will end up repeating it at the same time as you.

As for your main messages, it is not enough to say it to them once for everyone to understand and remember them. You have to say it to them again and again if you want it to really settle in your audience's mind.

Finally, it is the same thing when it comes to launching a media campaign, do not imagine that because you passed your message in a previous interview, everyone will have understood and retained it. Nothing is less sure. Refer to this passage on the virtues of repetition at the end of the first chapter. It is so easy to fall into this trap. "Memory is a faculty that forgets," right?

The collective memory retains even less. Don't tire of repeating your messages. It is not because we have been immersed in this or that situation for months, it is not because we have been repeating the same words for weeks, that everyone around us is aware of it in the same way.

See how women and politicians do it. See how advertisers do. They keep repeating. Some will even say that they ramble.

Be yourself

Have you noticed how certain people are depending on whether you rub shoulders with them in daily life or whether they are performing in front of a group?

I recognize that the profession of speaker and presenter has its requirements. We want to project the best possible image of ourselves towards an audience. when very often, everyday life does not require the same rigor from us.

The most important rule of thumb for communicating as well as possible is to stay simple and natural as you would be around a table with family and friends.

Of course, the larger the group the more you have to exaggerate your gestures to make sure everyone sees and understands. But what needs to be amplified is a natural behavior. Stay authentic.

If you are interested in the subject of the speech you are giving, if you really believe in what you are saying and want to share your message with others, your gestures will reflect it and be appropriate to your speech.

By staying yourself when you submit your message, you will be natural and spontaneous without having to think about it.

The exercise is not easy since it forces you to drop the mask. But to become an effective speaker, you have to drop that mask and share your feelings with your audience.

The latter wants to know if you are really convinced of what you say. If you want to convince others, you have to be convinced yourself and look like it.

Establish personal contact with your audience.

People came to hear from you. They just want to be charmed by you. From the start, establish a bond between you and your audience.

Tell them about yourself. Anything you tell them about yourself will improve your chances of making real contact with them.

In a few minutes, after thanking them for their presence, tell them who you are, what you came to tell them, and what you expect from this meeting.

Do not stay like a pure spirit, flying over his totally disembodied audience at the fourth level of abstraction. The more people identify with you and feel concerned about your message, the easier they will remember it.

Speak and articulate: pay attention to the end of the sentence

With stage fright, it often happens that we speak faster. We often lose clarity and effects there. The end of the sentence is particularly overlooked in such circumstances.

Become aware of this and force yourself to slow down your flow. Try to pronounce each of the syllables while remaining natural.

Throughput: 140 to 160 words per minute

For the sake of understanding, a normal rate should be 140 to 160 words per minute. Slower, they will fall asleep to your hearing. Speaking faster will surprise the audience who will have to make an extra effort to follow you. In addition, you will lose in quality of speech and pronunciation.

Avoid being monotonous

The monotone tone falls asleep. Since it is ultimately possible to speak in a lively way without changing your tone, many people do not realize that they have this type of problem.

Ask your friends to give you honest feedback about the tone of your presentation. Better yet, register. If you've found yourself boring, chances are you're not alone.

Breathe

Breathe deeply. This will give you many benefits. First, breathing well, bringing more air into your lungs, will help you have a better voice and speak louder in a safer tone.

Then breathing deeply will force you to slow down your flow. Finally, as we have seen, it is undoubtedly one of the best antidotes to stage fright.

Keep it simple in choosing the vocabulary and expressions used.

I remember one day chatting with a well known politician and known for his speaking skills, who had a disconcerting ability to explain the most complex things simply.

Doing my own work where I had to popularize the complexity of the parliamentary work of the Quebec National Assembly for the public, one day, I asked him to reveal his secret to me.

He replied, "When I speak in public, I always imagine that I am talking to my old mother, sitting with her on a couch by the fireplace in the father's house on Christmas Eve.

Warning! She is not stupid, my old mother. But she wasn't fortunate enough to have an education as advanced as mine and, although she reads a lot, I know she won't follow me beyond a certain level of language.

So when I speak in public and realize that my old mother no longer understands me, I change my language level."

This advice has proven to be useful throughout my career. I still like to say, "When you speak in public, imagine that you are talking to a 14-year-old teenager.

He will understand what you are saying, as long as you keep it simple in the choice of words, expressions, and examples that you will use."

Keep it simple in the choice of your words and do not presume to understand your interlocutors. Refuse to use acronyms unless you can be sure everyone in your audience knows them. If not, give an explanation.

We interrupt you during the presentation

Does someone interrupt you during a presentation to ask a question on a subject or an aspect that you planned to tackle later?

What should be done? You can, of course indicate to him that it will be discussed further and continue as if nothing had happened. I suggest that I be more diplomatic and flexible, and probably also polite, by giving a brief response before indicating that the subject will be discussed further.

If you do not respond, the audience will remain focused on this unanswered question rather than your presentation. So answer, but keep it short!

The famous memory lapse

If you have a memory lapse in the middle of a sentence and you find yourself completely lost in your presentation, don't panic.

It can happen to everyone. Smile, apologize to your audience, collect your ideas, find yourself in your notes, and start this part of your presentation again. Remember that people want you to make a good presentation, it is in their interest, and they are generally sympathetic to your cause.

We are ahead of you in your support document

You have prepared a document to support your presentation and have given it to participants before you start your presentation.

You expect them to follow you from page to page, as your presentation progresses. But now some have decided to get ahead: they have already gone much further and no longer pay attention to what you are saying.

A good way to avoid this inconvenience is to hand in your supporting documents at the end of your presentation. We have already mentioned this solution avenue.

However, since the damage is done, here is a way to catch the lost: refer to the page you are on and, as you progress, ask everyone if they are there. This diplomatic way of calling to order will help you regain control.

You are confused with someone else

You present an offer of services, and you realize that the main decision-maker confuses you with your main competitor.

In such a case, as soon as you realize it, repeat the name of your company as many times as you can until the end of your presentation. Stay positive, and don't try to decrease your competitor.

You don't make a reputation by crushing others, but by demonstrating that you are in the best position to help the interlocutor to solve his problems.

Parallel discussions

You try to convince your audience, and you notice that two or three people in the room are having a discussion outside of your communication. Not only do they not listen to you, but they disturb others.

Worse yet, they cause you to lose your focus. In such a case, start by looking at them insistently. They'll notice it, and it'll usually do the trick.

However, if their side continues, stop and ask the audience if there are any questions. If no one reacts, speak directly to the chatterbox and ask them if something is missing. They will usually stop talking from that point on.

If they still resume their exchanges, do not hesitate, ask them to please leave the room to end their conversation because they disturb the people around them. This will usually be the last warning.

Presentation of a speaker and thanks

You may have to present or thank another speaker for his or her performance, or publicly present an award to someone. You may even be the recipient of an award. The rules that prevail in this regard are simple, but you have to know them.

Introduce a speaker

The task is important and should not be underestimated. It consists of bringing the lecturer closer to the audience, establishing a general atmosphere of sympathy, and creating a link between the audience and the speaker. You have to manage to sell the subject and the speaker to the public in a minimum of time, without stealing the spotlight from the guest.

To achieve this, the best presentation will be the shortest. To be effective, it will, therefore, require careful preparation.

It is then necessary to gather useful information on the theme of the conference, to obtain references on the speaker and his skills with regard to the subject treated, and to check with the organizers of the event the interest aroused by the theme addressed.

This more personal information about the speaker can be obtained from several sources: the speaker himself, another person who knows him well, his or her superiors, colleagues, colleagues, family, or relatives. If possible, check all this information with the speaker himself before his performance.

The information gathered should be classified and presented according to three categories: the subject or title of the conference, the interest that this theme arouses for the presenter himself and for the audience, and finally the speaker, his titles, and main facts.'

The name of the speaker must be clearly and distinctly given (first and last name) as the last element before giving him or her the rostrum.

You have to arouse the interest of the audience and make them want to hear the conference. Also, adopt a dynamic, colorful, and lively style, without falling into excessive metaphor.

Be enthusiastic. Show that you are happy to introduce this guest. If possible, give your presentation in a crescendo, which will naturally bring applause from the audience when you get to the point of appointing the speaker.

Don't make "intimate" jokes; the public is not necessarily involved and may not understand. Go straight to the point and avoid verbal exaggerations like

"I have immense pleasure, great joy exceptional privilege,". These expressions are superfluous and clichés.

Always take a short break before saying the name of your speaker. This highlights it better. Make sure you pronounce his name, loud and clear.

Ask him before the meeting the exact pronunciation of his name if you are not sure. Finally, even if it is a short presentation, always have a small box or card containing the keywords for reference.

Thank a speaker

Again, the task is delicate, and all the more, so if the speaker was not very interesting and did not really raise the crowd.

Choose your words very carefully. Generally, the person succeeding the speaker or lecturer, in addition to the usual thanks, first briefly summarizes the speech by recalling the strengths and the main conclusions. Then, when possible, it seeks to bring them closer to the mission or activities of the host organization.

Finally, a bit like in an editorial note, it is desirable to project these conclusions into the future, making them stick as much as possible either to the news or to the directions chosen by the body before which the speaker is expressed.

For example, imagine a speaker who came to speak to the local chamber of commerce about the next generation of businesses and the rising labor force.

At the time of thanking him, in addition to the words of use, it will initially be easy to summarize the main conclusions of the speaker.

It will then be necessary to recall to what extent the Chamber of Commerce is concerned about the future development of a qualified and competent workforce.

Finally, we will conclude by wishing for example, that the government which is responsible for vocational training put in place the mechanisms to adequately train the workforce in collaboration with business people. To listen to their needs and expectations.

Give a prize or an award

This is a happy and solemn event. This general framework must guide us in the tone to be adopted and in the manner of acting.

Generally, in such a circumstance, you must first explain in simple words the nature of the award or prize awarded. It is then necessary to linger on the recipient by presenting his life and his work, by specifying how much the reward or the price is deserved and as all rejoice.

Finally, we must congratulate the person so honored by offering them all the best wishes for the future.

Putting too much on the risk of being perceived as satirical or, at the very least, will diminish the solemn and distinctive character that you wish to give to the event.

Accept a prize or reward

We all have in mind these award ceremonies, like "Oscars evening," where the thanks are sometimes endless, the words out of context and the general bill of the intervention unsightly.

The most important rule for success in this area is to keep it short. Do not try to thank all those who, throughout your career, have contributed to the success for which you are honored today.

First, it would be very long. Then you would surely forget about it. Finally, after a while, nobody would listen to you.

If you want to stay efficient - the nervousness and emotion often make you forget most of what you meant - get ready. Again the same advice!

It must be done so as not to forget anything, but also so as not to mumble a shy and inaudible thank you or a commonplace too overused such as: "It's the best day of my life ..."

Also, avoid the gag of the paper roll kind that we unroll by announcing a brief message.

The thing is worn out and not so tasteful. Finally, check with the organizers the duration allocated to acknowledgments and respect it.

Start by warmly thanking the assistance. Then briefly pay tribute to your essential allies and to those who, your associates, friends, or family members, are directly responsible for your success.

Then simply say what this award means to you by showing it to the audience and what it means for the continuation of your projects or your career. Finish with a new expression of gratitude.

MANAGE THE QUESTION PERIOD

Suppose that you have just finished your presentation and that you are still under the effect of adrenaline. You are pumped up and convinced that you have conquered your audience.

Besides, thunderous applause comes to show you the appreciation of your audience. Congratulations, that's a good job done. But in many situations, your task does not end with the last sentence of your communication.

Indeed, it is more and more common to authorize a period of exchange between the participants and the presenter at the end of a presentation.

In the past, this was seen regularly during a presentation to a small group, or during a training presentation. These days, it can even be seen at the end of speeches before larger assemblies.

A multitude of circumstances can justify the use of a question period at the end of the presentation, the first being that this period is particularly conducive to repeating, by the form of questions and answers, the judicious advice you have just given.

Other situations will require this type of exchange. You may find yourself in front of a single person, a customer, for example, who wants to know more about your products and services and their added value compared to your competitor.

Or, it will be a "Headhunter" interested in figuring out why you are the best candidate. Finally, let us suggest that you have been appointed to represent your organization as a media spokesperson.

In all of these cases, you need to prepare for your question and answer session as thoroughly as for your presentation.

Don't panic about having to answer questions. There is a way to prepare for it. This method is the same, whether you are speaking to a group at a conference or answering questions from customers or media representatives.

You should prepare for these sessions with as much care and attention to detail as your speech. You owe it to yourself in the first place if you want to avoid being unseated.

First, try to anticipate any questions that may arise from your conference. Design a list of possible questions and practice answering them, focusing on the most difficult ones.

In the preparatory stage, give yourself the opportunity to do all the useful research and consult all the specialists needed to articulate your answer. This is your chance. Do not wait until you find yourself unanswered or resourceless in front of a group or a person who questions you. What a disappointment!

If you're not sure, you've covered all of the questions in your preparation, first deliver your presentation to relatives and ask them which questions prompt your text with them.

Test your answers with this control group and see if you are convincing. If you can persuade your loved ones, you have done your homework well. If you can't make it, remember the maxim: "A hundred times on the job hand over your work!"

If you intend to allow a question and answer exchange at the end of your presentation, announce it at the start of your presentation and invite people to write down their questions along the way, so you don't forget them.

When the time comes, if you are speaking to a large audience, ask those who wish to speak to stand up first, introduce yourself, and use the microphones provided.

If nobody dares to break the ice, do it yourself by indirectly advancing the first question, for example: "I am often asked."

It will break the ice. The first question is important since it often sets the tone for the whole exercise.

Make sure you accept questions from the whole audience and treat all questions on the same footing. Choose your speakers by alternating between the two sides of the room, the front center, and the back.

Listen carefully to the question, without frowning and, in general, paying attention to your body language. Start by making eye contact with the speaker, then look at the whole audience. Give yourself a chance by repeating all of the positive questions in their positive form and paraphrasing the negative ones. You don't help yourself if you repeat hostile language.

Also, allow written questions either on-site or later by mail or email, to make it easier for shy people or those who want more intimate contact. This will give them an alternative.

Have a notebook and pencil yourself to write down the questions asked, making sure you don't forget the details and avoiding the "What was the question already?"

Finally, a final notice regarding the question period. Despite all your goodwill and your desire to give the maximum to your audience by answering their questions, there are three types of questions that you should never answer: hypothetical questions, questions that are addressed to someone else (the contact person must address them directly) and questions that you do not know the answer to.

The tips starting in the "What to do" section below apply to you, of course, for those cases where you will need to participate in a question and answer session with your audience.

But let us kill several birds with one stone, and know that these big rules can also be used for questions that will arise during a private interview or if you have to react to questions from the media. We will discuss these two subjects in detail later.

Listen to know the content but also the intention

Listen carefully to the question. Make sure you understand the content, but also the intent behind it. Make sure the audience clearly hears what it is about.

This is important in order to keep the group active and the attention focused on the subject. Repeat the question as needed.

Hear the whole question before you start answering, and don't think you've figured it out after just a sentence or two. Too often, we start answering a question before its author has finished asking it.

If you answer too quickly, you may give an answer unrelated to the question or fall into the trap it may contain.

Start by thanking the speaker. Make sure you do the same for everyone who asks you questions. To do otherwise may lead some to believe that you do not find their question as interesting or important.

Post questions out of context and personal questions to the end

What to do with personal questions and questions out of context? I suggest you never answer it in front of the audience.

If this is a personal question, respond that it would be improper to discuss details that relate only to the questioner, not the entire audience. Ask them to come and meet you in private after the session, so that you have more time to give your answer.

If it is a question out of context, it is a completely different matter. You have chosen to tackle a particular subject; you have delivered an inspiring performance for your audience, do not allow anyone to come and create a diversion, and dilute your message.

Say to your interlocutor that the subject he wishes to address goes beyond the scope of the conference, that other people have questions to ask on the subject on the agenda and that if there is some time left, in the end, we'll see.

And make sure there is no time left. If the other person insists, ask them to come to join you at the front to discuss their question while the room is empty. The same rule applies to questions from journalists. I've seen so many press conferences derail literally because the spokesperson decided to take questions out of context.

You went to great lengths to tie everything up before the conference, you defended your subject with flying colors, and now in the news for the next day, there is talk of everything except the subject you have dealt with. Be aware of the trap and know how to avoid it.

Ask for clarification to lower the tension if these are trick questions

You can see it by his attitude. Your interlocutor has this mine, which betrays his intention to trap you with his question. He's gone fishing and is sure to come back with a big catch.

Besides, everyone in the room can sense it, and the tension is escalating. All eyes are on you, and everyone is holding their breath, waiting for your response. Intimidating, isn't it?

It is seriously time to be diplomatic. If the person who asked the question seeks confrontation, this should not be your case.

Remain in control of yourself and resist the temptation to return her do her homework. Instead, smile. It will relax the atmosphere. Ask for details. Say, for example, "What do you mean by that?", "Give me a concrete example,"

"Tell me what you mean by ..." or use any other similar question. Gradually, you will lower the pressure, and the audience, taking the full measure of the intention of the one who apostrophes you, will soon take your part.

You have to know how to anticipate potentially difficult questions. It is indeed very rare that they come out of nowhere, without having been able to see them coming.

One of the most telling examples of this is provided to us by ex-President Ronald Reagan at the 1984 campaign for his re-election. Reagan's performance had been very poor in the first televised debate with his opponent, Walter Mondale.

The media immediately pointed to the president's age as a likely cause of his poor performance.

In his second televised debate with Mondale, Reagan was asked if he believed his advanced age could be a serious handicap to his performance as president during a second term.

Reagan had planned the coup. His response virtually had the effect of the last nail in the coffin of Mondale and definitively removed from the debate the question of the age of the president until the elections. Reagan replied, "I do not intend to use the whole age issue in this campaign.

I will not use my opponent's youth and inexperience for political ends. Some believe that this is the reason for his re-election. This pretty much illustrates the importance of preparation.

Although you have to take the time to answer these types of questions, don't be too angry either. As soon as you feel you can move on, call the next question.

Repeat the question

Repeating the question demonstrates your understanding of its content and allows you to ensure that the same is true for the entire audience. It also gives you two benefits. First, you will have a little more time to think about the answer.

This is not negligible, especially if it is one of these questions for which you know the answer, but for which you are still wondering how to answer it.

It also gives you the opportunity to rephrase the question more favorably, perhaps leaving out an aspect or two that you don't want to answer. This stuff is very often used by experienced politicians. When you feel you have answered it, look elsewhere for another speaker.

Do not remain to stare at this interlocutor because, as long as you maintain eye contact with him, he will feel authorized to ask additional questions. Obviously, we cannot use this trick every time we are asked a question.

Ask for details

Give yourself time to think before answering the question. This will help you to formulate your answer, which is especially useful for difficult questions.

You can even take the time to think about easy questions that you know the answer to. Answering easy questions too quickly will draw the audience's attention to the questions you find difficult.

Do not hesitate to ask your contact for details. This will show him that you are really interested in his question and that you are truly seeking to understand and understand his interest.

Cross out the "no comments" from your vocabulary

Here is the dreaded question set out, which you very much wish not to see coming. This question bothers you because either you don't know the answer or you can't answer, or you know the answer but don't want to touch on certain elements.

In either case, avoid the infamous

"no comments. " This is probably the answer from your lawyer who takes your interests to heart to prevent you from committing yourself.

However, especially when it comes to public relations, this is probably the worst answer. Whether we like it or not, rightly or wrongly, this kind of response will invariably provoke a reflection of the kind "Well, he or she has something to hide ..."

And, as you surely do not want to give the impression of plotting something, it will surely be your last choice of answer. Let's see how to do it.

Either you don't know the answer.

Here is a case where the "no comments" should be avoided. Above all, do not try to invent an answer if you do not know it!

Your interlocutor or someone else in the room may know it, and you will lose your credibility by trying to invent one. Everyone will respect you and understand if you admit not knowing the answer.

You might say, "You know, this question is important, and I don't have all the information to answer it correctly. I prefer to abstain from the moment, inform myself and get back to you with a complete answer. "

Obviously, you will not be able to use this tactic for all the questions that will be asked of you, or if the question concerns a subject for which you have direct responsibility, your credibility may suffer. Be prepared so that you know your subject better than any speaker.

Either you cannot answer.

You may not be able to answer the question. Moreover, when this is the case, it is always more or less for the same reasons: it is a case concerning private interests, a case under investigation or examination, an administrative inquiry, for example, or a case currently before the courts.

Everyone will understand that you did not want to deliver confidential customer information or information that could compromise the outcome of an ongoing investigation or trial.

If you are asked such a question, simply answer that you cannot provide the information requested and explain why. No one will hold it against you.

Either you know the answer, but there are some things you don't want to answer

Since I have been doing individual coaching, particularly in terms of exchanging questions and answers with journalists, I repeat that the question asked must become the pretext for the answer you intend to give.

Besides, on this subject, I remember the following anecdote. To a deputy dissatisfied with the reply provided by a minister during a question period at the Quebec National Assembly, the latter retorted: "You may not be satisfied. But let me tell you that if you have a choice of questions, we have a choice of answers."

Just answer, staying within the parameters you set beforehand, looking directly at the person asking you. Give simple answers to simple questions.

If the exchange comes after a presentation, you have just made, whenever possible, link the question to a passage in your communication. In fact, use these questions as an excuse to repeat your message, clarify and reinforce your point.

Even go back to your electronic acetates if you can link them to the answer you are working on. This will make your presentation even more credible.

Give a certain rhythm to the question period. Speak briefly and get straight to the point. Do not lie unnecessarily, and when you gave the items, you selected and decided to unveil, go to another question or Shut up and wait for the next.

Stay friendly, and stay calm if you are provoked. Respond as if the aggressor is a friend. Any attempt on your part to crush him with sarcasm will make you lose the sympathy of the public, who will then be directed towards the scoffed.

Do not place your hands or fists on your hips, and do not point your finger. This will weaken your position and make you appear belligerent or defensive.

Tell the truth, but not necessarily the whole truth. If you lie, you will almost invariably be exposed. Play fair, even if your position may seem uncomfortable at the time. At the end of your answer, summarize the elements of the message that you want to highlight. End the exercise on this note as this will be the last data that your audience members will leave with.

What you should not do

Don't show that you find the question stupid

Your audience will immediately give you some sympathy capital at the start of your presentation.

This capital will grow or, on the contrary, will melt during the presentation, according to your words. Obviously, you cannot please everyone.

But one sure way to make opponents is to get impatient with someone asking a question, or worse, to let them see that you find their question stupid.

Okay, you may have answered this question already during the presentation. This can be annoying for you.

Do not show your impatience by daring to finish the speaker's sentences. You are going to upset everyone. Be accommodating; it may be that the person was distracted during this passage. No doubt, other people were too and would love to hear your argument again.

For them, this question is not stupid. Keep calm, stay receptive, don't be afraid to repeat your explanation. Rather, take this opportunity to repeat your message. As we said, you have to repeat your messages continuously if you want them to be understood.

Do not answer two questions at the same time

It may be that the question posed calls for two distinct realities or that it consists of two or more components. Treat these as if they were, in fact, so many separate questions and tell your audience that this is what you are going to do. You will gain clarity and avoid any confusion.

Don't be fleeing

Some will have the reflex of being shifty when the questions become more delicate or even hostile. It is a normal reflex, which must be resisted. Your talent in resisting verbal attacks will strengthen your credibility and enhance public opinion about you.

Do not try to censor hostile interlocutors or limit their right to expression. Accept all the questions. In cases of hostility, let people empty their bags. As they let off steam, listen.

Then repeat the question without contempt or condescension, highlighting the main points without animosity. If you are unsure or if it is not clear, ask for clarification to understand the problem. Then say something like, "I understand what your problems are; now let me answer" Or again: "Let's work together to find a solution."

By doing so, you will demonstrate that you are paying attention to the feelings and words of the person (s) questioning you.

The audience will respect you for doing this, and, at the same time, you will manage to mitigate the expressions of hostility from your interlocutor, which makes everyone uncomfortable.

Don't answer without answering

This is what some call responses from politicians. Remember that all members of your audience, with some exceptions, are, as they say, "in the right bear average" and that they will see you coming.

Do not try to dodge yourself in empty words. If you don't want to answer, say so, and say why. You will gain credibility. Finally, don't say something like, "This is a great question!"

Twice rather than once, you will react to an unexpected question in this way, and answering it will draw the public's attention to your surprise, or even your discomfort with the question.

On the other hand, it is almost to insult the questions which preceded it. If you say that this question is good or interesting, does that mean that the previous ones weren't?

The adversarial debate

Obviously, the question period should not become cross-examination or, worse, debate. But it can, however, happen (politics is a breeding ground for this kind of situation) that you are invited to participate in a real contradictory debate. You will hardly be able to escape

it because according to a study carried out in 2002 on behalf of the University of Maryland, it has been shown that more than 55% of the people consulted would refuse to vote for a person who is running for elected office and who would have refused to participate in a debate with his opponent (s).

If so, be aware that very specific rules apply to such debates.

A debate is a discussion that aims to be constructive on a specific or substantive subject, announced in advance, in which individuals with differing opinions, ideas, reflections, or opinions on the subject take part.

The debate is, therefore, in essence, contradictory. A debate can take many forms, the most common being the meeting in one place of people called to confront their ideas.

It is important to understand that debate is the contradictory examination of a proposition that is either true or false. It is through debate that one can determine whether the proposition is true or false because, from a contradictory examination, the truth can come out.

However, for its part, the adversarial debate is most often exercised with two proposals, which are presented as the opposite. The objective of adversarial debate, especially between two or more defenders of opposing theses, is to succeed in triumphing "his" truth to the detriment of that of the other.

By preparing for it, you will, therefore, try to score a point by presenting your position; you will try to anticipate your opponent's reply on the question and, above all, to prepare a counter-offensive to respond to your opponent in order to make it credible again — your position.

A strategy often used by participants in adversarial debates is to manage to destabilize the opponent and make it look bad.

In other words, even if your argument is weaker, you can still "win the debate" because your opponent will appear to have been caught out. Because here is a great truth: in adversarial debates, even if we attach great importance to the content, it is often much more the container that will build the right impression.

Indeed, people rarely remember what we said in such circumstances, but will long remember the convinced, determined, competent allure that we had during the debate.

Obviously, this does not mean that the content should be neglected because one should not give the image of an empty soundbox. In addition, it is certain that experienced analysts will be happy the next day to demolish baseless positions.

However, the content is not everything and the way of being in the debates, the general impression that we will leave, is at least as important.

The debate of the chiefs during the electoral campaign can become one of the decisive moments for the fate of the participant in the debate who risks losing everything on this one deal and often, for questions of form.

As proof, what analysts, commentators, and political journalists describe as the very first debate, that between John F. Kennedy and Richard Nixon in 1960.

Richard Nixon, although competent and well-documented, had appeared badly in a debate. He looked tense, aggressive, and offered a general image that the electorate did not like.

The outcome of the poll confirmed this. John Kennedy, on the contrary, appeared confident, smiling, relaxed, and had performed much better than Nixon even if he was a neophyte in politics compared to the old truck driver.

In 1960, we were only in the infancy of mass television, and the politicians of the day were more used to the radio. You have to understand that the technique of expression is totally different on television, where we are seen as well as heard.

Spectators may be more educated, but political life today is much more complex than before. To form an opinion, people use very simple elements and easily stay in the emotional relationship with the politician. The non-verbal takes on all its importance here.

Recall that non-verbal communication is said to be based on the implicit understanding of signs not expressed by a language, such as gestures, colors, even clothes, or smells.

These signs and their understanding or interpretation are overwhelmingly culturally dependent. I refer you to the previous section of this book, where we deal with this issue explicitly.

If it is necessary to hold the comparison with a boxing match, the victories on points during the debates are more numerous than the k.-o.

Indeed, a decisive carpet rarely happens. On the other hand, what the public remembers is a host of little things that comfort them in their choice. And for politicians, it's important to know that again in this arena does not automatically translate into electoral gain.

If the debates seldom give a clear and clear victory to a chief, they are, however, always determining for the continuation of the things.

Finally, let us remember that it is imperative to score points at the start of the debate because, in an average television debate, half of the viewers disappeared after 45 minutes.

To be ready

That doesn't mean that the content doesn't matter. Here we are again: the famous preparation. In fact, if you really want to perform in an adversarial debate, you will need to own your content to the point that you will seem to improvise.

Spare nothing to go around the question. Do your research and carefully prepare the various elements that will support the presentation of your point of view.

Also, find the arguments that your opponent will want to use to defend the opposite thesis or his own.

See ahead of time how you might default him because of his earlier positions on the issue, or imagine the arguments he will want to invoke against your position. In short, prepare yourself.

Especially the introduction and the conclusion, where you will have all the space you need to show off.

Finally, be sure to model these interventions to suit the audiences you will be standing in front of.

But first, try to determine in advance what you want to do with the debate. Is it to consolidate your position, make your message better heard, or even to discredit your opponent?

Ask yourself what the strategic contribution of the debate in advancing your position or what you want people to take away from it, even before you start preparing for the themes of the debate is. Clearly, what is the title you would like to see in the newspaper the day after your debate if it were to be the subject of an article?

Know before you even begin to prepare for it what you want the debate to bring you in terms of strategic positioning. The rest will follow.

The general framework of the adversarial debate

Having become the focal point of electoral campaigns, the contradictory debate is not reserved only for political leaders.

You participate in a panel of experts within the framework of a conference or congress, you contribute to an exchange between several participants within the framework of a radio or television program, you agree to act as a resource person during an information activity, and you must defend your position against a hostile room.

In fact, all these situations and many others can lead to you in an adversarial debate.

The first action to take when we are invited to take part in an adversarial debate is to define the general framework in which the event will take place as well as the rules of debate, which will have to be respected.

Defining this framework is fundamental if you do not want this exercise, which you consider as an exchange of ideas and points of view, to turn into a rat race.

Everyone stands to lose from such an experience and, above all, our listeners or potential voters, whether live, on radio or television.

COMMUNICATE WITH A CONTACT PERSON

The interview

The human being is a social being. And since we are rarely really alone, since we are almost always in contact with someone else, every day of our lives, we must succeed in our interviews.

Some of us have even made it a profession. The job of any representative of an organization, for example, is precisely to conduct personal or telephone interviews.

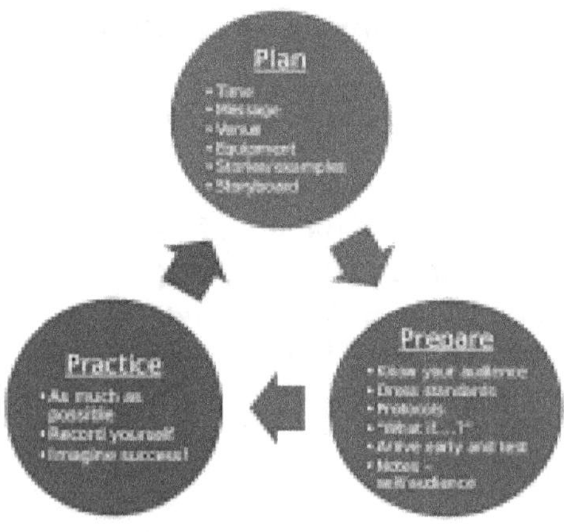

There is a distinction to be made between simple gossip and maintenance. The first is a friendly exchange between two people, often without great consequences.

Conversation, on the contrary, is an exercise that must be planned and organized, and which must aim at a very precise objective.

Whether it is a discussion, an interrogation, an interview, a debate, or a confession, each interview is unique.

In fact, each brings together two unique individuals who, together, interact, will have a relationship with no other comparable.

Of course, with experience, a good salesperson will tell you without much thought that there is nothing more like a sales presentation than any other sales presentation.

It's a bit true, but it's also a bit short. Because, if the beginning is often the same, the way in which the interview will evolve and conclude will be different from one occasion to another.

The interview allows the exchange of information. To maximize it, it must be carried out properly, and action is taken to encourage communication. An interview is not a monologue.

We usually approach an interview with simplicity without thinking too much. This is to ignore the fact that, in order to fully succeed in your interview, you must prepare yourself adequately.

During the interview, it will be necessary to establish contact, generate a climate favorable to exchanges, let the other speak, help him if necessary to progress by reformulating his words, resolve conflicts that may arise, and, finally, conclude.

In fact, almost the entire success of the interview rests on your communicator's shoulders.

In order to properly prepare for any maintenance, you must define the common thread. The latter must be concrete, precise, logical, and consistent.

What is the real purpose of the interview? What are the objectives, proven or not, pursued? Is this a selection interview? Should we welcome someone?

Is the interview intended to resolve a problem? Is it a matter of making a decision, assessing a file, a situation?

Is it a negotiation or sales meeting, or is it about gathering information? Obviously, our preparation will be different depending on the purpose of the interview.

Then you have to get information about our contact. A bit like preparing a speech before an audience, you have to know who we are talking to.

What's her name? His age? His homegroup? His nationality (this can indeed be of great importance due to cultural differences)? Is it your employer or your employee? Your advisor or your client?

What is his level of education? Does he know the subject on the agenda? What are his interests, needs, expectations? It is essential to know the answer to all of these questions before you go ahead.

Finally, it is important to understand the context in which the interview will take place. Will it take place in an official setting, such as a selection interview?

Or will it take place head-to-head over a cup of coffee? Will it happen in a public place? Will you be sitting or standing? Will you be face to face or on the phone? Obviously, the tone, the pace, and the form of the interview will change depending on the context.

"J" has arrived. Our speaker is in front of us, and we must now establish contact, that is to say, create a bond of complicity, collusion with this interlocutor.

Remember that the unspoken or not will work in our favor. I remind you that it accounts for 93% of communication. It's huge.

We need less than 10 seconds to get an idea of our opposite. The rest of the time spent together will be used to confirm or refute this first impression.

To project a good image, therefore, have at heart to respect the following essentials: stay in control; wear clean and appropriate clothing; take care of her hair; have good posture; occupy space; establish and maintain good eye contact.

We discussed these issues in Chapter 8. The advice and guidelines already given on appearance are appropriate in all interview situations.

Now let's give us some tools to help us get a handle on this unspoken reality and see how we can do it to maximize the impact of our interviews.

The look

Look, as we have seen, is one of the best communication tools we have. We all like a frank, direct, honest look. Supported but not rude. On the contrary, a fleeting glance, from below, inquisitive, displease everyone.

Smile

From our earliest childhood, we smile. And we are smiled for our greatest happiness. Smile is one of the first forms of communication we practice.

The smile reassures. The smile invites confidence. It helps to establish contact, even a bond between two people.

An overly persistent smile may seem forced, artificial, but, at the right time, a frank, loyal smile can only help to establish friendly and cordial contact.

A warm voice

After the eyes, the voice is probably the next communication tool you will use. We all feel good with someone who speaks to us in a warm, enveloping voice. This also invites confidence.

Practice placing your voice so that it becomes warm and cordial. The tips and advice discussed in Chapter 7 in this regard are still current. Record yourself on an audio cassette. Listen to yourself and correct what annoys you.

During the interview, study the voice of your interlocutor. Is she calm and calm?

On the contrary, is it an aggressive or disturbing voice? These are all hints that will tell you what to do to continue the interview.

The famous handshake

During a meeting between two people, the handshake was one of the first messages sent to our interlocutor. Too soft, it indicates weakness or lack of interest. With your fingertips, it says, "I don't want to be involved in your business." Too rigid, it betrays aggressiveness and impatience.

For a good handshake, you have to extend your whole hand, make contact with the other hand between your thumb and forefinger, tighten firmly but not excessively, and release without haste. Such a handshake demonstrates competence and authority.

Tame the other

I know there are people who are quick and direct and who get straight to the point. It's a style. Be aware of yours.

Are you direct in your approach, or do you like to take detours? And your interlocutor? Does he use the direct or indirect style in his communications?

Adapt your style to him. For my part, I believe that you must first establish a cordial relationship by taming the other. In the preliminaries, look for points in common with your interlocutor.

Seek to build on what brings you closer. Talk about children, sports, weather, familiar things. Yes, make the other speakers and know how to find points of convergence.

Locate the other

The above is essential since the next step, to succeed in an interview, is to locate the other, define him, determine his needs, his motivations, his situation.

How do you get there if that person hasn't said a word about themselves or, worse if you haven't really listened? The attention paid to finding information during the preparation for the interview may not have revealed everything to you.

The data we now have is vital because it will guide our message and, most importantly, how to codify it.

Remember that to reach its target, and our subject must have been coded so as to correspond to the decoding grid of our interlocutor (s). The first phase of our interview will, therefore, be particularly conducive to gathering useful clues for this purpose.

Practice dynamic listening

You have to listen to the other. It seems obvious, yet that is not always what we do.

Research at the University of Minnesota has shown how bad listeners are. In fact, without training, we only retain 25% of what the other says at the end of the exchange. Forget the rest!

How many times have you participated in an interview where you had trouble waiting for the other to finish before going from your dispatch?

Very often, no doubt. And yet, the most successful interview will be one where your interviewee will really have the impression of having been listened to, heard, and understood.

In such circumstances, if you have set your interview goal well and let the other speak fully, you have no doubt reached the target.

"If we have two ears and one mouth, then we have to learn to listen twice as much as we speak," said an old sage. Nothing is truer because, to communicate well, you must know how to listen to the other.

After putting him at ease, let him speak. Pay attention and show that you really want to listen, know, and understand.

Be empathetic, trying to put yourself in the other person's shoes, and avoid distractions. The interview provides a golden opportunity to practice what is called "dynamic listening" or "active listening."

Thanks to this approach, you will feed yourself from the words of your interlocutor to continue the discussion further. Pay attention to his style. How is it expressed?

What vocabulary does he use? What are its keywords? Are there expressions that come up often? Make an effort to understand their point of view. Be patient, and stay calm.

Make sure the other party does not feel rushed or, more importantly, does not feel rushed themselves. Do not make unnecessary criticisms, which will provoke a defense reaction in your interlocutor.

Ask questions, and try to understand. If necessary, rephrase what the other person has to say, the facts they are stating, their opinions, their feelings, and summarize what has just been said at each stage of the conversation.

Thus, your interlocutor will really have the impression of having been understood.

Avoid closed questions that attract only "yes" or "no." Ask only one question at a time and keep it short. Choose your vocabulary, do not provide the answer in the question, and ask questions that are linked to allow your interlocutor to find himself in his words.

Finally, let me slip a word to you about the silence. Although it is feared by many, silence is conducive to reflection. It also allows the other to gather his ideas if he hesitates to tackle the proposed subject.

Resuming the discussion too hastily can forever deprive you of this part of its history. Silence can finally indicate to the other that it is desirable to elaborate a little more on his last intervention.

Do not doubt it, if you leave the space of expression to your interlocutor, he will use it, and you will be able by listening to him to better understand his needs.

Use the language of the other

Thus informed by the words of the interlocutor, adapt your level of language to his. Take his keywords and try to integrate them into your own speech.

Analyze the results thus obtained and adapt your speech again if necessary. In this way, your contact will be sure to be greeted by someone who understands them and speaks the same language.

Be clear

Clarity is an efficiency factor. When speaking during the interview, try to be precise in the chosen vocabulary so that there is no ambiguity. Use short, clear, and explicit sentences. Use appropriate examples to make sure you are understood. Tell anecdotes.

Persuasion is important since it involves a decision to act, and it is, more often than not, the objective pursued by an interview. But now, we can persuade only on the condition of having been credible, coherent, consistent, and congruent.

Resolve conflicts

To obtain the maximum impact during the interview, you must ensure that no disagreement disturbs the favorable climate that you wish to create.

Along the way, be sure to identify the subject of any potential disagreement quickly. Are these the facts mentioned? Goals pursued by the exercise? Methods used?

Or even moral values likely to clash? Once you have identified the source of latent or emerging conflict, you should try to resolve it and clarify the situation, in order to give free rein to the real purpose of your meeting.

In this regard, see the "Conflict Management" section later in this chapter.

Conclude the interview constructively

Avoid hasty conclusions. A good interview is concluded when the people present have expressed everything they had to say and leave with the pleasant impression of having been understood by the other.

If this is not the case, it may be that your interview is not really finished. Take your time. Perhaps also you are unable, despite all your preparation and your goodwill, to create a favorable atmosphere for exchanges, to establish the necessary contact to achieve the goal.

In this case, do not be relentless. It's just not the right time or the right person.

At the end of the interview, summarize the main elements discussed and take stock of the results obtained.

If necessary, if one or the other person thinks that all has not been said, exchange additional information to answer the outstanding questions. If there is a follow-up, agree on the measures to be taken, the follow-up to be done.

In closing, here are a few tricks of the trade. Always stay in control of yourself. Control your emotions because they are a major obstacle to effective listening. Always make sure you stay on course before the match.

On the other hand, know what you want and make it clear. There should be no ambiguity in your words if you want your interlocutor to leave with the right message. Finally, watch out for chain reactions.

Avoid making comments which would have the effect of provoking a chain of divided actions triggered by the desire to defend oneself or to justify oneself. This would poison your upkeep and divert you from your run.

At the end of the meeting, shake hands with your interlocutor (s) and thank them, if applicable, for the welcome given.

Always have up-to-date copies of your business card. Present it at the start of the meeting, if it has not already been slipped into the presentation folder, if applicable.

Have your notes in order and your calendar with you to record the date of the next meeting, if applicable.

The selection interview

One of the best-known forms of interviewing is the selection interview. I do not pretend to replace, by a brief section on the question, the teaching that specialized firms can give you in this regard.

They have professional methods and resources that can provide you with appropriate support to help you behave well in a selection interview. Do not hesitate to seek this professional support; such an investment can bring you large.

There are also excellent reference works on this issue, and I mention a few in the bibliography at the end of this book.

However, I want to talk about the selection interview from the point of view of interpersonal communications.

In the context of the selection interview, the relationship between the two interlocutors is usually characterized by the high pressure placed on the candidate by his position of inferiority compared to the selector.

As for the latter, he must cross the jungle of voluntary or involuntary distortions introduced by the candidate, to discover his motivations and aptitudes, if any, to exercise the functions of the position offered.

In addition to the classic punctuality, straight but relaxed posture, appropriate dress, and firm handshake, there are some tips to help you get over the "test" with greater ease.

Again, you have to be ready and, as you know now, to be ready, you have to prepare.

Remember that the selection process begins upon receipt of your resume. It is from its content that we will want to meet you or not.

The recruiters will have read it, even studied it, and will have drawn questions from it to ask you. My first advice is, therefore, to invite you to memorize your curriculum vitae. Don't make a mistake, like many, of forgetting the details of your CV. Read it well before your interview.

Also, take the time to find out about the company whose job offer interests you. Try to imagine the questions you might be asked and try to answer them.

If the company is young and dynamic in its industry, there is a good chance that it is looking for a results-oriented person recognized for delivering the goods.

If, on the contrary, it is a very structured firm, working in a more conservative sector and having highly hierarchical management, it will probably be looking for a candidate who knows how to work in a team and operate in the respect for the established order.

Know how to present yourself accordingly. But, beyond the company, you will first have to please the person who receives you in a selection interview.

The latter will decide whether you should have access to the next step in the selection process. Pay attention to this person. He is not a robot, but a human being, with his prejudices, his opinions, and his feelings.

Arrange very quickly, at the start of the interview, to find at least one point in common with your interviewer, if only your opinion on a television program broadcast the day before.

Be warm to him. Show that you are paying attention. The more you are on the same wavelength as the coach, the more the latter will feel that you have the qualities required to fill the position. By talking to him, accentuate your positive sides and minimize your negative sides.

You must know yourself well when you are received in a selection interview. You have to know your qualities as much as your faults and not be afraid to answer questions about them.

Recognizing your shortcomings and saying what you have done to improve yourself will be to your credit. This question almost invariably comes up in selection interviews.

You may also be asked what you think are the skills useful for this position. We will, therefore, want to test your knowledge of the prior qualifications for this job. You may also be asked to describe the ideal pattern.

This will allow us to judge your expectations with regard to a superior and, above all, assess your compatibility with the already existing superior that the assessor knows.

If you're asked to describe your best friend, you want to know the profile of the people you love. If you are asked about the kind of employee you are, it is because you want to know how well you know yourself and the values that inspire you.

Other questions may come. Among other things, you may be asked about the reasons why you left your previous job or what you expect to find more in this new organization where you are applying.

You might want to know how you see the future of the organization you are looking for to work. You may still be asked to describe your leadership style, your greatest accomplishment, or your worst failure.

Take the time to think about the answers to give on these questions, because they will surely come. Anticipate brief, precise, and direct answers.

Stay open and attentive to the other person being interviewed, so as to provide them with the most favorable answers to your application. Again, practice dynamic listening.

Leave room for the interviewer. On the other hand, nothing prevents you from asking questions at the end, from obtaining details on the activities of the company, on the task which would be entrusted to you or on your new place of work.

These questions are very important because they inform the recruiter of your deep interests in the position. Again, take the time to prepare for these questions.

If this is your first interview, this is a bad opportunity to address the issue of salary. Wait. This will come during a subsequent interview, if applicable. Stay natural, look the recruiter in the eye and provide simple, concise answers to their questions.

It would be inappropriate to try to take control of the interview or, at this stage, to speak about your previous boss, especially in unfavorable terms, unless you have a direct question on this subject.

In conclusion, we must be aware of the resonance effect, that is to say, the effect produced by our words and our attitude on the coach.

During the interview, know how to recognize what is significant for your interlocutor and try to meet their expectations. Obviously, to achieve this, you must know how to observe yourself and control yourself.

Observe the evolution of the maintenance situation itself and, when appropriate, make the necessary corrections in case of deviation from the trajectory.

SUCCESSFUL NEGOTIATION

In our daily life, there are lots of situations where we have to negotiate. Negotiate with children to do their homework. Negotiate with our teenager the use of the family car during the weekends.

Negotiate a movie or theater outing with our spouse. Negotiate a salary increase with our boss. In fact, everything is subject to negotiation. In all cases, negotiation is first and foremost a communication exercise because it involves exchanges between two or more parties.

Good news: you can negotiate everything. You just need to have a little method and avoid the pitfalls that will inevitably arise in your path.

Of course, as a negotiator, everyone has their own style. Some will want to win at all costs: their approach is based on an extreme initial position, on the use of emotional tactics, on minor concessions on their part while they try to ridicule yours and assimilate them to brands of weakness.

In contrast, others will seek to negotiate so that both parties find mutual satisfaction.

Their method is based on the need to build a relationship of trust, characterized by a concern for resolving conflicts using an approach that seeks to harmonize or reconcile positions and needs.

Without making a value judgment on either of them, it seems to me that the second approach is more promising. It will always be easier.

Communicate with a contact person to adopt a solution in which we are winners, and we will always be quicker to reject an imposed position.

The three essentials of any negotiation

In any negotiation, there are three essentials: the balance of power, the time, and the level of information.

First and foremost, the establishment of the balance of power is essential to our negotiating position. Several elements can strengthen it. For example, the legitimacy that gives us all the authority we need to establish our position.

In the same way, there are elements such as morality, precedent, perseverance, the power of persuasion. Any negotiation involves a risk. Accepting this risk also strengthens our position, as does a knowledge of the other's real needs.

Time is the second most important factor because negotiation is not an event that occurs at a given time, but a process that spans a certain period of time.

In a negotiation, there is no hurry until the last minute. So avoid hasty concessions. Never reveal your date or your deadline and vice versa, try to guess those of your opponent because, whatever he says, he always has them.

Act quickly in the negotiation process only if it is to your advantage.

Information, finally, is the last element of our equation. It is essential to get as much information as possible about our "adversary" before even starting the process because its appearance and course depend on it.

In addition to the prior information you will have, several others will be added along the way, namely, unintentional information provided by slip-ups, non-verbal language, behavior, intonation, and tone. These are all elements you can use to supplement your situational awareness.

The negotiation technique

To succeed in your negotiation, focus on the substantive interests and not on the respective positions. Ignore personal considerations and focus on the goal of negotiation, which you must necessarily have established, even before the process begins.

Imagine solutions that are beneficial for all parties involved and choose solutions based on objective, verifiable criteria. To help you in your approach, choose the time and the field. Have a tactic prepared in advance that will allow you to suspend the negotiation process, if necessary. You will have the possibility to catch your breath during the course or to check new elements. Prepare meticulously, do I need to add it, and be the author of the final document. It is important, in fact, to be proactive in negotiations and to keep the initiative. Finally, here is a word on negotiation by telephone: choose this solution only in the event of last resort. Since you do not have visual feedback from your interlocutor, the risk of disagreement is increased.

Indeed, on the phone, you are depriving yourself of a host of information that the other's non-verbal language transmits to you. On the other hand, on the phone, it's much easier to say no than when the person is in front of us. Telephone negotiation is generally faster but gives us less time to share information and experience. The process is, therefore, more competitive, and, in any case, the advantage is always the caller.

He will indeed have taken the time to make up his mind, to gather his ideas before calling when we, preoccupied with something else, need some time to feel really "in the game."

COMMUNICATE IN BUSINESS

There is one area where communications are vital; it is the world of work, a world that is essentially based on contact with others. In an organization, internal communications are of primary importance.

As proof of this story, a man enters the shower at the precise moment when his wife leaves. It's also when the doorbell rings. The woman wraps herself in a towel, runs down the stairs and goes to open the front door where she discovers

John, the next-door neighbor.

Before she can say a word, John says, "I'll give you $800 immediately if you drop your towel." The woman thinks quickly and decides to drop the towel. He admires her at leisure, then hands him the promised $800.

A little dazed, but happy with the small fortune she has just reaped in the blink of an eye, she goes back upstairs. Her husband, still in the shower, asked who was at the door. "It was John," she replies. "Great," says her husband. Did he give you back the $800 he owed me? "

Applied to the field of communication, the moral of this story is as follows: if you work in a team, quickly share information concerning common files, you will thus be able to avoid bad publicity or misunderstandings.

In this chapter, we will focus on three particular situations that are constantly repeated in the world of work.

The first relates to the many meetings which often "clog up" our agenda and which must be optimized. The second theme will focus on the use of the telephone.

While the maintenance tips discussed above are helpful, the conversations telephone follow specific rules, especially if you use the telephone to support you in your sales process. This is what we are going to see together.

The third part of this chapter will deal with customer relations. Establishing contact, creating a feeling of trust, knowing how to listen, and responding precisely to the needs and expectations of your client are all extremely important actions that you must be able to carry out.

In addition, learning to recognize and deal with the various categories of customers, especially the difficult ones, can make the difference between success and failure. We will approach these subjects in mind the concern to equip you for success.

Effective meetings

"Oh, no! Not a meeting yet! "It may be the exclamation that will come to your lips as you read the advice just passed on by your supervisor.

Employees of organizations often suffer from what is known as acute "re-unionism." This evil occurs when meetings become too frequent without giving participants time to recharge their batteries between two meetings.

It is important that people are able to make new and meaningful contributions from one meeting to the next, failing which these quickly become unproductive.

And yet, any meeting should be an exceptional opportunity to communicate ideas, recharge your batteries, share your skills, learn more, and take part in a collective work that can go a long way.

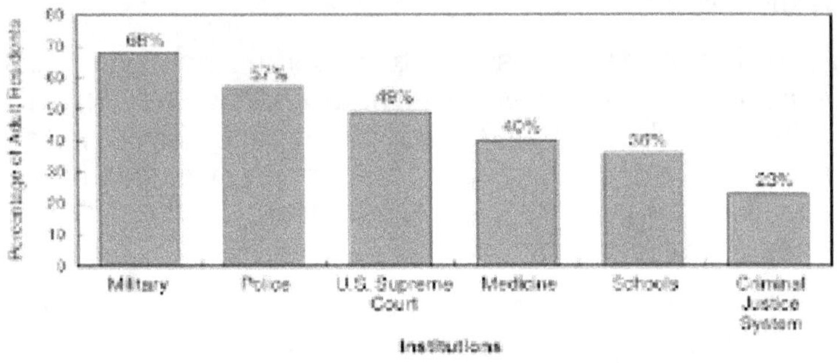

To be effective, meetings should be held as a last resort, when they have become unavoidable when all other means of information exchange have been exhausted.

In addition, organizations should quantify the cost of holding their meetings both directly (rental of the room, equipment, administrative support required) and indirect (the time of participants to attend the meeting, but also to prepare it) and only call them when it is possible to recoup the investment.

After such an exercise, firms, among the most, have reduced the number of their meetings from 25 to 50%. They don't get any worse.

Material organization

There are two types of meetings: those that take place in the conference room of your company or department, and those larger that will last one, two, or even three days, and that will take place outside the office to allow optimal participation by everyone.

In either case, the coordination and organization of this type of meeting must be carefully thought out. After having clearly stated the objective of the meeting, it will be necessary to establish the list of guests, invite them and, if necessary, make special arrangements for their transportation.

It will still be necessary to reserve the room (s), especially if the meeting is held outside, and in this case, a block of rooms for the participants, either in the hotel where the meeting will take place (which is nice - easier shot for everyone), either nearby if the meeting does not take place in a hotel.

Avoid overly large meeting rooms. We are lost, and they do not allow such a rich exchange between the participants. The distance is far away, isn't it?

Arrangements to ensure the logistics of meals, breaks, and any other activity likely to take place on the outskirts of the meeting must be made.

In addition, if the meeting must last more than one day, plan at least one activity outside the selected establishment. This will considerably enrich your program and encourage exchanges outside the formal framework of your meeting.

In parallel, it will be necessary to determine the agenda, make the necessary arrangements with the guest speakers (if applicable), establish a general program by timing each section and prepare the logistics of the reception.

Finally, it may be appropriate to prepare a participant's guide or, at the very least, to think about gathering the supporting information required for the smooth running of the discussions.

The role of the president or the facilitator

The meeting chairperson or the facilitator will have a central role to play. He is the guardian of the agenda, which will ideally have been distributed to participants at least 24 hours in advance and which will be the same for everyone. In this way, everyone can prepare their contribution to the meeting in advance and contribute to its success through thoughtful interventions.

It can be difficult to have a meaningful and constructive discussion when more than 12 people participate in the exchange.

If the group should be larger, divide it as many times as necessary, and appoint a leader for each subgroup. This nominee will also act as a spokesperson during the plenary.

Establish a precise discussion schedule, allocating a certain number of minutes to each portion of the agenda.

Whether it is a workshop, a sub-group, or the assembly, the role of the facilitator, the moderator, or the president is always to facilitate exchanges between the participants within the framework planned.

The purpose of the meeting must be clearly stated at the start of the meeting, as well as the procedure and rules to be observed.

The moderator will make it a point to present the operating ethics because non-compliance with such rules necessarily leads to unproductive and, therefore, unnecessary meetings. When everyone has understood their role and the course of the meeting, the facilitator's task is to encourage the expression of words and the emergence of ideas of each participant.

If the president must make sure to neutralize those who monopolize the exchanges and see, on the contrary, that the timid take their place and speak, he must also invite the participants to really listen to the words of their colleagues and to take into account in their own interventions.

In addition, the moderator is not there to impose his point of view but to seek the points of convergence and divergence, which must be clearly summarized at the end of each stage of the discussion.

It is, therefore, essential to be able to count on a secretary of assembly because it is very difficult to animate and note at the same time the results of the discussions.

The role of the participants

The chairman of the assembly alone cannot ensure the success of the meeting. Participants also have a leading role to play: they must speak and listen.

Speaking, each intervention should be as brief as possible. However, participants should be able to speak freely since all discussion is based on the exchange of ideas.

The richer and hindered the exchange, the more productive it is. Each participant has their own personality and background. Within the group, he is responsible for making his contribution.

During the discussion, the ideas exchanged are all interconnected and, as the proverb says, "you have to beat the iron when it is hot." When a topic is discussed, it should be cleared before moving on, even if it means a slight twist on the agenda.

On the other hand, you have to make sure that the discussion remains pleasant for all participants, even in the heat of the moment. Your point of view is important but not more than that of your colleague, whatever your opinion on it.

We must speak, but we must also listen. Everyone must feel that their right to speak is respected. No one should be subjected to ridicule, sarcasm, or the abuse of power. Act towards others as you would like them to act towards yourself. Courtesy and tolerance in the reserve of judgment are therefore required.

Telephone contact

Direct contact and personal contact are generally preferred to telephone contact, but the flexibility of the telephone allows for an often more productive schedule. Many people have died of stage fright at the idea of making contact through the telephone.

And yourself? Maybe you find it difficult to hold such an interview? Particularly when, because of your job or your duties, you have to do what is called in the profession of

"Cold calls," cold calls to strangers.

Are you a sales representative for your company, do telephone surveys, are you a recruiter for an organization or are you participating in a fundraising campaign? In all these cases, you are in the category of people who have to make cold calls and who generally do not like that.

But the phone is a dragon you can tame. If phone calls, especially those famous cold calls, cause you problems, it's usually because:

you are ill-prepared;

you tend to procrastinate or are a little lazy;

you are afraid of rejection, afraid of being told "no";

you do not have adequate training to succeed in your telephone contact.

Let's start with the fear of rejection because this is the most important. With adequate psychological preparation, it is possible to get rid of it.

At the outset, be aware of the following fact: you may get ten "no" before you get one "yes." Never mind! It's a sales process, not a heart surgery that has to work every time. And above all, do not feel taken personally: if your interlocutor answers "no," do not be offended.

It is not your person who is thus "attacked," but what you do, what you say, or what you represent. On the contrary, consider this refusal as a challenge and try to improve the average. And then, tell yourself that with each "no," you get closer to a "yes."

One of my good friends, a sales representative for a large organization, literally hates cold calls. Also, since he has to do his job well, he has developed some tricks. In particular, he always manages to work in a "hot" market, already prepared to receive it.

How does he do it? In two ways: either, it communicates beforehand with someone else who knows either the person or company they wish to approach, in order to obtain the maximum amount of useful information about them, or else they send them information in advance by fax, mail or email.

So he never makes a totally cold call. You, too, if you want to avoid cold calling, find ways to set the stage.

Finally, if you need to leave a message, here are some observations that may help you. Slow down your speed and clearly state your name, that of your company, the reason for your call, and your contact details.

Specify in your message when you can be called back to be sure to join you. Make sure you always make a professional impression by avoiding chewing gum or leaving a message that is too long.

On the other hand, record your own greeting message in your voice mailbox. To that end, here are some rules to follow. First, write your message before saving it. Among other things, make sure that the instructions for leaving the message are clear.

If you are in business, your welcome message offers you a great opportunity to sell your products or services.

Use it! By writing your screed, you will have the assurance of not forgetting anything important, and this will serve as a reminder when recording.

Practice aloud several times before recording it. Smile and speak in a friendly voice to create a friendly welcome. Finally, the little musical plot is usually in bad taste and frankly useless.

A few tips

As long as you put the following tips into practice in your phone procedures, you will quickly gain efficiency and relevance. Here they are in bulk: you must first get the attention of your contact, then introduce yourself, state the reason for your call, ask questions to obtain useful information, and finally if necessary book an appointment.

Respect this process; it will quickly become a convenient habit.

Prepare

Remember the motto of Scouts: "Always ready!" Make it yours! In this form of interaction, that is to say, with a telephone interlocutor, as in all communication, adequate preparation is the guarantee of a successful operation.

Look for an enabling environment. Make your calls calmly, taking care to remove anything that could distract you from your sight, because what you are about to do should get your full attention.

Establish your goal

As with any interview, the one we have on the phone is no exception to the rule. In this case, it is necessary to start by clearly establishing the objective aimed for: is it about informing, getting informed, talking to a specific person, getting an appointment to sell something?

Memorize a "script."

This is especially important, especially on the phone. Before opening your mouth, remember your text. Write it down if necessary.

You will first need to identify yourself and clearly explain the reason for your call. Then, you will need to establish your credibility: you have to be eager to listen to yourself, you can exchange or gather information, or get an appointment. Finally, you will need to complete the phone call.

Memorize the words prepared for each of these steps before lifting the handset. Of course, even if the frame is very precise, you still have to look natural.

There is nothing more annoying than these calls where, after having asked your attention, the representative reads his sales pitch to you also, exercise and even, record yourself, then listen to yourself and fine-tune your presentation until it seems natural to you.

Have your reference material close at hand

You have certainly already, during a telephone conversation, desperately seeking the answer to a question without being able to find it.

It happens to everyone. Give yourself a chance. Have all the documents you need ready to hand before you start your phone call. When the time comes, you will seem to really know your file by easily answering all the questions of your interlocutor.

Improve the average

Rather than suffer the famous "law of the mean," ten negative calls for a positive, see in this statistic a challenge to be met. This requires, of course, a good knowledge of the product or service that is the subject of your appeal.

And then, to put it mildly, to improve the average, you have to increase your chances first by increasing the number of calls. It's mathematical.

Here's another tip. If necessary, for your first calls, choose people with a profile close to that of the targeted client. The closer they are, the more likely your call will pay off. A good way to help you improve the average is to give yourself a minimum goal and a maximum goal for each of your calls.

The maximum objective will obviously be the full success of your approach. However, there may be a minimum goal that falls somewhere between the unanswered call and the goal fully achieved.

For example, it will be able to give the name of your company and explain what you do.

Even if you get a "no," another minimum goal could be to pique the curiosity of your caller, at least enough to make them want to know more on a next call.

Finally, if you want to improve your average, choose the time of your phone call. It's a safe bet that you will find it more difficult to gain the support of your interlocutor during mealtime than on a rainy Saturday afternoon.

In business circles, it may be easier to capture the other person's attention later in the morning than in the early morning while they are organizing their workday.

In the same way, it is useless to telephone an accountant and to think to hold his attention to two weeks of the deadline for filing tax returns or to call your parish priest on a Sunday morning.

Note the times of the day or week during which your calls best reached their target and the unsuccessful periods. See if there is a trend and act on it!

Mirror, oh mirror!

On the phone, your best tool is a mirror! It's easy to think of phone contact as impersonal. This is not the case. You transmit many messages by the inflections of your voice, your rhythm, and your flow. For those who believe that non-verbal does not exist on the radio or on the phone, think again!

Before dialing the number, look at yourself in a mirror that you have placed in front of you and make yourself the most beautiful smile.

During the conversation, take a look at your mirror and ask yourself if the image reflections of yourself is the one you want to project. You will see, it works every time.

Smile!

As with everything, even on the phone, attitude is important. Put a smile in your voice. And even smile effectively when you speak on the phone. This is an old trick used by radio hosts.

This will make you sound more welcoming, and we will want to listen to you more. This is a great asset when you consider that on the phone, you only have your voice to get your messages across.

State the purpose of your call quickly

Of course, if you are familiar, you will be allowed a longer start before the purpose of your call is stated. But, if you're making a cold call, don't beat around the bush.

In fifteen seconds, they have to know who you are and what you want. Do not make your interlocutor languish; he must be quickly fixed on what brings you and react accordingly. It's the same for you: you don't want to waste your time. The faster you will be fixed on the other person's intentions, the quicker you can go to another call.

Make an entry that arouses interest

Generally, people are interested in you if you are interested in them. Very quickly, your interlocutor will want to know how you can be useful to him or, more broadly, what he can get by speaking to you.

Make sure that this benefit is evident in your introduction. Again, don't beat around the bush. Go directly and know how to arouse the interest of your speaker if you want him to listen to you for more than fifteen seconds.

Ask thought-provoking questions

A good way to generate interest is to ask a thought-provoking question. It can be anything, but it definitely has to be related to the rest of your call and help you reach your goal. For example: "Are you concerned about your health?"

"Do you have children and, if so, have you ever thought about the best way to secure their future?" "Do you have retirement plans?"

"What is the most important thing for you in education?" These are just a few examples of questions likely to force reflection, and we could multiply the list endlessly.

Know how to generate useful answers for you

This advice is useful even if you do not work for a survey house. Obviously, you will understand, during a phone call, it is not only a question of maintaining the conversation.

The answers should allow you to determine the level of interest of the target customer for your product and help you understand their situation.

Check their level of knowledge or understanding of the effects of your product or service.

The answers to these questions are very important since they will help you to situate yourself in relation to your interlocutor and, above all, to adjust the rest of the conversation accordingly. They will even allow you to present yourself more effectively during your next call.

Difficult customers

Everyone dreams of having only easy customers. But now, the reality is sometimes quite different.

Some people have become difficult clients because of previous experiences. Others are naturally less open or more reluctant people.

In either case, they can be divided into seven broad categories. Difficult customers are not always unpleasant, although dealing with them is almost always unpleasant. Here's how to recognize them, what sets them apart, and how to respond to each one.

Hostile or aggressive

We all hate hostile or aggressive customers, and we could all do without them. We can divide them into two subcategories.

The first type of aggressive customer is what I call the "tank." People like this make direct attacks and go for it.

Some attack bluntly, others with more tactics. Tank type people have a very clear idea of what others should do, regardless of how they act. They have confidence in themselves and are indifferent to the feelings of others.

To deal with such a person, you must acquire the ability to defend your opinions while avoiding direct confrontation.

It's common to find that people like the tank type only respect people they perceive to be strong. So if you stay firm, they can even become friends.

You have to give them time to calm down or to express themselves to the full. When it's done, try to grab their attention carefully and express your point of view.

The second type of aggressive client is the one I call the "Maverick." People like this "target" others while staying safe. Their weapons include innuendos, allusions, inappropriate teasing.

Very often, the person who is attacked by a sniper has the feeling of being grounded, with no possible retreat. Snipers often have a very clear idea of what others should do. If their expectations are not met, they will need to feel that they are in control.

To deal with a person of the sniper type, you must "flush out" by revealing his tactics, his strategy. You can, for example, asking a question like, "What you just said sounded like a hint; was that your intention?"

After unmasking the attacker, you must direct the communication so that the exchange continues in a harmonious rather than in confrontation.

The furious person

People like this get angry because of frustration or after being injured. This behavior is similar to anger.

They are often suspicious, feel threatened, and are easily irritated or in a bad mood. And the person against whom this rage is directed often ignores the source of the problem.

When you are in contact with this type of person, you must listen to them and let them calm down. If possible, allow a break or a period of time to allow the person to calm down.

Then show him the seriousness of your intentions. Don't take her anger on you. Avoid reacting. You have nothing to do with it!

The chronic dissatisfied

People in this category complain, blame, and blame everyone. They refuse to recognize that they can have any responsibility in a situation that has become problematic. The search for solutions is not usually part of their discourse.

In the face of such people, I suggest that you try to establish an alliance to resolve the issues. After giving them enough time to empty their bags, take note of their main contacts.

Invite them, if necessary, to go back to clarify certain points. Then, when the exchange of information is complete, ask them to tell you what they think is a realistic way to make them happy.

If they can't, which will happen every other time, suggest one yourself? Get them to think in terms of solutions, not emotions, then finish the interview. Above all, do not ask them, "why?" Because you would find yourself back to square one.

The silent

People in this category are more than just quiet. They cannot or will not speak when you need their advice.

It is often difficult to understand the significance of this notable lack of reaction. You know, however, that the fire is smoldering under the ashes.

Your goal with this type of person is to break the silence. Make sure you have set aside enough time. Ask questions, try to guess things, and check for accuracy. Watch for any signs. The non-verbal will speak to you! At all times, maintain a pleasant attitude.

The super nice, the very nice

People in this category tend to tell you what they think you want to hear. The quality of interpersonal relationships is usually important to them.

Thereafter, they often have difficulty fulfilling the commitments they have made.

The first thing to do is to make them feel they can trust you. Then you can better help them focus on the task they have to do, such as filling out a form.

It is what they need to do that matters, not what they believe to be your expectations. Finally, you must help them honor their commitments and solidify your relationship. Force them to make commitments and keep them.

The negative

People in this category constantly raise the negative or unpleasant side of things. When dealing with these people, you must, above all, keep your own vision in order to avoid that they lead you into the same negative spiral.

Rather than trying to send them out for a walk, consider them resource people. Indeed, their negativism can be used to validate facts. So ask for clarification and approach things precisely.

Look for the intent behind their behavior. Do not try to argue with them to end their negative attitude. You wouldn't make it because that attitude is ingrained in them.

The expert

We all had, one day or another, to chat with someone who seemed to know more than everyone else, or at least believed. This type of person is no less unpleasant when you find him as a client.

First, there is the know-it-all type. These people do know a lot. This is part of the difficulty in dealing with them because it should be you, the specialist.

When you're in contact with people in this category, your goal should be to encourage them to open up to new ideas. In addition, when dealing with such people, you will need to know your subject in all its ramifications.

Be tactful, heed their doubts and desires, and offer solutions. Ask questions and, when you see fit, express your satisfaction in dealing with someone of their skill or knowledge level. Be sincere; however, it is crucial!

Another type of expert is one who thinks he knows everything. Unlike "know-it-alls," this one will prove, after a few questions, to know nothing at all. The difficulty with such people is that they still try to show you some.

Your goal should be to reject their misconceptions without making them uncomfortable. Come back to their ideas, ask for details, and give them the opportunity to get away with it.

Say what you think while giving them as much credit as possible. Build on the positives and avoid making them lose face by pointing out their mistakes.

The undecided

The undecided are afraid to make decisions. It will be, for example, the client who makes no decision without the presence of her husband. Or the consumer who does nothing without consulting his wife or a specialist friend.

Your goal should be to inspire these people to commit and to honor their commitments. Winning their trust will become paramount. Help them clear up conflicts, explore options, and make the initial decision.

Then make sure that the commitment will be respected by specifying what needs to be done and ensuring follow-up. Throughout this process, solidify your relationship with these people. Indeed, the "undecided" are people-oriented towards others, who will seek to have your blessing.

Gradually, a transfer of trust will take place; you will become the expert. Who knows? Maybe a friend!

CONCLUSION

Closing Credits

Nothing will give you more confidence than knowing that you have prepared yourself adequately to speak in public.

The fear of speaking publicly that many speakers experience is too often linked to their poor preparation.

It is important to start preparing early.

With the whole steps in this book **EFFECTIVE PUBLIC SPEAKING** *Self Confidence And No Fear, Persuasion, Nlp, Mind Programming And Mental Control To Influence behaviors,* you will be able to repeat and improve your communication until you are fully satisfied.

Practice in front of a mirror, it's very useful. Repeat your intervention in front of relatives or friends who are willing to give you an honest opinion on your performance.

This will help you more. If you have a video camera, take the opportunity to see yourself in action, and assess your performance. However, you have to learn how to use such video recordings.

First, watch your performance without paying attention to your faults. Listen to yourself and look at yourself as the members of the audience before whom you will be performing, as if you were seeing yourself for the first time, and try to assess the impact of your presentation.

When you reach the end of your presentation, give yourself a mark out of 10 while trying not to be too harsh with yourself. Remember that the audience wants to have fun hearing you and will be forgiving of you.

Then bring the tape to the beginning and play it a second time, without the sound. Pay attention to the visual elements that bother you and write them down.

After this step, replay your recording, this time without looking at the image. Focus only on sound. Pay attention to your flow, pace, volume, and tone of your voice, then return to your rating grid.

Several people have never even heard a recording of their voice. Get used to the sound of your voice until you can hear it as others hear it. Take note of what you like and what you don't like.

When you have listed the visual and audio elements that are enjoyable or annoying, ask one or two family members to watch the recording with you and provide their comments. See if they match yours.

As for your weaknesses, do not try to correct them all at once. Find your most apparent defect and try to fix it first, then move on to another.

Self-improvement often involves emulating an admired person. Trying to imitate seasoned speakers is a great way to improve.

Go see them and hear them. See how they behave, how they speak and walk on stage, what voice effects they use, what structure they give to their performance. Take note of what they have in common. Try to take ownership of these ways and integrate them into your style.

Obviously, none of these "stage effects" can replace good content.

The following models cannot guarantee that your audience will agree with you.

But, you can borrow from the ways to make sure your audience will hear you, understand you, and remember your message.

Imitate them, but remember that it is through practice and sustained effort that they reap the results that you yourself seek to achieve when you speak in public.

"To be ready, you have to prepare." It is by preparing adequately that you become a champion in your communications and that speaking in public becomes easier.

COPYRIGHT BY TED ROBBINS 2020

DARK PSYCHOLOGY AND MANIPULATION WITH HYPNOSIS

MIND CONTROL & EMOTIONAL INTELLIGENCE SECRETS, ART OF PERSUASION, EMOTIONAL INFLUENCE, NLP & BODY LANGUAGE TO WIN PEOPLE WITH SUBLIMINIAL MANIPULATION

WRITTEN BY:

TED ROBBINS

TABLE OF CONTENTS

COPYRIGHT

The author is not obliged, directly or indirectly, to assume civil liability for any restoration, damage, or loss resulting from the data collected here. The respective authors retain all copyrights not kept by the publisher.

The information contained herein is solely and universally available for information purposes. The data is presented without a warranty or promise of any kind.

The trademarks used are without approval, and the patent is issued without the trademark owner's permission or protection.

The logos and labels in this book are the property of the owners themselves and are not associated with this text.

INTRODUCTION

The mind is one of the highly complicated aspects of human nature. The functioning of the mind has perplexed and intrigued humanity for as long as we can remember. Philosophers, psychologists and scientists have tried to unravel the mysteries of the mind. It is widely believed that the human mind influences our behavior and actions. Hence, a lot of research work has been devoted to understanding the mental process a person undergoes before acting, both for good and evil.

Some attempts to study the human mind have focused efforts on the brain. These studies examine the brain's physical aspects, focusing on how information is acquired, processed, interpreted, and stored. Essentially, they hope to understand better how the brain can affect a person's way of thinking. Analyses like these have paved the way for progress in managing debilitating conditions such as Alzheimer's, perception difficulties, and even memory loss.

The most familiar aspect of the study of the human mind is psychology. At some point in our life, we consulted a psychologist or met someone who had to consult with one to face our most challenging emotional battles. Many times, life's experiences destroy us in ways that we cannot fix on our own. Sometimes, the failure is the result of some biological markers we inherited from our parents. Emotions such as depression, anxiety and fear obscure our daily experiences making growth difficult. With a blend of medication and therapy, we can protect ourselves from the inner darkness.

But what about the darkness in others? Everyone can do great good. We also possess the ability to do great evil. Underneath emotions such as sadness, depression, joy and happiness is a deep seething desire that can lead us to deliberately hurt others if these impulses are not kept in check. These darker desires are rooted in more primitive instincts, such as our flight or combat response, promoting our survival. Sometimes, there is only one word that qualifies the human response to these evil dark emotions.

Dark psychology is a research of the individual state of human beings' psychological nature to prey on others. In secular terms, dark psychology explores that aspect of human nature that allows us to deliberately and voluntarily take actions that harm our fellow man. Mind you, the use of prey in this context does not necessarily translate into physical harm to a person. However, there is a branch of dark psychology devoted entirely to this. Subsequently, we will briefly touch on these areas to better understand the subject.

Those cases are just triggered responses to external situations. The pot was stirred, and those dark emotions that lurked beneath it boiled to the surface. They usually withdraw once control is exercised. Everyone has a latent tendency to be a little mean or just plain evil if the right "buttons" are pressed. Some other individuals, on the other hand, are in full control of these dark emotions. They feed them, feed them, and voluntarily release them at the expense of another person when it serves their purposes.

Sometimes, these emotions are cured at an early age. A child learns that if he cries a certain way, the adults in their life rush to follow their orders. If the parents don't impress the child early enough about the mistake of this, the child grows up thinking that the people in their life can be manipulated to do their bidding. Crying would cease to be a weapon as they grow up, but they would continue in their manipulative ways. Where they don't use tears, they use emotions to blackmail their victims. Thus, what began as innocent childish behavior becomes a dark need for control.

The lengths this individual would take to exert their control would define the intensity of their actions. Dark psychology is based on studying the thought process of a person like this. It tries to understand the reason behind these actions. The patterns exhibited before these acts are performed after and shed more light on how a person can intentionally see those actions to conclude knowing the pain and pain they might cause to another individual. Dark psychology illuminates the dark side of human nature.

CHAPTER 1: DARK PSYCHOLOGY AND MANIPULATION

It is of primary importance to establish a clear definition of manipulation. Without understanding what constitutes manipulation, there will be many difficulties separating manipulation cases and other forms of influence.

In a broad sense, manipulation is the effort to influence the behavior or perception of others. Most definitions extend it to include "through the use of abusive, deceptive or otherwise exploitative means" or something similar, as a means of differentiating between manipulation and other influencing behaviors, such as persuasion. It raises even more questions, such as what constitutes "exploitation." Deception is relatively easy to define as intentional concealment or distortion of the truth. But does deception preclude persuasion?

It could be argued that anyone taking on a job is already operating with the knowledge that people are likely to highlight their positive traits and divert attention from the negative. In this sense, it is not necessarily dishonest to omit certain information in that situation. So, expectations can also play a role in determining the ethics of manipulation and where the line is drawn between manipulation and other forms of influence.

There is another word in that broad definition worthy of attention. Defining manipulation as an "effort" suggests that manipulation is still manipulation regardless of success or failure. The act of manipulation is defined as attempting. Ironically, those who are less successful at manipulating others, who are discovered more frequently are more likely to gain a reputation as manipulators than those who are successful.

You can probably point to someone in your orbit, perhaps a relative or colleague, who you consider manipulative. However, consider how others view them. Are they known as manipulators? Does this affect their success? The answer to this can also be complicated. If colleagues see someone at work as a manipulator and yet dominate the boss, they could still be judged successfully. When thinking about manipulating others, it is vital to set clear goals. It will allow you to make rational and objective decisions, which is the key to success.

Manipulation vs. Influence

The modern world has adopted the term influencer for people with a large following on social media, able to influence others with their content. It doesn't take a particularly critical mind to recognize the source of this term as advertising. As consumer behavior evolves, advertisers have noticed and seek increasingly to harness influencers' power to draw attention to products. It is done in various ways through paid or unpaid sponsorships, promotional deals and agreements.

In some cases, influencers disclose these deals while, in others, they don't. Ethical issues are raised again, mainly if an influencer is just a happy consumer but secretly on the company's payroll selling the product.

The goals of many influencers, especially those who work with advertisers, are fundamentally manipulative. It's not even a gray zone problem. Influencers aim to pass products to their followers to make money. It is impossible to know whether everyone they influence would benefit from the product, nor is it possible to know their financial situation or specific circumstances. In this case, the influencer puts their interests first.

Manipulation does not necessarily include an attempt to harm others. However, to some extent, efforts must put to goals and interests first. It is part of the puzzle.

Furthermore, it is safer and more logical to refer to the flu as a parent term of manipulation, including manipulation and other influence methods, such as inspiration and emulation.

Manipulation vs. Persuasion

These terms might seem opposed, with persuasion serving as a form of "honest" manipulation, in which the actor is at the forefront of his own goals and opinions. However, it will be more useful to consider persuasion at a lower level than manipulation. Persuasion, therefore, becomes a method of manipulation, which is a form of influence. Persuasion is also one of the least effective methods of manipulation. How many times have you been in a debate with someone else to raise your hand and say, "I admit, you're right"?

It is probably possible to count these instances on one side. It can be easy to convince someone that smoking is unhealthy, but is it easy to get them to quit? If so, governments would see no need or benefit to imposing heavy taxes on tobacco products to discourage their use.

And what about other forms of flu? And other methods of manipulation? Well, manipulation must have intent, and it should have some form of goal, even if the goal is to create anarchy. A great director can influence the work of many others, but it is different from manipulation. The director does not set out to influence others (although they can). Instead, he gains influence through others' reactions to their work, resulting in inspiration and even emulation. Persuasion, likewise, is not the only method of manipulation that could be employed.

An easy alternative is to lie, a form of deception. Lying and being believed will inevitably change the perception of those who believe the lie. As has already been established, it is still a manipulation, whether successful or not. Persuasion, like influence, does not suffer from the same image problem as manipulation. It is seen as a good thing to be able to make a "persuasive argument." Even if it has a sinister tinge; the phrase "I can be very persuasive" implies an effort for power over another party - perhaps even abuse. Furthermore, when employers refer to the soft skill of "persuasion," it is correct to interpret it as a euphemism for manipulation.

Definition of Manipulation

Manipulation is a form of intentional influence. It is characterized as an attempt by a person or party (the manipulator) to change another person or party (the target), typically to achieve an objective in the manipulator's interest.

This definition is useful because it is objective and transparent. Also, it's useful because you'll learn manipulation techniques that will help you achieve your goals.

However, two problems remain. The first refers to the "desired influence." The intent is problematic because it implies responsibility. Everyone manipulates everyone around them all the time, even from a young age. It would be wrong to exclude a child's whims from the manipulation umbrella, just because they are not old enough to rationalize their behavior. The same goes for adult outbursts, after all. The intent, therefore, does not imply conscious behavior, but it can also be instinctive. It also allows for the authentic presence of "naturally manipulative" people.

The second problem is the disappointingly vague ending: "typically to achieve a goal in the interest of the manipulator." Not only is it problematic to define "the interests of the manipulator," but there is also a general ambiguity in the inclusion of "typically." This part only creates a normalized idea of manipulation and would not fit into a more general definition. After all, how can anyone know their interests perfectly? Of course, it is possible to manipulate someone successfully, and the result is still one's death.

By successfully manipulating others, you can change their behavior, opinions, and achievable goals to promote your interests. It's that simple. Effective manipulation, however, is about improving the success rate. It could be that everyone is manipulating the boss, to some degree, to get that promotion, but only one candidate will get the job. Working hard is the right place to start, and working effectively is even better. However, letting it be merit alone may not make it. How can you make your boss want to promote you, rather than anyone else? Understanding this will give you the edge.

Beware of The Manipulation of Others
The more you understand manipulation, the better equipped you will be to avoid being manipulated by others. Recognizing manipulative behaviors in other people will not only protect you from their influence, but you will learn more about their goals by feeding your mind with the information you can use to manipulate them. It is not hard to be conscious of the situations you can expect to encounter manipulative behavior. The hardest thing is always identifying how you are being manipulated.

A vital part of this is understanding other parties' goals and how they attempt to achieve those goals at any given time. With this information, you can not only recognize and capitalize on the behavior of others, but you can develop the ability to predict the future actions of your opponents. It requires emotional intelligence, as it is necessary to put yourself in your target's shoes. In developing this ability, a good starting point is to evaluate one's behavior through one's actions and learn to understand one's choices from an objective point of view.

Your Goals

Since you are probably already manipulating the people around you to some degree and being manipulated yourself, the first significant step in achieving effective manipulation is understanding and defining your goals. Without setting goals, it's impossible to measure the effectiveness of your current manipulation efforts. It is not to say that you are not already manipulating with some level of effectiveness. Some people are naturally more manipulative, and some people are natural manipulators; however, the two don't always overlap. Start by thinking about your actions and behavior towards others.

Consider who you see positively at work or in your social circle, and who you see negatively. Also, consider how you deal with different people and whether it aligns perfectly with your opinion of them. There is a good chance it isn't. What you are probably already doing is working to gain others' reasonable opinion who you believe hold power and influence. It is a very general approach that everyone in society takes. To use an obvious example, your behavior towards your boss is likely different from that of your peers, regardless of your personal opinion about them.

You May Also Set Goal

Otherwise, you might just be trying to impress. You might also try to carve out a comfortable work-life by shedding responsibility and doing what you can to obscure your low productivity. Maybe you are taking action to get closer to a colleague you are romantically interested in. These are just ideas. Every day before going to be, think about your behavior. What have you been thinking about and trying to get the day too? These are the goals you are already naturally working towards. When you truly understand what your current motives are, you may be surprised. To start manipulating effectively, it's time to clearly and consciously define your goals. If you have already done this, that's great. Make sure you have something with a clearly defined ending point.

Power Is the Ability to Help Other People Succeed

It is an interesting definition because it seems to subvert the typical idea of power to exert force on others. However, breaking it down, the two are closely related. Having the ability to exert force on others can mean not harming them, not invading their country, not throwing them in prison, not creating laws that have a negative impact on them; these are all forms of power. The power to help other people succeed is very similar to the power to make other people fail, if not exercised.

What can you provide to people that will help other people achieve their goals? The most obvious are extraordinary skills. Talent is precious in every aspect of life, from sports competitions, business, and raising children. If you have talents that other people can use, that's a powerful thing. Another form of power is authority. The boss decides who gets promoted and who fired. A police officer can arrest you or let you go with a warning, thanks to his or her legally authorized authority.

A judge can decide your sentence, based on specific constraints and their opinion of your nature. However, there is a problem: you may have the same or more extraordinary talents as another person. Still, they may be more successful than you, be valued more, and enjoy more significant benefits. The other aspect of power is reputation. It refers to the belief, held by others, in your power. Reputation is often the key to manipulation. The judgment of others regarding your abilities and authority.

CHAPTER No 2: DARK PSYCHOLOGY

Given the little we now understand about dark psychology, we know that some of the most shocking crimes are rooted in some personality traits related to dark psychology. But this is a broader side effect. We need to fetch it nearer to home, to you and me. How does this dark psychology affect us, if it even affects us? We can ensure you that there are no "ifs" to this question, and in a few moments, we would understand how. The effects of dark psychology are experienced by both the author and the victim. To know the impacts, we need to explore some elements of dark psychology. Folks who display specific behavior characteristics that are considered obscure such as narcissism, psychopathy, and Machiavellianism, are prone to experience difficulties in all aspects of their relationships. If all three traits are present in a person, they have a greater propensity to commit a crime. The three personality traits mentioned have specific characteristics grouped under them.

Narcissism, for example, is characterized by a sense of entitlement, feelings of superiority, deep seething envy for the success of others, and exploitative behaviors. Psychopathy has an absence of guilt, a lack of empathy, destructive impulsive behavior, self-centeredness, and an inability to accept responsibility as some of the characteristics. Selfishness, cruelty and manipulative behaviors are indicators of Machiavellian traits. Separately, these traits are problematic but put together; they can cause trouble. Especially in a person's relationship with others. In the office, for example, that individual would do it;

- Insufficient performance in the office, even with the most mundane tasks
- They disrupt the flow of work due to their inability to get along with others
- Others would intensely detest him
- Their impulsiveness would lead them to make questionable and unethical decisions
- If placed in an administrative capacity, they are more likely to commit white-collar crimes
- But it's not just their working relationships that suffer. In their relationships, they are bound to encounter the following problems
- Their constant need for attention and validation can be exhausting for their partner, resulting in faster relationship expiration dates
- They resort to physical and emotional blackmail to manipulate their partners
- They tend to be verbally, emotionally, or physically violent with their partner or children

People who come into relationships with them pay a high emotional cost. If you've met someone whose relationships are characterized by these experiences, for the sake of your sanity and general well-being, avoid them. But if you are the one experiencing this, seek the psychological help you need to get better. No matter how ingrained these problems are, you can improve your behavior and experiences with the right form of therapy. The initial phase is to recognize the situation for what it is, recognize that you have a problem, and seek help promptly. For our respite, exchanging with people who have the traits I mentioned above leaves us emotionally and mentally drained. Sometimes, the effect can be physical and, in extreme cases, fatal. His home, his business, his finances, but his loss was much more profound and more significant than these. We did not have a relationship with the author of the act, but we also became victims. Our losses weren't as monumental as yours, but we also suffered losses. For starters, we've lost our sweet neighbor. She is not dead, but she never recovered from the experience. We have lost our ability to trust strangers. Our mutual relationships also seemed to require an additional layer of trust to thrive.

The most significant impact of dark psychology on anyone is that it produces a strong sense of loss. We lose our valuables, we lose relationships, we lose ourselves, and for those who are extremely unfortunate, they lose their lives. It is secure to say that the impact of this darkness is profound.

If a person exhibits one of the dark personality traits, there is a very high tendency to exhibit others. In society at large, if the larger members of society display these traits, it is safe to say that the crime perpetration rates in that society would be significantly high. It is not to say that people living in cities or towns with higher crime rates are more prone to crime. There are other contributing factors to consider. But not even the prospect can be excluded entirely.

However, one thing that cannot be ruled out is the ripple effect of actions directly related or as a result of dark personality traits. Some destructive behaviors even turn victims into predators, and this cycle continues well into the future until someone takes courage and takes the courageous step to break free. Children from abusive families, for example, more often than not grow up to be abusers. In some cases, in an attempt to break away from their parental mold, they find themselves trapped in equally abusive relationships, even if they are not the abusers themselves. It is virtual to have an influential gravitational pull towards the violent elements that characterize their childhood homes.

For others, becoming victims can have such a tremendous impact on their psyche that it triggers something inside them. I have read that the "click" can be temporary. In a short moment, they lose all control over their primitive instincts and act exclusively on the strongest emotion that emerges, which is usually anger. This condition is what causes some people to declare temporary insanity. But some people embrace the dark emotions that arise when they "snap." The absolute sense of morality comes out of the window. The consequences of this are usually devastating.

Manipulation of Dark Psychology

Put, manipulating someone means controlling or influencing that person intelligently or evilly. Like it or not, we've all manipulated a person or situation to achieve a desirable result. It sounds grim but let me lighten the mood with a story from my mischievous childhood.

The art of manipulation is part of our nature. However, when it comes to psychological manipulation, things get darker and more sinister. In this situation, a person's actions or thoughts are influenced by the use of underhanded tactics that are offensive, deceptive, or even both. In this context, the manipulated person does not choose to accept or reject the manipulator's will. They are forced to comply.

Manipulators have their reasons for doing what they do. Sometimes, it's something as fundamental as making financial gains like the fictional soldier who cheated my neighbor out of all her life savings. In the workplace, these people are committed to promoting their agenda, even if that would mean banging a few heads against each other. Their principle is straightforward; if you want it, you have to reach out and take it. In relationships, it's usually about gaining power and staying in control. The need to be responsible fuels everything they do, and sometimes they can go out of their way to achieve this. And then you have those who love to manipulate people for recreational purposes. They are just bored and use their manipulative games to pass the time. It's crude and vicious, but that's just the way they think.

One of the usual utmost tactics used by manipulators is lying. A master manipulator is well versed in the art of deception. They are adept at making up fantastic stories that have no bearing on the truth. Or they subterfuge and lie by omission. Some people are so good with their lies that you rarely notice until it's too late. Another tactic employed by manipulators is guilt and shame. When confronted for something they did wrong, they would immediately deny it and then promptly change the situation, making you feel bad for questioning them in the first place. To further strengthen their grip on the victim, they denigrate her, turning the victim into a rapist. You will find this type of manipulative technique in domestic cases where the abuser would claim that the victim's character, words, or actions are what prompted his behavior in the first place.

Other subtle techniques used in manipulation include the use of evasive and undemanding responses to the questions posed. Rationalize actions if they are captured and rotate reality to fit their narrative. Some manipulators use sex and seduction to accomplish their ambiguous goals when trapped, anger and guilt projection are quickly used to manipulate the situation in their favor.

However, manipulators are not always casual in their selection of prey. There are specific traits in their victims that attract them, and some vulnerabilities also make it easier for the manipulator to perpetrate their crimes. Lonely people with low self-esteem and a desire to please are more comfortable to control than the bold social type. However, some people show similar characteristics to later ones who end up being manipulated. For these people, manipulators study their personality flaws and weaknesses before using them against them. Impressionable people are likely to be fooled by appearances. Cheeky people who tend to make compulsive decisions are more likely to be manipulated to make quick decisions with a long-term impact. Greedy and materialistic people have a greater tendency to be scammed.

Hypnosis

The idea of hypnosis has been relegated to the world of belief. That the swing of an object can control a person's mind, and a finger's snap was considered an incredulous idea.

No amount of denial can change the fact that hypnosis is real and used far more frequently than we care to admit. In today's modern psychology, hypnotherapy has effectively treated certain skin conditions and manage pain associated with childbirth, dental procedures, and even rheumatoid arthritis.

Hypnosis and psychology are described as a cooperative interaction in which participants respond to suggestions from the hypnotist. That is to say, when a person is hypnotized, the hypnotist firmly guides his actions. In films, we are led to believe that a person under hypnosis becomes sleepy and disoriented. In reality, people react differently under hypnosis, but they are not as clueless as they seem. Indeed, psychologists refer to this as a state of hyper-awareness. In this state, they experience focused attention, heightened suggestibility, and vivid fantasies. People are brought into this state through the use of visualization and verbal repetition.

Here are some of the most common misconceptions we have:

- Hypnotism Puts You Under Complete Control of Your Hypnotist In the movies, and we are made to believe that a depressed person would have their actions controlled by the hypnotist. It is not valid. Although hypnosis relies heavily on suggestions, if your mind disagrees with these suggestions, you would openly reject it. Then no. You won't crawl on all fours and moo like a cow, not unless you want to.
- The brain is more complicated than we think it is. The same self-protection mechanisms that make it nearly impossible for your hypnotists to control your actions keep you alert, and if there is immediate danger, you can get rid of it in an instant.
- Hypnosis is a kind of pure science. It is based on the research work of renowned psychologists such as Sigmund Freud. There are a method and a process, and none of these require wooden dolls and red candles. All it takes is your consent.
- Hypnosis can improve your skills. It dangles on what you are viewing. Hypnosis can improve your memory, but it can also give you false memories or even distort that memory itself. Hence, the results are not as great as you would have hoped. It has also been linked to improved

performance but doesn't expect to run the 5km marathon overnight.

Hypnosis does not always imply that you enter a trance state for it to be effective. The critical elements of hypnosis are the power of suggestion and the repetitive use of words that resonate deeply with the victim. Politicians, for example, exploit this aspect in their campaigns. They use words like change, make a difference and so on. These words trigger a more in-depth search within oneself, and unconsciously we find ourselves longing for that change.

Problematic Behavior

The subject of criminal behavior is not our focus, but it cannot be overlooked because it constitutes an aspect of dark psychology. Profilers, criminologists and law enforcement agencies benefit immensely from studying criminal behavior. In psychology, criminal behavior is not often thrown around because it is believed that crime is behavior. However, engaging in a crime doesn't necessarily make you a criminal. Sure, there's a lot of debate about this kind of thinking, but we should leave it to the experts. Our focus here is on those elements that cause a person to commit a crime.

Some people do things merely because they can. Not because they were driven by some childhood wound, by the need to take revenge for an offense you may or may not have committed. They do it simply because they can. As individual persons, it is in our nature to try to understand why. We want to make sense of our situation rather than believing that we are just victims of random acts. However, we should be prepared to accept that sometimes the situation is just as it appears. A person guided by his desire to hurt others. If you are trying to find answers to such questions, you should also open yourself to the possibility that this person was just plain evil.

For a person to commit a specific type of crime, there are usually some characteristics that indicate that this person may be capable of this. It goes beyond judging a book by its cover because prolific criminals are often mastering of disguises. They fascinate you before they disarm you. In our daily life, these people disguise themselves as one of us by pretending that they have your best interests at heart. Given what we now know about manipulation, deception and hypnosis, we know that predators are not always strangers. So, how can you identify those things that help you make better choices in relating to people?

We will explore the traits in detail.

Family and Friends
In addition to yourself, examine the circles in which this person runs. Do they come from a close-knit family? How is their relationship with the family? Have you met their friends? If this person has no friends, it could be a red flag.

History
We like the idea of a person being wholly reformed and, in all honesty, this happens. However, it would help if you didn't ignore that a person with a horrible history has a greater tendency to become a repeat offender. If the person was abusive in their previous relationship, there is a possibility that they would be the same as you. No, unless they have undergone or are actively undergoing treatment.

Problems with Control
People who cannot control themselves in situations that cause them to have a propensity to inflict harm on others. Likewise, people who have trouble giving up control have the nerve to snap and lash out at the

closest victim when they lose it, and that person could be you.

Antisocial Values

In social settings, monitor their interactions with others. People who don't generally like everyone are red flags. If the person is generally obnoxious, rude, and low at getting along with people, you may have a problem on your hands.

Substance Abuse

Addiction to any form of drug or alcohol is a clear indicator that this person struggles with specific problems. Substance abuse negates their ability to reason correctly and make correct decisions. An individual who misuses drugs or alcohol may not be able to make your relationship a priority in their life. And unless they have a way to support that lifestyle, you may end up paying for it directly or indirectly. It can lead to years of abuse and neglect.

These are just indicators of criminal elements in the people we relate to. As with all human things, there are exceptions, and there are variables. However, the major fault you can make is seeing precise pointers and then rationalizing them. We tend to make excuses for others. The first thing we rush to tell ourselves is that no one is perfect. But that ideology can quickly take us to warm waters. Get informed, be aware, and then make informed decisions. These do not guarantee that you would stop these types from hurting you and taking advantage of you. But you can protect yourself from them 100% better than if you were acting from a place of ignorance.

Some of us are inherently hard-wired to want to fix the people in our life. We see someone who is broken, and we think that if we love him strong enough, we can bring him back from the edge of whatever precipice he is in and begin our journey to a happy ending.

Areas Vulnerable to Dark Psychology

The chances of things getting this creepy are pretty slim. But never make the mistake of assuming that you are immune to the powers of dark psychology. Its influence is much closer to you than you think. The most common place where elements of dark psychology manifest themselves

Love and Relations

Love is a universal language. It is a primal emotion that we all instinctively desire. As human beings, we are designed for love. We want to love and feel loved. Nobody is as content as a man or woman in love and knows that he is loved in return. Some people mate for procreation purposes. Some people mate to deny social pressure. Some even mate to promote the alliance of powerful families. But the main reason for relationships, namely how to get a mate, is love. That said, it is easy for things to degrade to the point where love is used as a bargaining chip to have more power over another individual. And this is where the elements of dark psychology come into play.

Social Conditioning

Social conditioning refers to the impact society has on your life as a whole. While social conditioning looks more at your social status in terms of income, living conditions and so on, its reach can go deeper. Your society can and does affect your beliefs and your religion. You may not be a direct practitioner of those beliefs, but you are indirectly affected by them. In certain cultures, certain days are considered sacred. It means that doing business in those days could be considered a crime.

There is a general misconception that being part of a more advanced society makes you impervious to cultural influences. How can a company that gave birth to characters like Albert Einstein and Neil Armstrong be influenced by something as ridiculous as culture, right? Well, you're wrong about that. If nothing else, you are even more vulnerable.

The most significant advance our society has made today is in the field of technology. We exist in a world where things get done in a flash. Money transactions are completed at the push of a button. If you are working out a business plan in this era, your products and services need to match the same speed we are all used to. Otherwise, you are preparing for failure. Unfortunately, this speed that characterizes our daily life makes us vulnerable to get rich quickly with schemes. We hear all these fantastic stories of people who became millionaires overnight, and, on a subconscious level, we want the same thing.

The only logical explanation we can give for a situation like this where a company with almost no recorded documentation of its existence comes in and scams the hard-working people who are usually smart in their relationships is social conditioning.

Ambition and Personal Aspirations
We altogether have a to-do list. Occasionally, this list is just a group of activities designed to help us get through the day. And sometimes, it's a roadmap towards where we would like to be soon. Draw up a business plan for your startup? It is an entirely different game. You are trying to prepare yourself for the future financially and, most likely, by providing a product or service that influences people's lives. In today's terminology, we call it "head moves." Ambition is what drives you towards the goals you have set for yourself. Do you want something? You strive to achieve it, and for the more ambitious people, when they reach their goals, they push a little more. Ambition is an attractive trait in every human being. The aspiration to be better than who, what and where you are now often putting you behind the wheel that directs your life. Nobody needs to

be with individuals who are content to sit on the couch all day and do nothing but eat chips and browse the channels. People want to be with someone genuinely excited about the beautiful future they envision for themselves and who are working meticulously to achieve it.

However attractive as ambition is, it can attract the wrong kind of people into your life when put into overdrive because it leaves you open and vulnerable. It may seem like a contradictory statement because ambitious people are described as anything but vulnerable. Where ambition drives your goals, your aspirations can instead be seen as indicators of success. There are many similarities between aspirations and ambitions, but the main difference is the successive ones' magnitude and intensity. Your ambition may be to move up the managerial ladder before the end of the year, and your aspiration may be to open up more job opportunities when you reach that position. Ambition is more concrete in its desires, while aspirations are those noble notions, we nurture to make us feel better about ourselves. By themselves, neither ambition nor aspirations should harm you, but when other elements come into play, they can be expended to operate and deceive you.

Most organizations believe that ambition is one of the most desirable qualities in a potential employee. And this is usually because ambitious people are more willing to do what needs to be done to move the company forward than their seemingly more docile counterparts. People like these are very focused and have a one-sided mind regarding fulfilling their responsibilities, sometimes not considering what it would take to do it even if it would mean stepping on some colleague's foot. In some contexts, this can be good. After all, the workplace and the world at large aren't a playground where the rules of what's right for everyone to apply. But this attitude can quickly create a hostile work environment that makes it difficult for employees to grow. The organization's goals can be achieved consistently but at the expense of its employees. But that's not the immediate danger, even if that doesn't mean a situation like this isn't a cause for concern.

A person who does not reign in their ambition can be persuaded and manipulated to do morally and ethically wrong things to achieve their goals. The people with high ambitions and aspirations are most likely to fall into the manipulative techniques that involve blackmail. For example, a young career man with an excellent reputation and a good position within a company is more likely to do anything to maintain that status quo if he is ambitious. However, those things he is required to do would further taint his reputation if knowledge of those actions came to light. It is not to say that the rest of us are less likely to become victims of blackmail and other forms of manipulation.

Manipulation is not about physically wielding a large and dangerous ax on a person to force them to do somewhat they typically would not do. It is a game of fraud and deception. The manipulator acts as a mirror that captures the victim's desires, ambitions, and aspirations and then threatens to realize that vision by showing its weakness. The victim is forced to falsely believe that his only hope of saving his dreams is to fulfill the manipulator's wishes. The stronger the ambition, the more likely the victim is to obey, especially if they believe they can get away with it.

The acts that could be manipulated into performing could be anything from undermining the authority figure in their life, committing an act that could be offensive or any of the other things the manipulator may have in mind. Let me resize it to relatable proportions. In all our relationships with people, there is a measure of trust. No matter how unreasonable you may be, the working relationship you have with your tailor is also an indication of a certain level of trust as you trust them to help you cover up your nudity without being harmed in the process. But as there is trust, there is also distrust. Nevertheless, we strive to process these feelings to maintain the bond/bridge between the people involved.

Emotional Scars

One of the most significant residual effects of any experience we have is emotions. They say experience is the best teacher in life. Having used above than a period trying to understand human nature. There are some experiences in life that would promptly cause you never to react again. Those experiences are so deeply etched in our minds that we immediately interpret sure signs as a precursor to the event that scared us in the first place. And the second we observe these signs, our fight or flight instincts are unleashed, especially if those experiences threaten us. This predictable pattern of behavior is meant to protect us in times of perceived danger. Think of it as a biological defense against what could harm us or that emergency exercise your body goes through when your brain feels you are in danger.

A woman in love memorizes her lover's scent. And every time he smells that perfume, his mood changes. Sometimes it induces joy, and on certain occasions, it can trigger lust. If that relationship builds up, the scents could induce sadness or anger, depending on how severe the breakup was. All I'm saying is that emotions are part of the human experience. When we feel a certain way, we act a certain way. Some events can trigger emotions that cause us to react abnormally. People can disguise themselves and turn into something they are not. They wear clothes and perfumes that look rich, and because you have a strong emotional connection to wealth, you look past the other warning signs and make a sorry decision. Whether they are good or bad, your emotional scars can make you vulnerable to deception and manipulation.

CHAPTER 3: MIND CONTROL

When we try to rise above being human animals, we are animals under human skin. We are subject to the wishes and desires of any being with a genetic makeup and vertebrae. To rise above this is an admirable aspiration and one that we encourage anyone to undertake as a worthy spiritual endeavor.

But to deny that we are genuinely animals is to lie to ourselves. We need to interact in a social environment and deal with people who may not be enlightened and spiritually advanced. They may want what we have and secretly be filled with envy and contempt. The worst event is having these suspicions satisfied and then being drawn into the politics of man.

In this case, what are the options? Do we deny this is happening and hope others will be touched by our honesty and goodwill enough to change? Or do we abandon our higher spiritual ideals and play their game? We could like to advocate for a fundamentally different approach. Take the manipulation game and mind control and make it part of your spirituality.

In this way, we do not deny manipulation and mind control or give up. As an alternative, we comprise it and see it as a tool for our growth. We describe the spiritual life of the warrior who embraces life and sees each battle as an expression of life, not death. For this warrior, every moment is an opportunity to live fully and aspire while walking in the world but guided by something higher. If you are courageous and daring enough to embrace mind control in this way, each interaction is lifted above the mundane and mundane and becomes a vehicle for your spirituality. You will be relieved and remain intact even in the most vulgar of human politics. Your war will be your temple.

You should be warned. While reading, there is nothing that will be held back. Like the combatant, there are many unpleasant things you need to learn about this life you choose. Although you are obligated to learn these secrets, you are not obliged to use them.

What is Mind-Control?

Mind control, when you hear these words, a myriad of images come to mind. You could imagine a sneaky man using the power of his mind and the will to control the acts of some unsuspecting and innocent women. You might think of some clandestine cabal of world leaders secretly planning the next steps towards a unified world economy. Or maybe you are the cult leader with a gathering of loyal followers ready to hear every word. You are not likely to have in mind a loving parent who reads to their children or an alcoholics anonymous meeting that helps its members live a decent and sober life.

Likewise, improbable that you will recognize the hold that mind control has on you while in your favorite church of worship. Or, as you sit down with your psychiatrist, you are unlikely to be aware of the subtle acts of mind control being used on you. But there is. Any attempt to cause a change in your thoughts and feelings, and therefore in your actions, is an act of mind control.

It may sound shocking because most people see mind control as a bad thing done by bad people. So, let it be clear; the controller's intention and motives do not apply to this symposium. The regulator may be encouraged by the most altruistic ideals, or he may want your money.

We will try to find out how these thoughts and feelings are instilled to achieve the controller result. Mind control is different from vulgar actions and coercion tactics. Coercion is when all a controller wants to take a specific action and don't care about their motivation. Threats, guilt, and humiliation usually do their job. But pressure lacks any form of grace or elegance.

Pressure does not care about the thoughts and feelings of the people who are forced. It is the main difference between coercion and mind control. As many so-called cults use coercion to gain compliance from their followers, the topic will be discussed, but the goal is to aspire to something higher, namely mind control.

It requires knowing how people think and react and knowledge of individuals' impulses and weaknesses. More importantly, you need to know yourself and be able to control your impulses to react. Your goals, your highest ambitions, must be kept secret and every action measured by how close you are to your goal. One way to distinguish the way people reason is in footings of sequential, linear, and non-linear reasoning. Sequential thinking is the act of thinking and replying automatically. Serial thinking is the result of our evolution and is very useful. Simply reacting to the current situation prevents us from having to overthink. It is also the way sheep are led to slaughter.

Linear thinking is a step forward and requires foresight and the ability somehow to predict the consequences of the activities and numerous ways to advance our objectives and wishes. For the regular chess player, the game is an excellent example of extending linear thinking to its limits.

Non-linear thinking doesn't stop at the chessboard. In its pentacle, it incorporates all the dimensions of space and time. While a linear-thinking chess player may aim to win every game and become a world champion, the non-linear player will see how losing a game will position him to play an opponent who will be easier to beat and thus give himself and the game more significant publicity. A player who thinks non-linear can also see so far, knowing their limits and the limits of the game, that at some point they will stage a considerable outburst promising never to play again and the player's exposure to one of their ambitious others.

The ability of mind control is more than just responding to the situation (serial thinking) or having a structured plan to get your result (linear thinking). It is the capability to be smooth when responding to a fluid environment. You have to know your goal, you have to know yourself, you have to know your environment, and you have to know the people you influence in every possible way. And you have to do everything while appearing to be like everyone else around you.

It is not an everyday task, but it is worthy of your efforts. To aspire to these ideal promises that you will learn something about yourself and your world at every turn. Of course, if you are concerned in mind control, it is perhaps rational to discuss mind control ethics. I am not one to preach morality, and you will not read how you should use mind control.

If you're not bothered by Mind Control being used on you and generally a happy person, then it's possibly okay to do similar things with others. As a common rule, if you decide to use mind control and are motivated by anger or grief, you will likely hurt people in the process. Maybe that's not a problem for you. So be it. It would help if you were cautioned never to underestimate people's desire to equalize and change your actions accordingly.

What you will find is that sleep (metaphorical sleep) is the natural state of mind. People will parallel your attempts to arouse them with an attempt to change them. While people don't mind changing, they resist being changed. Consequently, it is finest to stick to your advice. Do people need to wake up? Sure, but let them do it when they want. Until then, it will be you and I who benefit from these insights.

Assuming you are an insignificant energy source subordinate to an enormous machine dominating the world, would you have swallowed the red pill like Neo's main character, to be "woken up" and realize it?

Introduction to Mind Control

To understand the Mind Control process, it is necessary to understand the human mind. People make decisions at every level in a way that is unique to each of them. These determinations are centered on mind dribbles that are spent to identify the self and its situation. These filters are best comprehended in the form of questions people ask themselves. Preserve in mind that these questions are asked unconsciously because people are not aware of them, but they can be inferred from their behaviors and how they respond to events.

These inquiries are not the same in every perspective. A person can make essential relationship decisions based on the query "Would this person arrange me with security?" but from the perspective of buying a car, the question might be, "Will it get me consideration?" or vice versa.

These questions can be numerous and have a hierarchy of priorities. For example, defining whether to consider someone as a sexual partner may involve answering the following questions.
- "Am I attracted to their looks?"
- "Do I feel unharmed with this individual?"
- "Can I see myself having aroused with this individual?"
- "Can I view myself being intimate with this individual more than once?"
- "Will I feel good about me if I have sex with this individual?" etc.

People will reply contrarily to the same situations depending on the questions (filters) they ask. A person facing job loss may ask, "What did I do wrong?" in which case they noticed, found, or created what they have done wrong. In the same situation, another person may subconsciously ask, "How is this a chance for me?" and view the same position as an opportunity.

To the astonishment and enjoyment of many rational thinkers, there is no end to people who routinely focus on problems rather than solutions to the thing's life throws at them. None of these queries are asked on an awake level. Many of these queries /filters are so deeply entrenched that it could upset people if they are asked to view the situation in any other way possible.

The grade you can express a person's filters and the unconscious questions that arise is how you can direct their thoughts and actions. In other words, Mind Control. By understanding this, you can begin your mind control learning journey by examining your filters/

queries that lead you to make conclusions and, at the same time, also perceive the people around you.

A pair of filters/questions you could add to your personal repertoire to learn mind control are: "What can I assume is true for this person that is not overtly obvious?" and "How can I be through their attentiveness to get my result?" Mind control has many names, persuasion, seduction, manipulation, sales skills, politics, advertising, etc. The desire to change the minds and behaviors of people was the only thing.

It is one of the main tasks of communication. Yes, even when you talk to yourself, your motive is to direct your thoughts, actions and behaviors. The sour truth is that we use mind control every time we open our mouths to speak. While these two words, "Mind Control," may have a grinding ring to very of our ears, it doesn't avert it from being a reality of everyday life. Many people will violently deny using it.

It's time to lift the phrase "Mind Control" from its misplaced sewer and subject it to scrutiny as a mere fact of human nature. It means being truly honest with ourselves by keeping our intentions close to the vest. While this is ideal and few people will enthusiastically tell you otherwise, the opposite is usually true.
To show that all you have to do is be completely honest about your intentions every time you go on a first date. Maybe you have visions of marriage in mind with your date. Or maybe your only goal is to bring your date into an unbridled expression of sexual debauchery. Truth, it turns out, is a caustic and volatile chemical when added to most human interactions.

When administered without limitation, the only specific result is that the result will be uncertain. Thankfully, the truth is also very malleable and relatively safe when administered with caution in deluded forms. Therefore, it is best to be judicious with your expressions of honorable intentions and feelings until a reliable answer can be concluded. In the interim, we can look for proof of how pervasive Mind Control is in our daily life.

Mind Control is Used Universally

Here is how mind control is worked in ordinary life:

- Motivate a child to improve in school enthusiastically
- Create obedience to a religious or political figure
- Create a feeling of superiority towards a group
- Motivate a potential customer to purchase a specific product or service
- Create panic to sell a particular stock
- Instill confidence in the authority who is speaking to you on television
- Create contempt for competition by establishing greater customer loyalty
- Bring more revenue
- Bringing an attractive person to a romantic or sexual encounter
- Selling an undervalued product at a higher price
- Discuss a cop about a fine
- Make a viewer believe in psychic abilities
- Get someone to reevaluate their previous beliefs

The list can go on and on. In all these cases, the controller knows his results and objectives. It is safe to say that whenever you want something that involves motivating someone to do something or when people do something without asking why they are doing it, some form of Mind Control is involved, whether deliberate or not. So, we are applying Mind Control all the moments. Even the function of having your partner take out the trash couldn't happen without some form of preparation, conditioning and mind control.

If in doubt, ask a stranger to take out your trash and see what kind of agreement you get. As you will study, mind control requires thinking at a higher level than the subject and veiling the strings of control with everyday life's daily distractions. When one tries to control the higher levels of a power hierarchy, something interesting happens. The visibility of control becomes less evident to individuals as they become more involved in their daily concerns.

Mind Control is around us. Once you understand the intensity of Mind Control in your life, your only option, outside of paranoia, is a calm, almost Buddha-like omniscience that recognizes the ubiquitous presence of Mind Control and sets out to use it to your advantage. Although this mentality can be encouraged, no one can teach it. Only through patience, effort and a little bit of suffering can you get this priceless prospect.

Mind Control Models

If mind control controls others' thoughts, emotions, and actions, several functional models will help you do this. To determine how mind control creates the degree of compliance you want, let's consider some standard mind control models.

Behavioral Modification/Conditioning Model

As in any case of Mind Control, the controller identifies what he needs people to do and needs them to do it willingly, and for what they think, it is their reasons. The behavior modification/conditioning model works with stimuli in rewards and punishments based on their behaviors. In much the similar way you would train a dog to do tricks, you can train a person to take part in some action voluntarily. Behavior alteration/taming needs a sequence of steps that repay good conduct and penalize lousy performance. But let's speak. You want your follower to steal candy from a store (or worse). Using the behavior modification model, you would first reward them for "thinking creatively" outside the norm of social, ethical behavior.

After they have gotten used to thinking outside the norm, and you reward them with every step for it, it's time to move on to the next level. In this next phase, rewards are given for taking actions outside the norm but sanctioned within a social structure or group. University hazing is a good example. It wouldn't take much more than many of these exercises to get them to do something even more harmful. When an action is not taken, a punishment could be as mild as having group members scoffing in contempt. They will also be allowed to deal with the consequences of not acting as required. It creates the illusion of free will.

The controller must make the remunerations huge and the punishments mild but memorable to use the behavior modification/conditioning model skillfully and stealthily. It will prevent the follower from believing that he has been coerced in any way. Scientology has an extensive behavioral conditioning process called "The Training Routines" or "TRs." TRs are presented as communication training at the beginning of someone's interest in Scientology.

Wired Pattern

A doctor can tap your knee, and this is often reflected with a snap of the leg, so we, as humans, also are programmed to answer. The hard-wired human answer to the present is one among conformity and a sense of gratification. The scapegoat is that the fundamental human got to know that our problems aren't our fault, albeit they're. There are tons of conversations among the Human Potential Movement to "take responsibility for one's life," On an understanding level, it makes perfect sense.

If we glance at our life as something that we've complete control over, we feel more empowered, and that we tend to act more decisively and be happier people just because we elect it. However, the planet has other plans and can often throw us a curveball that we didn't expect; people we trust will rob us, we'll affect bills and financial worries, and love relationships will end. It's still a relief to understand that "it's not our fault" altogether these cases. We'll gladly take the side of strangers who will support us by throwing stones at our enemies.

NLP Model
NLP stands for Neuro-Linguistic Programming. It's a field of study developed within the late 1970s by two scientists, Richard Bandler and John Grinder. They wanted to work out why some therapists could affect their clients and obtain speedy results were other therapists seem to require months and years. During this way, they found that we all undergo specific mental processes to form decisions and make changes. If someone (someone) knows about another process to form changes, they need to conform to that process, and therefore the change will happen. It's essentially having the road map for someone's mind.

You can guide the person to try too many things without even knowing what you're doing. As a result, many of us have applied NLP to sales and persuasion, while others have applied it to seductions. What makes NLP unique as a mind-control model is that it treats people as distinct individuals, not as a mass of wired robots. It means everyone has their change processes and these processes are unique to them. The central key to using NLP as a mind-control tool is finding ways to stimulate people's processes. These processes are often within ideas, personal assumptions, trends and values, and their strategy for creating decisions. Once the unique processes of a private are discovered, the doors are wide open for mind control.

Environmental Control Model

The environmental control model is often tons of fun and challenging. It requires the controller to think about everything the topic will experience so that he can, of course, conclude what the controller wants and, consequently, achieve the controller's goal without considering other possibilities or options. It's essential to ascertain a way bigger picture of what's happening. Believe how wizards control the environment to form you think the effect. an honest magician won't tell you, "This may be a normal deck of playing cards." Instead, he'll fan them out for you and even cause you to manage so you'll find out what he wants you to believe on your own. The bridge might be marked, rigged, or support of 1 kind.

To use the conservational mind control model, consider this sentence: "Nobody can resist what they cannot detect." The environmental control model is additionally a favorite of scammers. Suppose you substitute a hospital parking zone and see a person during a white coat with a stethoscope dangling from his pocket. This label says, "Samuel Wallis, MD, Urology," posing for jumper cables to start his car, of course. In that case, I assume that's a doctor. More importantly, don't suppose he is not a specialist.

The pentagram of the control model is that the film "The Matrix." For people that lived linked to the Matrix, everything was even as they thought it had been with everyday life's worries and desires. All the while, they were shielded from discovering that they were nothing but AA batteries won't power a worldwide machine. To effectively use the Environmental Mind Control model, you initially got to ask what you would like your follower to try and what to believe and then create the environment that will naturally make him finish what you would like.

Doing this on an outsized scale can prove difficult thanks to the various variables required to be controlled. On a smaller scale, however, it is often relatively straightforward. Let's take the instance of getting to a spiritual retreat. Participants are isolated from the remainder of the planet. No TV or newspaper. No cell phones or computers. They're then asked to require off their shoes and shut one's mouth when in certain places as a symbol of reverence.

After doing this for any length of your time, it doesn't take long to believe what they're told to believe. A scammer will also use isolation by ensuring his brand is continuously occupied by his scammer co-workers, whose job is to ensure the brand's attention is continually directed where they need it. These are Mind Control models only, not techniques and tactics. As models, they supply suggestions on possible strategies that make mind control possible.

Memes and Mind Control

It signifies a replicator of cultural information that one's mind transmits (verbally or by demonstration) to another mind. Examples of Dawkin's memes are melodies, slogans, dress fashions, ways of making vases or building bows. Other examples include divinities, concepts, ideas, theories, opinions, beliefs, practices, habits, dances, and moods propagating within a culture. A meme propagates as a cultural evolution unit analogous in many ways to the gene (the unit of genetic information).

Memes often propagate as more or less integrated cooperative ensembles or groups, referred to as memeplexes or meme complexes. The theory itself proved to be a successful meme, gaining a rare penetration into a scientific theory's popular culture. Some meme theorists argue that memes most beneficial to their hosts won't necessarily survive;

instead, those memes that replicate the most effectively spread the best, which allows for the possibility that successful memes could prove harmful to their guests.

An instance of this is the meme of a faith that states, "something wonderful is about to happen." This belief can benefit all rational analyzes regardless of its truthfulness, but stronger beliefs such as the "Everyone wants to get me" idea can win. Suppose this is true when designing a meme (or belief system) for Mind Control purposes. In that case, one must consider increasing the meme's ability to replicate itself and increase the belief system's lifespan.

Some memes' supporters propose that they develop through natural selection, very similar to Charles Darwin's biological evolution ideas on the premise that variation, mutation, competition, and "heredity" affect their replicative success. For example, while an idea may become extinct, other ideas will survive, spread and change for better or worse through modification. It has some practical applications when applying your mind control skills. If the beliefs you instill in people are beneficial to you, you need to find a way for them to persist and replicate.

Give sense, not just to the faith, but to the maintenance of the idea. For example, a religious group can call itself a "believer" to emphasize the value of their beliefs, especially of particular beliefs in the leaders' words' correctness. So, because they appreciate calling themselves "believers," they appreciate the leaders' words as truth without stating it. Perhaps a more straightforward process for making a meme replica is the initiation process. During a typical initiation, the initiate is subjected to emotional stress. This procedure inspires in the new initiate a deep sense of personal worth for the group and initiation. It makes him eager and willing to participate in the subsequent initiation ritual of initiates.

Only Idiots are Suffering from Mind Control

When human behavior's extremes are considered, the foremost brutal actions to know are seemingly ordinary people acting in ways contrary to even what they might think they're capable of. Cults are the simplest example. No average person would tell you that he plans to become celibate and kill himself in hopes of reincarnation on a spaceship journey by angelic space aliens.

But this is often what Charles Manson forced many of his followers to try. Once we attempt to add up to those acts, we are often amazed and quickly classify them into one among two categories; they're "crazy" or "monsters." therein act, we inadvertently prevent ourselves from learning the foremost valuable lessons of Mind Control. So, we enquire you to think about what if they weren't crazy?

What if They Weren't a Freak?

It is where we run into the most crucial obstacle to understanding how Mind Control works, which is morality. Whenever we use our morality to gauge an action, event, or situation, we unconsciously block our ability to know it and involuntarily limit our ability to speak effectively. The very fact is that anyone is often influenced, moved and manipulated by Mind Control. Like Archimedes, who realized that he could move the world if he could stay within the right place within the universe. No man can't be moved with the proper pressure within the right place at the proper time.

So, Would You Use Mind Control?

On many levels, the study of mind control can benefit anyone. At the main basic level of our needs and desires, it seems straightforward that the more quickly we will influence the people around us, the more comfortable we'll meet our needs for money, love, sex and security. But this is often only the foremost obvious. It's also the smallest amount necessary. While I've managed to urge everyone studying the topic in my life, the foremost significant benefit I've gotten is that the hardest to quantify.

It is the peace of mind that will only come from long years of using and using power. Most humans are hungry and crave the facility that Mind Control can give. That hunger, though irresistible, is additionally the result of lack. Not enough money. Not enough sex. Not enough certainty. Not enough security. Just like the child who continually tries to convince their parents that they're okay while they enter the third, fourth and fifth decades of life.

After maintaining power and influence over others for a short time, you quickly find out how simple it's. It seems that most people go around with their duct in their hands, trying to find someone to attach it to. Power and influence are not any longer goals to be achieved but become tools to be used. A bit like a drill in the hands of an honest carpenter learning to hammer a nail with the smallest number of blows, so too power becomes something you employ less and fewer to indicate your skill. It's just a tool. And just like the carpenter and his hammer, you'll earn a living using it effectively. Once you first start using mind control, your goals are usually predictable and straightforward; usually more sex and money. But eventually, all of this becomes old and familiar.

The goal then becomes to work out the minimum amount of power (and mind control) is required to urge what you would like. Another advantage may be a quiet detachment from the foremost significant suffering of humanity. It's noted in particular because of the smug feeling of superiority from knowing something forbidden from others. Superiority later gives thanks to a way of fun within the way people do "little things" about life and death. They panic about renting, relationships, and seeking approval.

Eventually, people will come to you wondering how does one stay so calm and poised during the turmoil that seems so evident to them. In truth, all they need is to be within the presence of that calm because there's nothing you'll tell them, which will give them what they need.

What if You Do Not Learn Mind Control?

It is an honest question, and that we can say that if you never learn the art of Mind Control, life is going to be more or less an equivalent. You'll run with an equivalent sort of people doing equivalent belongings you have always done. You will have equivalent frustrations you've always had and, therefore, the same rewards. It's very likely that outwardly you do not seem to miss everything. Your life will be like prominent people, thinking that what you see is real, and you'll not be curious or disturbed by the subtle and sometimes devious things that happen beneath the surface.

You will see people as people, and that they will inevitably live up to your expectations. If you do not learn mind control, you'll still be distracted and bothered by politics or advertising, but you'll never realize or consider why. If you never learn mind control, you'll evaluate yourself and confidently conclude that you simply are very almost like most people, you know, and you'll be right.

Why Do I Need to Learn Mind Control?

We distinguish between learning mind control and being good at it. Mind control learning falls into two categories. Reading it and studying it. As far as we do know, you're only willing to examine Mind Control. It means you'll be ready to tell folks that you recognize somewhat about mind control. Learning mind control is an order of significance beyond reading. Studying means dedicating oneself to understanding the concepts of Mind Control, a minimum of on an intellectual level.

Studying will cause you to an honest commentator on the topic. Being good at mind control is another quantum jump. You do not realize it at this level, and you'll mention it. You are doing it on every occasion. You see each social interaction as a chance to witness some aspect of Mind Control in action or, better yet, to check something about Mind Control that you simply have learned. So, if you would like to be good at Mind Control, it'll take time and study, reading (of course) and learning concepts, but even more, it requires an adventurous attitude and a desire to attach deeply with people.

It is a decent idea to revise everything you'll consider about hypnosis, NLP, social influence, brainwashing, cults, unclassified government interrogation documents, and more. You'll also strive to ascertain mind control in action. You'll visit and join cults. You would possibly also attempt to climb the cult's hierarchy to ascertain how far you'll go and the way much you'll learn from experience. You'll make every plan to enrich your life with differing individuals' types to find out from experience the principles and exceptions that apply to human behavior and thinking.

To be truly good at Mind Control, you've got to swear to measure your life, trying to know and control people in ways in which make them enjoy your presence and are grateful for your attention. When you're wrong, you objectively review the results and make changes. There's a mindset that anyone who wants to find out mind control is probably going to evolve.

Curiosity

Mind control information does not have any boundaries, which will be studied and tested. Its why curiosity is so important. Curiosity is that the quality that will allow you to check everything you study mind control.

Gregariousness

If you're getting to learn mind control, you better enjoy being with people. It doesn't suggest you will not have a personal life. A life crammed with personal self-discovery will surely benefit you. The chance to be within people's presence is usually taken as a chance to check your ability to steer and influence. Your goals do not have to be great during these interactions. Sometimes it's just a matter of observing which individuals answer your influence.

Scholar

Mind Control is limitless. You'll study. It's inevitable that as you delve into the depths of research and experimentation, you'll discover new and unedited information.

Strategically Not Just Tactically

The tactic is about the items you are doing to urge a result. The strategy is to regulate the items that influence the achievement of the result. A simple strategy will make it appear to be the planet that offers you everything you would like as if it were a present, but you've seen the critical picture of what affects things. A small push using the strategy will produce even as much like an active push using the tactic and make your power feel almost magical.

Quiet

It may seem contrary to the mentality of sociability, but it turns out that creating a balance between these two extremes offers excellent strength. It is perhaps the most challenging part to learn: keeping quiet about things you know. Several who have just acquired their first magic trick are often inclined to reveal the secret in exchange for short-term attention. In the long run, however, we forgive because the sense of awe you can create is replaced by the awareness of being a cheater from that moment on. Thus, you learn that keeping a secret has power, and giving it way limits that power.

As an insight into the purpose and power of emotions, this exemplary act of parental heroism testifies to the role of selfless love and every other emotion we feel in human life. It suggests that our deepest feelings, passions and desires are essential guides and that our species owes much of its existence to power in human affairs. That power is extraordinary: only powerful love, the urge to save a beloved child, could lead a parent to ignore the urge for personal survival. It is viewed from the intellect, their self-sacrifice was arguably irrational, and seen from the heart, it was the only choice to make.

Sociobiologic emphasizes the heart's prominence over the top at such pivotal moments once they speculate why evolution has given emotions such a central role within the human psyche. Our emotions, they say, guide us in dealing with difficult situations and too important tasks to go away the intellect alone with danger, painful loss, persevering towards a goal despite frustrations, bonding with a partner, building a family. Each emotion offers a particular readiness to act; each point us during a way that has functioned well to handle human life's recurring challenges. As these eternal situations are repeated and repeated throughout our evolutionary history, our emotional repertoire's survival value has been attested by the very fact that it's imprinted on our nerves as the human heart's innate and automatic tendencies.

A view of the attribute that ignores the facility of emotions is, unfortunately, short-sighted. The actual name humans, the thinking species, is misleading in light of the new appreciation and new view of the place of emotions in our lives that science now offers, as we all know from experience, when it involves shaping our decisions and actions, feeling matters the maximum amount and sometimes quite thought. We've gone too far in emphasizing the worth and importance of the purely rational of what measures IQ in human life. Intelligence cannot achieve anything when emotions dominate.

Passions Above Reason

When our emotions are wise guides within the long evolutionary period, the new realities that civilization presents have arisen with such rapidity that evolution's slow march cannot continue. As Freud pronounced in Civilization and Its Discontents, society has had to use rules from the surface to subdue emotional excess tides that run too freely within.

Despite these social constraints, passions overwhelm reason over and once again. This fact of attribute arises from the essential architecture of mental life. In terms of biological design for the essential neural circuits of sentiment, what we are born with is what has operated best for the last 50,000 human generations, not the last 500 generations, and positively not the last five. The slow and deliberate evolutionary forces that have shaped our emotions have done their beat in the last 10,000 years. Regardless of having witnessed the rapid rise of human civilization and the explosion of the human population from five million to 5 billion, we've left a touch footprint on our biological models for emotional life.

For better or for worse, our assessment of every personal encounter and our responses to that are shaped not only by our rational judgments or personal history but also by our distant ancestral past. It leaves us with sometimes tragic propensities. In short, we are confronted with postmodern dilemmas with an emotional repertoire adapted to the Pleistocene urgencies. This example is at the guts of my topic.

Impulses to Action

All emotions are, in spirit, instincts to act, the moment plans for managing life that progress has inculcated in us. The very origin of the word emotion is "motere," the Latin verb "to move," plus the prefix "e-" to connote "to move away," suggesting that a bent to act is inherent every emotion. Emotions cause more alleged actions when observing animals or children; it's only in "civilized" adults that we frequently find the many anomalies within the Animalia, emotions - radical impulses to act - separated from the apparent reaction.

Each emotion plays a unique role in our emotional repertoire, as revealed by their distinctive biological signatures. With new methods of peering into the body and brain, researchers are uncovering more biological facts of how each emotion makes the body for a different sort of response:

- In anger, blood flows to the hands, making it easier to grab a weapon or hit an enemy; pulse increases, and a rush of hormones like adrenaline generates a surge of energy strong enough for vigorous action.

- With fear, the blood goes to the massive skeletal muscles, like the legs, making it easier to flee and turning the face pale when the blood is diverted (creating the feeling that the blood is "running cold"). Simultaneously, the body freezes, albeit just for a flash, perhaps allowing time to measure whether hiding could be a far better reaction. The brain's emotional centers' circuits trigger a flood of hormones that put the body on general alert, making it nervous and prepared for action. The eye is fixed on the threat in situ to gauge better which response to offer.

- Among the many biological changes in happiness is increased activity during a brain center that inhibits negative feelings, promotes a rise in available energy, and quiets people who generate troubling thoughts. But there's no particular change in physiology except inactivity, which causes the body to recover sooner from the natural arousal of upsetting emotions. This configuration gives the body general rest, and therefore the readiness and enthusiasm for whatever task is at hand and to strive towards the right sort of goals.

- Love, tender feelings, and sexual satisfaction involve parasympathetic arousal, the physiological opposite of the "fight or flight" mobilization shared by fear and anger. The parasympathetic pattern, nicknamed the "relaxation response," maybe a set of whole-body reactions that generate a common state of calm and contentment, facilitating cooperation.

- Surprise brow lift allows for a broader range of vision and allows more light to hit the retina. It offers more information about the unexpected event, making it easier to know what's happening and develop the best plan of action precisely.

All over the planet, an expression of disgust looks an equivalent and sends an equivalent message. The countenance of disgust - the upper lip curled to the side while the nose curls slightly - suggests an early attempt, as Darwin observed, to shut the nostrils against a noxious odor or to spit out a toxic food.

One of the sadness's primary functions is to assist adapt to a significant loss, like someone's death close or a perfect dissatisfaction. Grief brings a drop in vigor and eagerness for life's activities, mostly leisure and pleasure, and because it deepens and approaches depression, it slows down the body's metabolism. This introspective withdrawal creates the chance to mourn a loss or frustrated hope, grasp the results for your life, and plan for brand spanking new beginnings when the energy returns. This loss of energy may have kept the first humans saddened and vulnerable closer to family, where they were securer.

These biological propensities to act are shaped further by our life experience and our culture. For example, universally, the loss of a beloved elicits sadness and grief. But how we show our grieving—how emotions are displayed or held back for personal moments—is molded by culture, as are which particular people in our lives fall under the category of "loved ones" to be mourned.

When these emotional replies were beaten into shape, evolution's protracted period was undoubtedly a stricter certainty than most humans tolerated as a species after the dawn of recorded history. It had been a time when few infants survived to childhood and a couple of grownups to thirty years when hunters could attack at any moment when the whims of scarcities and floods meant the transformation between hunger and existence. But with the approaching of agriculture and even the foremost primitive human societies, the chances for survival began to vary dramatically. Within the last ten thousand years, when these advances took hold throughout the planet, the aggressive anxieties held the human population in restraint relieved gradually.

We Have Two Minds

We've two minds, one that thinks and one that feels. These two fundamentally alternative ways of knowing to interact to construct our mental life. The lucid mind is the mode of understanding. We are typically aware of more prominent in awareness, thoughtful ready to ponder and reflect. Nevertheless, there's another system of knowing: impulsive and powerful, if sometimes illogical—the emotional mind.

The emotional/rational dichotomy approximates the folks (the distinction between "heart" and "head"; knowing something is right "in your heart" may be a different order of conviction, somehow a more profound quite certainty than thinking so together with your rational mind. There's a gentle gradient within the ratio of rational-to-emotional control over the mind; the more intense the sensation, the more dominant the emotional mind becomes. Therefore, the more ineffectual the rational. It's an appointment that seems to stem from eons of evolutionary advantage to having emotions and intuitions guide our instantaneous response in situations where our lives are peril and were pausing to chew over what costs us our lives.

Therefore, the emotional and rational, these two minds operate in tight harmony, for the significant part, intertwining their very alternative ways of knowing to guide us through the planet. Ordinarily, there's a balance between emotional and rational minds, emotion feeding, and informing the rational mind's operations. Therefore, the lucid mind is filtering and sometimes refusing the efforts of the sentiments. Still, the emotional and lucid minds are semi-independent capabilities, each, as we shall see, reflecting the operation of distinct, but interconnected, circuitry within the brain. These minds are exquisitely coordinated; feelings are essential to thought, thought, and feeling. But when passions surge the balance tips, the emotional mind captures the whip hand, swamping the rational mind.

How Did the Brain Grow?

To better grasp the powerful hold of the emotions on the thinking mind—and why feeling and reason are so readily at war, consider how the brain evolved. With their three-pound approximately of cells and the human heart's natural juices, human brains are tensions of these in our nearest cousins in evolution, the nonhuman primates. Over many years of evolution, the brain has grown from rock bottom-up, with its better centers evolving as amplification of lower, more primeval parts.

The oldest root of our emotional life is the sense of smell or, more precisely, the cells that absorb and analyze the smell's sense in the olfactory lobe. Every living entity, be it nourishing, poisonous, sexual partner, predator or prey, has a distinctive molecular signature that can be carried by the wind. In those primitive times, the sense of smell was praised as a fundamental sense for survival.

The ancient emotion centers began to evolve from the olfactory lobe, eventually becoming large enough to surround the brain stem's upper part. In its primitive stages, the olfactory center was composed of little more than thin layers of neurons collected to analyze the sense of smell. A layer of cells absorbed the odor and divided it into relevant categories: edible or toxic, sexually available, enemy or meal. The second layer of cells sent reflexive messages throughout the nervous system, telling the body what to do: bite, spit, approach, run away, chase.

As the limbic system has evolved, it has perfected two powerful tools: learning and memory. These revolutionary advances have allowed an animal to be much more intelligent in its survival choices and fine-tune its responses to adapt to changing needs rather than having invariable, automatic reactions. If a food causes illness, it could be avoided next time. Decisions such as knowing what to eat and what to refuse were still determined mainly by smell; the correlations between the olfactory bulb and the limbic system now took on the task of making distinctions between smells and recognizing them, comparing a present odor with past ones and thus distinguishing good from the bad. It was done by the "rhinencephalon," literally, the "brain of the nose," a part of the limbic wiring and the neocortex's rudimentary base, the thinking brain.

This new addition to the brain allowed for the addition of nuances to emotional life. Get love. Limbic structures produce feelings of desire and sexual desire, the emotions that fuel sexual desire. But the addon of the neocortex and its correlations to the limbic system has allowed for the mother-child bond that underlies the family nucleus and the long-term commitment to child-rearing that makes human development possible. (Species with no neocortex, such as reptiles, lack maternal affection; when their young hatch, babies must hide to avoid being cannibalized.) In humans, the protective bond between parent and child allows much of the maturation continues throughout an extended childhood, during which the brain continues to develop.

Emotional Intelligence and Destiny
IQ offers little to explain people's different fates with more or less equal promises, education, and opportunities. When ninety-five Harvard students from

the 1940s classroom - a time when people with a broader IQ prevalence attended Ivy League schools than they currently do - were followed into middle age, the men with the highest scores senior in college were not incredibly successful compared to their peers with lower scores in terms of salary, productivity, or status in their field. Neither have they had the most excellent life satisfaction or pleasure with companionships and passionate relations.

A related follow-up in middle age was done with 450 boys, most immigrants, two-thirds from assisted families, who grew up in Somerville, Massachusetts, and a "slum" a few blocks from Harvard. A third had an IQ below 90. But again, the IQ had little bearing on how well they had done at work; for example, 7% of men with IQs below 80 were unemployed for ten or more years, but so were 7% of men with IQs above 100. There was a usual link (as always) between IQ and socioeconomic level at forty-seven. But childhood skills, such as the ability to manage frustrations, control emotions, and get along with other people, made the most significant difference.

It also considers data from an ongoing study of eighty-one valedictorians and salutatorians of 1981 in Illinois's high schools. All had the top-grade point average in their schools. Nevertheless, while they continued to perform well in college and achieved excellent grades, they had only achieved average success levels by their late twenties.

And this is the problem: academic intelligence offers virtually no preparation for the turmoil or opportunities that life's vicissitudes bring. However, even if a high IQ is no guarantee of prosperity, prestige or happiness in life, our schools and culture fixate on academic skills, ignoring emotional intelligence. Some might call it a character that is also immensely important to our destiny. Emotional life is a field. And how proficient a person is at these things is vital to accepting why one person prospers in life while another, of equal intellect, dead ends: emotional aptitude is a meta-skill, which determines how well we can use any other skill. We have, including raw intellect.

There are great ways to thrive in life, and many domains where other abilities are remunerated. In our progressively experience-based society, technical skill is undoubtedly one of them. There's a children's joke: "What do you call a nerd in fifteen years?" The answer: "Chief." But even among "nerds," emotional intelligence offers an added advantage in the workplace, as we will see in the third part. Much evidence shows that emotionally adept people - who know and manage their feelings well and who read and cope effectively with others' feelings - have an advantage in any domain of life, whether romantic and intimate relationships or grasping the unspoken rules that govern success in organizational politics. People with well-developed emotional abilities are also more likely to be content and effective in their lives, mastering the mental habits that promote their productivity; people who cannot exert some rule over their vibrant life fight internal battles that disrupt their work's attention and think clearly.

CHAPTER 5: ART OF PERSUASION

A persuasion is an additional form of mind control that will be discussed. While there may not be as much media hype about this form of mind control as there is with brainwashing and hypnosis, it can be just as effective when done correctly. The problem with this module is that there are so many different forms of persuasion present in daily life that it can be difficult for any source to reach the topic and make a difference.

While persuasion works to change the follower's thoughts and beliefs like other forms of mind control, it looks like everyone is trying to persuade you of something, so it becomes easier to ignore the follower's persuasion. For example, commercials on television, when there is an argument going on or even when a conversation is going on, there is some form of persuasion taking place. People will often use persuasion to their advantage without realizing it.

What is Persuasion?

To begin with, is the definition of persuasion. When people think about persuasion, they often come up with many different answers. Some may think of the commercials and advertisements they see around them that prompt them to purchase one particular product over another. Others might think about persuasion in terms of politics and how candidates can try to sway voters' opinions to get another vote. Both are examples of persuasion because the message is trying to change the way the follower is thinking. Persuasion can be found in everyday life and is a compelling force and a significant influence on followers and society. Advertising, mass media, legal and political decisions will be influenced by how persuasion works and, in turn, will also work to persuade the argument.

As you can see, there are some key differences between persuasion and the other forms of mind control that have been discussed so far in this guide. Brainwashing and hypnosis require the individual to be in isolation to change their mind and identity. Manipulation will work even on one person to achieve the ultimate goal. While persuasion can be done on one subject to change your mind, it is also possible to use persuasion on a larger scale to persuade an entire group or even society to change the way they think. It can make it even more effective and possibly dangerous because it can change many people's minds all at once rather than the mind of just one follower.

Many people have the false impression that they are immune to the effects of persuasion. They consider they would be able to see any sales pitch launched in their way, whether the agent is selling a product or some new idea, and then understand the situation and find the conclusion. Their logic. It will be true; no one falls in love with everything they hear as often as they use logic, especially if it goes entirely against their beliefs, no matter how intense the argument may be. Most people will also avoid messages about buying TVs and luxury cars or about the latest product on the market. Often, the act of persuasion will be much more subtle, and it may be more difficult for the person to form their own opinions on what is being said.

When it comes to the act of persuasion, most people will see it in a negative light. They will think of a salesperson or scammer trying to get them to change all their beliefs and push and annoy them until the change occurs. While this is undoubtedly a way to think about persuasion, this process can often be used positively rather than just a negative way. For example, public service campaigns can encourage people to quit smoking or recycle can be forms of persuasion that can improve a person's life. It's all about the way the persuasion process is used.

Elements of Persuasion

As with other forms of mind control, there are a few things to look out for when it comes to persuasion. These elements help define what persuasion is so that it is more recognizable. According to Perloff in 2003, persuasion is defined as "A symbolic process in which communications seek to convince other people to alter their outlooks or behaviors about a problem by transmitting a message in an atmosphere of free choice."

It is one thing that makes persuasion different from other forms of mind control; the follower is often allowed to make his or her own free choices on the matter, although the persuasion tactic will work to shift the follower's mind in a particular direction. The follower can choose which way he wants to think, whether he wants to buy a product or not, or whether he thinks the evidence behind the persuasion is strong enough to change his mind.

- There are some elements present in the persuasion that help define it further. These elements include:
- Persuasion is symbolic, which means it uses sounds, images and words to make the point.
- Persuasion will involve the agent deliberately trying to influence the follower or group.
- Self-persuasion is a vital part of this process. The follower is usually not forced and instead is given the freedom to choose its own decision.
- There are many ways that persuasive messages can be conveyed, including face-to-face, the Internet, radio, and television. Communication can also take place non-verbal or verbal.

Let's take a look at each of these points in a little more detail. The first element of persuasion is that it must be symbolic. To get somebody to think or act a certain way, you need to show them why they should change their thoughts. It will include the use of words, sounds and images to make the new point understood. You can use words to start a debate or discussion to show your point. Images are a eminent way to show the evidence needed to persuade someone to go one way or another. Some non-verbal cues are possible, but will not be as effective as using words and images.

The second key is that persuasion will be used deliberately to influence how others act or think. It is pretty apparent, and if you're not intentionally trying to influence others, you're not using persuasion to get them to change. The persuader will try different tactics to get the follower to think the same way he does. It could be somewhat as modest as having a debate with them or presenting evidence to support their perspective.

The unique thing about persuasion is that it allows the follower to have some form of free will. The follower is allowed to make his own choice in the way. For the most part, no matter how hard someone tries to persuade him of something, he doesn't have to. The follower might hear a thousand commercials about the best car to buy, but if they don't like that make or don't need a new vehicle right now, they won't go out and buy it. If the follower is against abortion, no matter how many people come out and say how big the abortion is, the follower is unlikely to change his mind. It allows for much more freedom of choice than is found in other forms of mind control, which could explain why many people don't see it as a type of mind control when asked.

A persuasion is a form of mind control that can happen in many different ways. While brainwashing, hypnosis and manipulation have to happen face to face, and in some cases in complete isolation, persuasion can happen in other ways. You can find examples of persuasion everywhere, including talking to people you know, on the Internet and through radio and television. It can also deliver persuasive messages through non-verbal and verbal means, although it is much more effective when verbal techniques are used.

Modern Persuasion

Over time, the persuasion has been able to evolve and change from its original origins. The persuasion has been around for many years; in fact, it has existed since ancient Greece. It does not mean that the art and persuasion processes are the same as they were then. Certainly, some changes have been made to the art of persuasion and how it is used in modern times. Some of the critical elements of modern persuasion will be discussed in this section.

The use of modern persuasion is different from how it was used in the past. These five ways include:

- The number of messages considered persuasive has grown by leaps and bounds: in ancient Greek times, persuasion was only used in writing and debates among elites. The occurrence of persuasion wasn't a significant thing, and you wouldn't see it very often. In modern times, it's hard to get anywhere without a persuasive message following you. Think about the diverse types and sources of advertisements available; the average adult in the United States will encounter up to 3,000 of them every day. In addition to that, there are always people knocking on your door trying to get you to buy something, believe their ideas or try something new. Persuasion is much more a part of modern life than it has been at any other time in history.

- Persuasion travels very fast: in ancient Greek times, it could take weeks or more for a persuasive message to arrive from one point to another. It limited the impact of persuasion because most people would not be able to get the message. Most of the persuasion had to be done in the context of face-to-face communication. In modern times, persuasive messages can cover a great distance in no time thanks to the Internet, radio and television. Political candidates can reach voters all at once in seconds, and any message can be spread easily. Persuasion takes on a much more critical role when it can be spread so quickly.

- Persuasion can mean a lot of money: Now that companies have discovered the power of persuasion, they are doing all they can to make it work for them. The more effective they are at persuading consumers to buy their products, the more money they will make. Some companies are pure because of the persuasive process, such as public relations firms, marketing firms and advertising agencies. Other companies will use these companies' persuasive techniques to reach and exceed the sales goals they have set for themselves.

- The persuasion has become more subtle than in the past. At the beginning of the persuasion, the agent announced his opinions aloud for the whole group to hear them in hopes of changing everyone's mind. Those days are over, and the persuasion process has become much more discreet. While it is possible to find persuasions that are still very loud and, in the face, many others follow a more subtle path in some forms of advertising.

An instance of this is when businesses create a specific image of themselves, such as being family-friendly, to achieve consumers to buy their products. You may also notice that instead of getting into a debate with your friend about going to a party, they will use peer pressure or just list some facts to get you to come with them. Despite being more subtle, persuasion is even more significant today than ever.

The persuasion process has become more complex: Along with persuasion, which is more subtle and sometimes more challenging to point out, it is also going to become more complex. The topics target more diverse than in the past, and they have many more choices to make. If an individual went to a store in town to buy everything they needed, they could now choose from different stores for their needs, from the hardware store to the grocery store and the convenience store. Clothing. Additionally, there is often more than one option available for each shopping category in the area. These choices make it harder for the agent to develop an excellent persuasive message for the consumer or any other topic.

Methods of Persuasion

Persuasion methods can often go by other names and be referred to as persuasion strategies and persuasion tactics. Resultantly, there is no specific approach that can persuade someone to think or act in a certain way. The agent may be able to speak to the follower while presenting evidence to change the follower's mind, may be able to use some sort of force or pull at the follower, and may perform some sort of service for the follower or use another tactic. This section will detail the different persuasion methods available and how they could be useful in persuasion.

Use of Force

Depending on the situation, the agent may decide that it is good to use some force to persuade the follower to think his way. It can happen if ideas don't match up correctly, if regular talking doesn't work, or if the agent feels frustrated or upset with the conversation's turn. Force is often used as a scare tactic because it gives the follower less time to think logically about what is happening than when a normal conversation occurs. Force is usually used when the agent has been less successful using the other means of persuasion available, although it is sometimes initiated using force. Other times, the force can be used if the agent feels that he is losing control or when the follower can present contradictory evidence to the agent, and the agent becomes angry.

It is regularly not the best idea to use force when it comes to the persuasion process. Many people will see the use of force as a threat due to the agent giving no other options to the request they are making. The whole appeal of persuasion gives the follower choice of paths, but the force has entered the mix, freedom of choice is gone, and the follower is more likely to feel threatened.

Once the follower feels threatened, they are less likely to listen and take into account everything the agent is saying and therefore, the process will not go further. Because of these reasons, the use of force is generally discouraged and avoided in the art of persuasion, unlike the other forms of mind control discussed.

<h3 style="text-align:center">To Influence</h3>

Another method that can persuade the follower to lean in a specific way is to use the available points of influence. We discuss the art of persuasion and define the six points of influence that can make the agent succeed in his goals. The six influence points are reciprocity, commitment and consistency, social proof, sympathy, authority, and scarcity. These six points of influence are critical to the agent as they are part of their subjects' change. Each of these six points will be discussed below:

Reciprocity

The first point of influence is the principle of reciprocity. This principle states that when a person, the agent, provides the other person, the follower will attempt to repay the agent in kind with something of value. It means that when the agent performs some service to the follower, the follower will feel that he should perform a similar service to the agent sooner or later. Although the two services may not be identical, they have the same kind of value so that the obligation of each is equaled. The act of reciprocity ends up producing a sense of obligation in the follower, which the agent can then use as a powerful tool when he wants to use persuasion. The reciprocity rule is very significant because it helps the agent bring the follower into the right frame of mind for the act of persuasion by instilling and overwhelming the follower with a sense of obligation. The agent may be more likely to persuade the follower to act somehow because it will have that sense of obligation hanging over him.

Another added benefit to the agent in using reciprocity is that it is not just a moral position that will put the follower but also a position supported by social codes. The agent will not worry if the follower has the right moral code to return the favor. If the follower does not feel the need to do so, the agent has some tools to spur him to action.

As a society, people don't like negligent people about returning a favor or payment when offered a gift or service. If the agent has not considered that the follower will reciprocate with them, they will hand it over to their social group. They can do this by telling other friends or colleagues how they did the follower a favor, but the follower never returned it when needed. Now the agent has imposed social standards on the matter by declaring favor, making it even more likely to persuade the follower to do something.

For the most part, the follower will be happy to reciprocate with the agent without external forces. When the favor is granted, the follower will begin looking for ways to repay the agent so that the score is even and does not seem greedy or selfish. The agent will then provide an easy solution to repay this debt; the follower will be grateful for this easy solution and will be more likely to go the way the agent wants.

Commitment and Consistency
The next weapon of influence that needs to be discussed is that of commitment and consistency. The agent will need to use both if they want to persuade someone to change their perspective. When things are consistent, they are easier to understand and help individuals make their own better decisions. It is not suitable for the agent to always change the facts he uses or change

other information necessary to help the follower process the information. Rather than helping with the persuasion process, consistently staying out of consistency will make the agent seem like a liar and cannot be trusted, failing the persuasion process.

Dependability is one of the significant features of the persuasion process. It is why:

- Consistency is highly valued in society: People like things to stay a certain way most of the time. People feel safe knowing that things will remain fairly consistent overall. It allows them to remember what happened, know what to expect, and be prepared should changes occur. If consistency weren't available, things would be complicated to plan, and there would always be chaos issues around. If you want to persuade a follower of a particular thing, you need to ensure that your facts are consistent and make sense to them.
- Consistency benefits most people's approach to daily life. Have you thought of trying to plan a day out when something unexpected happens? It can make things nearly impossible to do, and it will end up looking like a disaster. People like consistency because it lets them know what to expect and what to do. They know when it's time to eat when it's time to work, and when other things will happen throughout the day.
- Consistency provides a very valuable shortcut through the complications present in modern existence. Life has been hard enough without having to add other things they haven't done since. When people can have a coherent life, it makes things a lot easier.

Consistency is a great tool because it allows the individual to make the right decisions and process information. If the agent is to persuade the follower successfully, he must ensure that his message is consistent. There is no room for false evidence that can reveal itself later and ruin the whole process. Keep the facts truthful and concise, and it is much better to persuade the argument.

Something that binds to consistency is the act of commitment. It is good to know that the follower is persuaded and that the effort has paid off. It is essential to have some commitment. In advertising, this can mean that the follower will buy the product or politics; it can mean that the follower will vote for a particular candidate. The commitment made will vary according to the nature of the persuasion. According to the consistency concept, if a person undertakes, in writing or orally, he is much more likely to honor the commitment he has made.

It has been found that this is even more true in terms of written commitments as the topic will be psychologically more concrete, and there is some hard evidence that they have accepted the commitment. It makes much sense; many people will promise that they will fix something or do something, to turn around and not do it. Sure, some people will do what they said, and they are more likely to do it if they promise orally. They don't promise, but it is often difficult to achieve the desired results this way. Plus, there's no way to back it up as an oral agreement will just become a disagreement, she said, and no one will win. On the other hand, if the mediator can produce a written commitment from the follower, he has the proof he needs that the thing has been done.

The reason it is so essential for the agent to get the follower to accept a commitment is that once the follower has committed to the new position, they have more of a disposition to act in a way that fits that commitment. After that point, the follower will continue and begin to engage in self-persuasion for the cause. Various justifications and reasons for supporting the commitment will be provided to avoid any problems with the agent. If the agent can bring the follower to that point, they will have much less work to tackle.

Social Proof

Persuasion is a method of a standard interface and will have to follow social rules where it occurs. The people around it will influence the topic; they will be more likely to want to do what others do rather than do their own thing. The follower will base their beliefs and actions on what others are doing around them, how they act, and how they believe. For example, if the person grows up in a city, he is more likely to behave like others who come from that area; on the other hand, those who grow up in a very religious community can spend much of their time praying, learning and helping others.

Under this influence, the saying "crowd power" can be beneficial. The follower will want to know what other people around them are doing at all times. It has become almost an obsession in this country to do what others do to fit in, even though people will say how they want to be different and be individuals.

An example of how people will do something because others can be found on the phone. If the host says something like "Operators are waiting, call now," the follower may assume that operators sit with nothing to do because no one calls them. It will make the follower less likely to call because they imagine that if someone else isn't calling, then they shouldn't either. If the host changes only a few words and instead says, "If the operators are busy, call again," the result can be very different. The follower now assumes that operators are busy with many other followers' calls, so the organization must be reasonable and legitimate. The follower is much more likely to call if they can get through right away or have to be put on hold.

The social proof persuasion technique is most effective in situations where the follower is unsure of what he will do or when there seem to be many similarities in the situations. In ambiguous or uncertain situations that require multiple choices or possibilities, the follower will often choose to conform to what others around him are doing. The choices are so similar that each one will work, but they will assume that the choice others are making is the right one. The other way social proof can be used is when some similarities occur. For example, the follower is much more likely to conform and change around those similar to them somehow. If someone is similar to the follower responsible, the follower is likely to listen and follow him more than if the response is very different from the follower.

The agent will be able to use the idea of social proof to help with their persuasion process. The first way they can do this is to look at the words they are saying. With the given an example from the game show, both quotes said the same thing, but they got two different meanings by changing the wording. Neither was a lie; they were only useful in eliciting a different kind of response. If the agent can observe the way things are expressed, he can get the right answer from the followers and persuade the follower to follow the same ideas and beliefs.

Additionally, the agent will find that there is more successful if he can persuade those like them to share ideas. It is why politicians will try to campaign against like-minded groups. If they need to reach a larger group, they will modify their ideas to make them more attractive to these new groups.

Liking

There is a straightforward reason or this; if the follower likes the agent, he is much more likely to say yes. Two main factors will contribute to how well the follower likes the agent. The first is physical attractiveness, and the second is similarity.

First, if the agent is physically more attractive to the follower, they will feel more persuasive since they can get what they want more quickly, also changing others' attitudes. This pull factor has proven effective in sending encouraging messages and impressions of other traits the agent may have, including intelligence, kindness, and talent. These work together to make it more likely that an attractive person will more easily persuade the follower.

The second factor, the similarity, is a little more straightforward. The idea states that if the follower is similar to the agent, they are much more likely to respond in the affirmative to what the agent is asking. This process is quite natural, and most of the time, the follower won't have to think about whether it's the real thing to do when they like and are similar to the agent.

Authority
One of the ways the agent will be able to persuade the follower is to become an authority. Resultantly, there is an inclination for most people to believe that something an expert says about a topic is correct. The follower is more likely to enjoy listening to a reliable and competent agent; if the agent can bring these two things to the table, he is already well on his way to getting the follower to listen and believe them.

Studies have been conducted to show how this authority technique can persuade the follower to listen to what the agent says. Of course, when it comes to persuasion, pain isn't always needed to change the way people think. Conclusion This study illustrates how the follower will react to the agent if the agent can prove that he is authoritarian. Keeping this in mind can help the agent reach their agenda.

Shortage/Scarcity

Scarcity is another form of persuasion that people may be familiar with but is often underestimated. When a product or idea has limited availability, it is more likely to be assigned a higher value. People want more of what they can't have. While it might sound like it describes a child trying to get into the cookie jar when said no, it could also describe how normal adults will act. When there is a question of scarcity to consider, the context will also matter. It merely means that, within specific contexts, the idea of scarcity could be an advantage.

The agent of persuasion will be able to use the idea of scarcity to his advantage. A way is needed to be defined to make the follower believe that the object is scarce by explaining why that object is so unique and what it does that nothing else can do. The agent will have to work on the topic right. The agent can also choose to go to the other side; instead of explaining what the customer will gain from the item or idea, they can explain what they will lose by not having the item.

There are two reasons why this principle of scarcity works. First of all, when items or products are challenging to obtain, they usually gain more value. The more value an item has, the better the quality it will appear to have, even if this is not true. The second thing is that when something is not as available as it once was, the follower will realize that it will lose the ability to acquire it in the future. Once this begins to occur, the follower will begin assigning the service or item in short supply a higher value only because it will become more challenging to acquire.

A significant deal behind this principle is that the follower will want things out of their reach. If something is easy, no, sometimes ill want it as much as when the object is more complicated. If the agent can plant the idea that his thoughts, beliefs or objects are scarce and hard to find, he will have a much greater chance of seeing success in his persuasion efforts.

Appeal to Social Needs

After that, the agent could appeal to the follower's social needs. Although social needs are not as significant to use as primary needs, they are still an important tool that can be used. People like to be wanted and to be part of the crowd. They like the prestige that some objects can give them and feel like they belong to a higher social position. The idea of appealing to the follower's social needs can be found in most television commercials on the air; in these commercials, the viewer will be encouraged to purchase an item so that it can become famous or be just like everyone else. When the agent appeals to the follower's social needs, he can reach a new area that might interest the follower.

Use of Uploaded Images and Words

When it comes to persuasion, the choice of words that are made can make all the difference. There are several diverse ways to say the same thing, but one way might push the follower into action while others don't. Telling the correct words in the right way will make all the difference when using persuasion. The example on the telephone at the beginning of this chapter is an excellent example of how words can persuade followers to take action.

Persuasion is a powerful mind-control tool that is often underestimated and overlooked. Perhaps this is because it offers more choice to the follower than other forms of mind control. In the other options, the follower is forced into submission, sometimes in isolation, by the agent and does not have much choice about what is going on in the process. In terms of persuasion, the facts are presented so that the follower can make a decision, even if the facts are posed in a certain way to show them in the best light.

CHAPTER 6: NEURO-LINGUISTIC PROGRAMMING (NLP)

NLP is brief for Neuro-Linguistic Programming and is the most modern mind control system available to the public. NLP was born of therapists who could achieve their therapeutic goals in a brief time. Not only has NLP proven to be a useful therapeutic tool, but it is also a powerful hidden instrument of persuasion and inspiration. If an analyst can delicately encourage a client to accept a new solution to their problem, similar methods can be worked to sell a product or even infuse a new list of principles. Considerably NLP is a science. It is also an art and requires a good understanding of the NLP model and techniques and the time to practice it.

To understand the NLP model, one must first accept that people are both the same and different in many ways. We are the same in that we only have an inadequate numeral way to comprehend our knowledge. We are distinctive in that each person has a particular way of creating the logic of their knowledge. For the person who distinguishes how someone else makes the logic of their world, they can customize their message to be accepted. With the power implicit in NLP, it has been picked up and tapped into the realm of sales, advertising, and helping men to stay courageous.

Sensory Acuity

Sensory acuity is NLP jargon for "pay attention!" it basically means that when you work with somebody, you have to pay more responsiveness to how they are responding than whether you are doing things right or not. When you do this, "pay attention!" You will observe that people reply to you in very subtle ways.

Relationship

For the purposes of mind control and NLP, the best place to start is the beginning. All NLP teaching begins with the topic of the relationship. The relationship is more than just having someone like you. It is probable to have a connection with someone who doesn't like you. What's important in the relationship is that the other person perceives that you are very similar to her on a deep level. It allows the person to feel comfortable and willing to respond to you with a certain recognition feeling. (yes, even if they don't accept you, they can be sensitive to you. Think of this as respecting enemies.) It has been told, and correctly so that without the affiliation, nothing is possible. Everything is possible with relationships. "mirroring and matching" are the first techniques learned to create a relationship. Mirroring means moving and talking like the other person and doing it in a way that doesn't seem to mimic. It creates an unconscious influence on the other person that you are like them.

You can see people subconsciously mirroring each other among those who are already in a relationship. They sit in a similar way. When one varies his position, the other person will change his position to match the other person. It is a very typical result of having a relationship. Many NLP courses spend long hours doing mirroring and matching exercises to help attendees learn how to quickly get into a relationship. The exercises are beneficial, but there is an easier way.

The simplest way to achieve a relationship is to think that you are mirroring yourself as a result of the relationship rather than its cause. When you like someone and feel like this person, you are in a relationship, and you will do all the reflecting and equaling without believing concerning it. Suppose the relationship is already there and that you both are deeply familiar with other people's thoughts and habits. At first, this can take some mental gymnastics, but it's a lot easier than paying close attention to people's movements and then moving your body to match theirs.

Stimulation and Guidance

Stimulation and guidance can be used in any situation in many different ways. Stimulation and guidance consist of the first stimulation, which essentially means that the controller does what the other person is doing, followed by the guide, doing something that takes the initiative to follow. Using rhythm and guidance is an essential part of traditional rapport exercises, as mentioned above. In the case of intercourse, the controller will follow the follower's movements and then lead him. Stimulation and guidance can also be used in almost any situation to take the initiative. Linguistically, stimulation and guidance take the form of rhythm that is true and verifiable by the follower. A clue is a statement on which the controller wants the follower to agree.

Stimulation and Entertainment

It refers to something a little more intense than pacing and driving. It requires strong sensory understanding and the ability to force the follower to follow your lead much sooner than generally with rhythm and guidance. Stimulation and entrainment require several things from the operator.

Focus

Focus means that the operator is wholly focused on the follower and intentionally ignores any personal concerns, whatever they may be. As a controller, this means that bills, mortgage payments, quarrels with spouses are put aside wholly when you are with your dependent.

Concern

As a controller, Concern means making the dependent the most critical individual in your world as you are with him. It can only be done using your focus and sense of care, even if you have to pretend.

Excitement and Principle

Excitement and principle is the expertise that what you are fixing it right. To rekindle this influence, consider all the benefits of what you're doing that involves the topic. These benefits include reasons why it matters and also includes the values or things it gives you. By combining these qualities, rhythm and dragging are made more accessible. Sensory acuity will be heightened by concentration and worry and can be used to see if the follower is somehow resisting the drag. When resistance is detected, the controller can make instant improvements to their performance.

The Influence of Functioning

Functioning in NLP terms means how the body is used to create and lead emotional and mental states. By changing the physiology, it is much easier to access individual emotional states. An excellent example of this is the act of simply sitting with your back straight and looking up. It is complicated for anyone to maintain a depressed state while doing so. On the other hand, one will find that collapsing, looking down and taking very short, shallow breaths are easy to achieve. It is a fantastic wonder that more people have not applied it.

But suitable Mind Controllers do. Consider how churches can have very high and ornate ceilings. It forces people to look up and access pleasant emotional states more easily. Another way to use physiology is for the controller to simply tell the follower what to do and how to get into position. Rites, contemplations, and breathing exercises are all designed to secretly influence the followers' physiology to aid in a consequence. By solely asking, "Can I show you something about how your body affects your mind?" a controller may then ask the follower to change posture or movements to prove the fact.

The critical factors of physiology under conscious control are posture, breathing, eye movement and activity. Thus, by making any combination of these, a change in emotions can occur.

Sensory Modalities and Sub-Modalities

In NLP, the reality is interpreted through the feelings, and commonly, one of the feelings is domineering. Graphic/sight, auditory/hearing, and kinesthetic / sense are the primary modalities (or modalities) that people use. These are the preferred ways of thinking that people use, and in the NLP literature, it is referred to as VAK for visual, auditory, kinesthetic. People who think predominantly in visual terms will refer to something as to how they "see" things and use phrases like "It seems right," "it's clear to me." "I have a good picture of what you say."

An individual who thinks in auditory terms will say things like, "Sounds like a good idea." "Let me intervene." "

All you have to do to determine someone's dominant sensory modality is to listen to them speak. Therefore, sensory understanding is critical. When you use a person's predominant sensory modality, you increase the ratio and gain a more significant foothold to guide them.

Learn More About Sensory Modality

Ask somebody how they determined to make their latest buying and hear what they say. In making choices, people will go through a mental process that they mention to the sensory modalities they use. For example, if you show someone a coat to buy and ask them how they got their latest coat and say, "I saw (visually) the coat at the window, and I said (audibly) to myself, 'It looks good.' Then I had this (kinesthetic) feeling that I had to have it. " To maintain a relationship, all you have to do is use the same process. For example, "Take a look (visually) at this coat, and when you do, listen (audibly) for" Looks good "and tell me how good you feel (kinesthetic)."

Sub-Mode

Sub-modes are more specific distinctions than various sensory modalities. When these sub-modes are changed, the impact of the message is also altered. Of the visual mode, some of the sub-modes are image distance, size, position, whether it is color or black and white, image position is the most prominent and common and sufficient for most to use effectively. Auditory sub-modes include volume, whether it is a voice that is heard or said (usually it is), the gender of the voice, emotional tone, direction position, whisper, speed of the voice. Kinesthetic sub-modalities include heat, heaviness, position in the body, tingling.

To comprehend how sub-modalities are used therapeutically, consider how someone might describe being depressed. Their head drops, and their physiology collapses (kinesthetic). They listen to a rambling, oppressive voice in their mind saying, "you are useless!" then hear your voice say, "I'm nothing." Then see a picture of yourself standing two feet tall and staring at them with contempt by all who see them (visual).

The NLP therapist should elicit this information, which the follower is not consciously aware of, and then consciously alter these sub-modalities. The follower would start by imagining themselves, standing very tall and seeing people seeing them and smiling (visually). Internal voices would turn into laughing murmurs with noisier, more optimistic voices saying, "you are the finest!" added. It will immediately affect the follower, but may only be temporary unless practiced as an ongoing project. Sub-modes can be used as a mind-control tool in stealth using some general rules about sub-modalities that affect most people.

Visual sub-modes tend to significantly impact people when pictured in the foreground, large, and color. So, describing your product or service as "great" and seeing it "up close and colorful" will tend to have a more significant impact. For example, note the difference between these two rental apartment listings: two bedrooms and one bathroom. Dining room with kitchenette. "Or" Spacious apartment with two colorful bedrooms and sunlit dining area. "Notice how the second description makes the apartment seem more real.

It can be used for Mind Control by adding more visual sub-modes to your product or service description. TV commercials and print ads often use this by showing their product the greatest and most colorful as possible and comparing their competitor in smaller black and white images. Describing auditory sub-modes as loud and echoing will tend to have a substantial impact. Still, you have to be cautious with this as some people will not respond positively to a "strong description" The kinesthetic sub-modalities of "warm," "soft," "comforting," and "enveloping" tend to be considered favorable for most people. To be considered negative.

To add effect to any message, a Mind Control practitioner can use a beneficial process to incorporate visual, auditory, and kinesthetic sub-modes into all of their communications. It will ensure that people will see, hear, and feel the message's impact regardless of their dominant sensory modality.

Values Elicitation

Values are at the heart of our decision-making process. They are profound and oblivious until they are satisfied or dared. Standards are strong enough that when someone tells you that your values will be met by purchasing their product or service, it's nearly impossible to resist. For a seller, finding someone's values is the same as finding the buy button and pressing it again. Using values as a mind-control tool is powerful enough that if you don't keep them as you promise, you will become a sinister enemy, so use this tool wisely. The process of using values as a mind-control tool is to discover a person's values and then link them to your achievement. Both steps are surprisingly simple and straightforward.

The Excitement

First, understand that everyone has criteria that must be met before accepting anything. If it's a new car, it may need to be fast, or a new model or color, or within a specific price range. Once these criteria are met, the person feels their value. Most individuals try to persuade by trying to meet all criteria. The elicitation of values bypasses it and goes straight to that motivating value. Achieving value is achieved simply by asking the question, "What is important." For instance, if you attempt to enroll someone in a communication seminar, you would ask, "What is important in connecting with individuals?" From that, you will acquire their first answer. Then ask them, "What's important in this (their first answer)?" giving you their second answer. Then ask, "What's important in this (their second answer)?" You will usually have reached their highest value by then. Don't be astonished if they show some strong emotion.

Let me give you some assistance on how to ask these questions. Keep in mind that you don't want to learn because only what's essential about "it" matters. The reason is that "why?" it causes people to get defensive. To keep it simple, don't ask, "Why is _ important?"! While asking these questions, it is essential not to craft it sound like an examination. You can do this by combining your questions with conversations about life and relevant issues. You will notice that people become interested when you show genuine curiosity about what is essential to people. To put it another way, asking these questions builds rapport because people like to talk about what they think is essential.

Another way to get a recall of values is to listen. Many people will quickly start talking about what they like. If you simply give it to them and ask them to elaborate, you will find that they "turn on,"; a strong indication that you've come to something they appreciate.

Delivery of Elicitation Values

Once you have their principles, the rest is pretty simple. All you require to do is reference these values as you describe your service or product. Saying, "Do you think having X, Y and Z are important enough to take part in this seminar?" Or, even though this may be crude, you can say, "This seminar shows you how to have more X, Y and Z. Sounds like something you'd like to take part in?"

This process is so robust that you have to try it to test its efficiency. You should also notice that if your product or service doesn't meet that value as you implied, you may have a very ready person. In reality, enemies are made by deceiving them in this way. Be careful.

To uncover people's values on a large scale, some people will employ a survey asking various questions about certain aspects of their lives. From this information, you can customize your responses and presentations before individual meetings.

Emotional Elicitation

Emotional elicitation is NLP's process of fetching out the emotions you need a person to sense. It will be of enormous worth in the next section on anchoring. To begin, determine what your follower's emotions might aid tip to your result. These emotions could be eagerness, joy, fear, worry, frustration, despair, love, certainty, curiosity, etc.

There are several ways to arouse emotions. The simplest and most direct way is to ask, "What is it like when you hear X?" or "Do you remember a time when you felt?" Keep in mind that the relationship is vital to this process because these are pretty weird questions to ask a stranger. So, earn a report! As you ask these questions, observe how they respond. You should be able to witness the emergence of emotion. Another way to do this is to talk about the feeling of telling a story that describes the emotion.

Use your sensual insight when doing this as it doesn't promise your description will match your followers, so pay attention to how they react. By successfully performing emotional elicitation, the follower becomes a little more flexible. If they can provoke emotions to which you lead them, it is an indication that you have a great relationship and make them even more responsive to your driving. It is often done on TV shows and what makes watching particular series so compelling. Yes, the media know the power of mind control.

Emotional Elicitation in Writing

Emotional processing always occurs in writing and is more common in fiction because it allows the reader to identify with a character and be emotionally involved. You will also see emotional stimuli in the best advertisement.

Anchoring

Anchoring is the next step once you have learned how to arouse emotions. Anchoring is a very Pavlovian practice that links emotion to a gesture, a touch, an object or setting, or whatever. It is a very natural process that we humans have anchors. We adore our beloved restaurant because they treated us well and left us feeling warm every time, we think about it. Commercials use the anchoring process by eliciting emotion and then connecting the sensation to a product. By using anchor, your sensory acuity must be sharp enough to notice when someone is experiencing the emotion you are trying to elicit. As the emotion rises to its peak, you "fix" the anchor, meaning you bring what you want to associate with the sensation. Think about how anchoring happens in a romantic setting. The relationship is built, and warm, confused feelings begin to build as you look at the person. It alone connects those feelings to the person so that all you have to do is think about the people they are dealing with and have those feelings.

But you can use it to speed up those thoughts by using the anchoring method with an aware purpose. It can be achieved by eliciting the sensation by asking how it feels to feel "a connection" with someone or describe the connection (or both). When you notice the feelings inside the person grow, you uniquely touch them. Here is a literal example of a romantic anchor that is often used in romantic contexts.

The solar plexus touch will anchor that feeling of connection (called "fixing the anchor"). So, whenever you want to bring that feeling back, all you have to do is touch the solar plexus, and the feeling will come back. You can fix anchor without contacting physically. Create a unique gesture, and it will work. In NLP jargon, that second touch that brings back the emotion is called "firing the anchor."

Built-In Commands

The built-in commands are incredibly useful as a mind-control tool because they send messages to the unconscious mind without the conscious mind being aware of them. You can consider them almost subliminal except that when you are trained to listen to them, they become quite apparent. Thankfully, hardly anyone spends enough time learning how to use or listen to the built-in commands. To learn how to use built-in commands, first consider how we talk. We tend to say things in a specific voice or tone of voice. We usually get excited or get anguish, and our voice pattern changes by intensity or in volume. Still, mostly our voice pattern does not get significant changes in our modulation and rhythm.

The built-in commands work by using our voice to highlight certain words and phrases in our speech to send Messages conscious and unconscious. The conscious message is the necessary content of what we are saying. It would be the information conveyed to write our words and read them from a script. Oblivious messages are the brief words and expressions you mark as commands by changing your words' delivery.

There are several ways to pronounce sentences differently from the rest of the paragraph so that the unconscious mind begins to recognize the tapping. The simplest way is to pause before the built-in command, lower your voice, and then pause after the command ends and resume speaking typically. Try re-reading it this time and notice that the signs indicate a pause and when you read the command, read it as if you were giving a command and let the pitch go down as if you were giving an order.

Using built-in commands will seem awkward and unnatural at first. Get over it. It is a tool that people have paid a lot to learn for good judgment; It works. If you understand the steps below, you will become very good with the built-in commands, and you will see people respond to your commands without even knowing what is going on.

- State your result not only in terms of actions but also in terms of the emotions that motivate the action.
- Write a short 2 to 4-word commands that lead to your result. The more, the better.
- Write a maximum of these commands as probable.
- Make sure they are in the command form.
- Start writing commands in a monologue about anything you would usually talk about.

- Read it aloud.
- Practice, practice, practice.

Using a single built-in command will not be effective because the follower's unconscious mind will not have enough samples of the commands to distinguish it as different from the rest of the speech and determine that they are instructions. So, the instruction is to use a lot of them. Since the built-in commands are hidden, you can send them to one person in a group by marking the commands with a candid look at the follower.

Meta Programs

A Meta Program is an NLP text that describes the possible ways in which individuals order the information they perceive. Thus, they can bring about an appropriate reaction. It has been claimed by some that there are over 30 different Meta Programs that people use unconsciously. The NLP Model Meta Programs demonstrate that we will best interact with (and control) people if we treat them as they're rather than forcing them to be what we expect they ought to be.

Keep in mind that each one Meta Programs are context-dependent and not necessarily universal to the individual. So, someone could use a meta program towards (see later) to settle on a romantic partner but could use a foreign meta program to shop for tuna. So, people aren't considered "types" of meta-programs. Meta programs depend upon the context, not the person.

The key to using Mind Control Meta Programs is straightforward and easy. You employ the meta program your follower is using for the context you're discussing. Period.

When someone says "I want/don't want to try to to it because " what follows will tell you whether or not they are motivated by getting something (a meta program towards) or avoiding something (a distant meta program). Consider this, counting on the context and, therefore, the situation, and each folk is motivated either by eager to avoid something we do not like or by getting something we would like.

When given the selection of the way to do something, people will have two ways of responding. They're going to prefer to respond by choosing a predetermined procedure or deciding from a spread of options. People that tend to procedures will tend to possess a group way of doing things. They do not need much for motivation, just a process they will ask and believe. Those who tend towards options will always be looking for a better way to do things and will love to respond creatively with new ideas.

For example, when you ask, "How did you choose your current job?" an Options response will sound like "I wanted to be in a position that gave me the ability to travel. I went through my choices, started at the top of my favorite possible jobs list and went down until I got one. "A response to the procedures will be very systematic and procedural! Something like this: "I went to a friend of mine, and he told me about the work the flight attendants do, so I researched and talked to some people. One of them worked as an assistant and told me where to apply, so I looked at some training courses and "This kind of story can last for a while.

Meta Program: Relationship

This Meta Program helps determine how many similarities and differences contribute to people's choices. When asked, "What is the relationship between the (service or product) you want and what you have now?" the follower will respond by saying that it is similar or different. There is a standard test that NLP professionals use in which they show three coins, two heads and across.

When this question is asked about what the controller is trying to offer, the controller will adapt it to the meta-program of the relationship between followers. In other words, if the follower were asked about the ratio of his current car to an ideal car and he replied that it had to be completely different, the controller would emphasize the difference in the car he offers, even if he offers a very similar car.

You will notice that the follower is underlining an exception to "all the same" and "all different." In this case, the controller would also give an exception, thus matching the Meta Program followers.

Processes of Changing Influences

NLP is an incredibly valuable therapeutic tool to help people re-evaluate the influences that have held them back from achieving their goals. Since NLP is often used as a secret tool of persuasion, it can secretly change people's beliefs for mind control purposes. To understand the process of belief change, it is easier to see how it is used in an overt therapeutic context. In a therapeutic example, the follower reports that he is reluctant to go back to school because he believes he is too old to resume his education. Here the sub-modalities are used, and four different images are elicited and followed by the NLP process that will create the change they needed.

1. The person is asked to create an image of the idea, "I am too old to learn." Then, the sub-modalities of that image are asked; location, distance, black and white color, moving or still, etc. The NLP practitioner/controller takes note of these.

2. The person is then asked to imagine a new positive idea that could benefit him, such as "I can learn at any age, " and the same sub-modalities are raised.
3. The same is done for "something true but is no longer true." It should be something mundane that has no emotional content.
4. The last image that is elicited is something the follower knows to be true.
5. The person is then asked to move the image of the idea quickly "I am too old to learn." in the position of "something true but is no longer true." and make sure it assumes all related sub-modalities of "something true but is no longer true."
6. The image of the idea "I can learn at any age." it is then moved very quickly into the position of "something true."
7. The person is then asked to try to see these changes. If done right, the influence is permanent.

Secret Change of Ideas

Changing an idea on the sly is a little more complicated because it requires many relationships and becomes very adept with anchoring. To do this in a converted way, the controller will perform the same procedure mentioned above but embed hidden anchors. The controller's first step is to get the thing that was true or could be something they know as "wrong." Then drop anchor when the discussion moves to their current idea that the controller wants to remove. The next anchor is for something they know to be accurate and for shooting that when the discussion turns into the idea that the controller wants to be accepted. This process is performed regularly in many TV commercials.

Simple operant conditioning will also work (see Behavioral Conditioning). Reward any movement that is indicative of the new idea and give a hard look to opposing ideas. Using the light mouth is also useful in fighting an existing idea (see Gaslighting). Another method is to use the voice where any reference to the old idea is referred to with a whimpering tone, sarcasm, or contempt. A healthy relationship is significant as a warning because it can quickly be taken as an insult.

Timeline and Time Manipulation

Chronology refers to how people perceive time as a linear series of events from the past, leading to present events and being followed by future events. It can be drawn as a line in two dimensions.

To understand this, tell someone to assume they are on a timeline and ask them where they perceive the past and ask them to point it out. Then invite them to indicate their future. With this information, you will understand how they perceive the past and future.

A controller can elicit a history of people, or simple use of gestures can suggest it; the right hand extended to the side can represent the future, and the left hand extended can represent the past. The center is present, and it can be kept secret by talking about the past while extending the left hand and the future while extending the right hand. To suggest a future answer, the controller can simply point to the future and suggest the feeling of being there.

Time manipulation refers to the process of secretly suggesting that a response or feeling from the follower will occur in the future. It can also help the follower imagine that a sensation or event has happened in the past. An example would be to elicit a feeling and use linguistic patterns (mentioned below) to suggest it in the future.

Linguistic Patterns

Linguistic patterns are phrases, stories, and metaphors combined with other NLP practices (such as anchoring and built-in commands) to secretly elicit a response from the listener. The desired response is usually something emotional so that it can be anchored in some way. Linguistic patterns are a unique form of secret hypnotic suggestion. In old-fashioned hypnosis, the hypnotist will give direct suggestions, tell the follower what to do, and respond. Linguistic patterns differ from traditional hypnotic suggestions in that they are not direct. Instead, the operator often describes a process. For the follower who is listening to the pattern to understand the process, he must go through it in his mind, doing it to himself.

The popularity of hidden language models evolved from NLP professionals who wanted to fuck. Then they were packed into "fucked" NLP products and seminars designed for consumption by the horny male masses too busy to take an NLP class and figure it out for themselves. If you can control the emotions of others, they are very likely to follow the suggestions. It is because people almost universally make their decisions based on emotion rather than reason.

Using emotions, a nation can be pushed into war or the construction of giant monuments. Individuals in a one-to-one are no different, and because a controller can get instant feedback, control is often more straightforward. When using linguistic models, the relationship is essential. Most people who learn language patterns first start memorizing existing patterns and, if they are intelligent, practice them. After some practice, most people understand the theory behind language models and start generating language models independently.

The Model of Depression

This model is very advanced because it employs Elicitation and Anchoring of Values. The beginning of the model is to arouse the life values of the follower. In other words, the process begins with the relationship, and the practitioner asks, "What is important to you in life?". It will lead the follower to reveal what those values are finally, and, for this example, let's say the follower replies, "Family, Faith and Work" in that order of importance. The operator will then ask the query, "What are you not considering?" This question will cause a deep state of confusion in the follower. At that time, the operator will secretly anchor the misunderstanding with touching or gesturing.

The operator would talk about the values of the followers of "Family, religion and work" and shoot the anchor of confusion that links the confusion to these values, effectively canceling them. The most damaging use of this or any "Dark" model would be to have the follower practice this response and predetermine it as a result. Now consider why this type of pattern is so harmful. If done effectively, every time the follower thinks about what it had value in; Family, religion and work now feel confused.

Elements of Dark NLP Patterns

Some obscure NLP patterns are not bad and are often used to help in a therapeutic NLP situation. It is forming an anchor for "things that were real." The hypnotic type of this would be to have the follower create a place or even a box in his mind in which he puts things that are no longer true to him. They can put habits, compulsions, and cravings in the box to no longer be valid. The result is very significant and positive for the follower.

The Linguistic Scheme as Storytelling

When someone tells a story, especially a vivid and compelling story, they use metaphors to influence and hypnotize covertly. Since a story is not about the people it is told to, they can listen without feeling preached. But to truly understand the story, they must, at some level, experience the emotions of the characters. It is where storytelling is an excellent tool for mind control. Many good examples of this can help a beginner understand the mind control process. The first example is quite common and happens every time someone reads a story or watches a movie and gets involved in the plot that they forget that they are getting involved in fiction. Although they may be sitting on the sofa reading or watching a TV show, they react as if they were in the story. In other words, they are influenced by what they are reading/watching.

If It Was True

Mind Controllers have used it throughout history, and many shamanic cultures place the narrator as the central person in their rituals. To learn this skill, the controller should enter their story first and remember the moments when they were reading or watching a show and got involved so intensely that they lost track of time and started taking care of the characters in the story. What made it so enjoyable? How did you forget where you were and "make history"? What emotions did the tale involve? By relying on these queries, the controller can understand what kinds of stories move them and create stories they can tell equally engaging. How do you create a story that conveys a hidden message? There are a few influences that you need to understand and try to incorporate.

- Tell a story with a listener-like character. The main character must have something that the listener can relate to regardless of whether the main character is a turtle or a human.

- If you tell the story orally (aloud), get involved. The more desire, energy and enthusiasm you can put into the story, the more the audience will react.
- Discuss the topic sometimes. The more convoluted a story becomes, the harder the listener has to strive to follow.
- Design a message in the story. The message in the story can be a moral of the story like Aesop's fables. The message can also be much more hidden. The hidden message is one of emotion, which means that there is an emotion that the main character feels that motivates him. This emotion must be justified in history. In this way, the follower who listens to the story can relate to the emotion.

CHAPTER 7: BODY LANGUAGE

Many of us may have spent a long time in our life without even realizing that we have been persuaded and manipulated so often. The damage from this manipulation can last forever and can be challenging to improve. Once you become conscious of how others might subliminally convince you, you can better protect yourself from these tactics in the future to maintain your independence and stay out of the influence of others. It is imperative to recall that you are better equipped to identify and defend yourself against them by understanding these concepts. Your new knowledge should not be about how you can use the same strategies to influence other individuals.

There is a variance among evil manipulation and trying to persuade someone of something. You don't want to get someone to do things for you when they're not going to benefit from it. You only need to use these tactics when you need to persuade someone about something and not openly ask for help. Some people are more challenging to convince than others, so you may need to use persuasion strategies. Who might need to convince? You certainly do not want to take the benefit of someone who doesn't already have much to give. The ones you should try to persuade our people who hold power. You may want to learn how to get your boss to get a raise. Maybe you want to try to get your girlfriend to move in with you. Maybe you need to borrow from your parents. You don't want to "punch," but instead, "reach out."

Body Language

One of the easiest ways to analyze other people is to look at their body language. The way a person holds himself, moves and even talks can tell you a lot about him. Everyone has many variations in their ways, and there is no exact way to tell what constitutes a person. There are still many similar clues between groups of people that can give your insight into how someone works. It's not easy because it begins with becoming aware of your body language. To understand and attempt to overcome the riddle of body language, you need to be hyper-aware.

Now is the time to work on becoming aware of your body. To learn what makes a person different from others based on their body language, you first need to look at yourself and analyze how you hold your body. Some people may be more aware of their movements than their thoughts are. Women will likely be more aware of their bodies and their space, mostly due to the patriarchal society we grew up in. Everyone may still find it challenging to cope with the way they hold their body. You can lose focus while maintaining awareness and becoming too insecure about your body and your movements. Once you get to know another person's body movements better, you can also understand what makes them unique. The more you know about a person, the better you can conclude the best persuasion strategy.

Cultural Differences

Each person is different, and sometimes the way a person holds their body has a different meaning than someone who is the same way. There are many ways that a person's body language is different, so it's important to remember that not everything about a particular body movement is 100% true for every person. It is especially important to remember when talking to people from different cultural backgrounds.

There are some cultures that practice modesty, so touching could be forbidden entirely. Other cultures may be more open to expressing their feelings through their bodies, so the culture is vital to remember when thinking about how they might use their bodies.

Learn the Movements of Others

Once you become more aware of body movements and what they might represent, you can start studying them when interacting with different people. Anyone who comes into contact uses their body to represent different things. Some people are closed, and others may be more open. These are some small differences you might notice just by looking at someone's body language. When you study other people and yourself, it is essential to try to act naturally as well. It can be comfortable to befit hyper-aware of your movements but know that you don't have to hold your body a certain way. Not everyone is aware of body movements as others might be, so don't look too much at your movements at the end of the day.

However, once you start studying others' body movements, you will begin to realize just how much you can learn about them. Some things may start to make sense after meeting a variety of people. You may notice that one of your friends is quite pretentious in how he holds himself or talks. Other friends may show how insecure they are with themselves, even if you thought they had been incredibly confident since you've known them.

Knowing a person's body language and getting an idea of why they might move a certain way can allow you to understand them deeply. It gives you better influence when it comes to persuading them. You may want to match your boss's confidence when you make a deal for a raise. You may have noticed that you need to be more relaxed with certain friends who seem shy or nervous. Becoming aware of your body language can be scary at first, but you will eventually feel comfortable with the way you move.

To start practicing being comfortable with your body, try spending time in front of a mirror. When you dine, watch TV, or even relax in bed, set up a mirror so you can see how you hold yourself back. Once you get a stranger's point of view on how you move, you will be able to see how others move as well.

Visual Contact

Eye contact is one of the most significant clues you can use to determine how someone is. It is also essential to become aware of your use of eye contact, as it gives others clues about your personality and true nature. Maintaining eye contact is vital in letting a person know that you are interested in what they are saying and that they have your full attention.

However, it can also be abused, and you let people know that you are trying too hard to convince them that you are listening. Too much eye contact can sometimes be intimidating to others too, so if you notice that a person is getting nervous due to the amount of eye contact you have with them, change it up every so often.

Pupil dilation can be a direct indication that a person is interested in what you are saying. Studies have shown that when a person's pupils begin to dilate with the person, you're making eye contact with, they're more interested in what you have to say. They are listening to you with their full attention and are thinking deeply about what you are saying. When a person's pupils are dilated while talking to you, you know that they are legitimately interested in the conversation.

The receding eyes will indicate otherwise. Someone who looks your eyes back and forth is probably trying to convince you that they are listening. They are aware that they need to make eye contact, but they are entirely excluded from what you say. Those with shifty eyes may also lie to you or try to deceive you in some way. They may have a hard time maintaining eye contact with you because they know they are deceiving.

Movements of The Mouth

What someone does with their mouth is very crucial to understanding their personality as well. Someone with pursed or pursed lips may be trying to focus, or they may even be trying to hide a sour face. You can also analyze a person's smile. If the corners of their eyes aren't bent, they could force you to smile.

Someone faking a smile isn't necessarily evil. May be thinking of something else and too distracted to pay full attention to what you're saying. Sometimes, smiles are also reactions to uncomfortable situations.

When monkeys smile, it is not because they are happy, but mostly because they show their teeth to threaten them. When they feel frightened and nervous, they open their mouths, showing that they have teeth that they could use to hurt. The same goes for dogs. They only show their teeth when they feel threatened. For humans, this can be true at times too, but on a subconscious level. Laughing nervously and smiling are just one way for a person to relieve their tension. You can tell someone is smiling sincerely when they have creases in the corners of their eyes.

A healthy person who covers his mouth all the time is also usually nervous. They might bite their lip, finger, or punch their mouth. Knowing when a person is uncomfortable or nervous can sometimes be helpful when trying to persuade them.

Nodding

The way a person turns and tilts their head can be a subtle movement. Most of the time, others are not so aware when they move their heads. The movements of the neck and head of the person you are talking to can give you an insight into what they might be thinking on a deeper level. Someone who nods their head rather quickly while listening to you may be anxious, trying to get the conversation going as quickly as possible. They are trying to set a pace for you so that you can speak faster. They want you to know that they listen to you, but you don't speak fast enough. If someone is doing this to you, try speeding up your words to get their attention.

Someone who tilts their head to the side may have a legitimate interest in what you are saying. They are trying to turn an ear towards you so that they can hear you better, whether they are aware of their movements or not. They are also indicating that they are listening to you and want you to keep talking. It's a way to get closer to you in conversation without having to do any interjection or interruption. If someone nods too artificially, they may just be trying to convince you that they are interested in what you say. They may be aware that they should be paying attention, but they may have lost interest.

In an attempt to keep up, they pretend to nod their heads. They may not even understand what you are saying, so they nod to make you think they are keeping up. If you notice that others around you are artificially nodding their heads, it might be worth changing the follower to regain attention or better explain why they may be confused. Imitating someone's head movements can be beneficial in using persuasion. A slight tilt of the head while listening to them can show that you understand what they say. It can also display that you are empathetic with them, especially if they seem to be talking about difficult things.

Hands and Arms

The way someone uses their hands and arms is another way that body language can be interpreted to understand better the people you interact with. Our hands represent so much of ourselves. They are a way to express stories, placing a different emphasis on various parts. If someone tells a story, they will use hand gestures to keep people interested. Think of someone engaged in conversation as someone conducting an orchestra. They will raise their hands to maintain the rhythm and pace of the listener. Someone's hands and arms can also express how open or closed they are. They can be like the door in someone's body. If they are crisscrossed tightly in front of someone's chest, that person maybe a little more withdrawn, not wanting to engage too much in conversation. Having your arms crossed doesn't always mean someone is necessarily closed. They may also want to rest their arms, so if they're hanging loosely in front of your chest, they're probably listening to you casually.

Someone who has their arms outstretched, perhaps above their head, will likely be very open and perhaps even seek to exert power over a situation. Someone with their hands on their hips might even try to assert their power.

Signals

Everyone has different body language questions that they use as signals. Across cultures, genders, and ages, the different movements someone makes with their body can be conscious or unconscious signals they are giving to the people around them. Signals allow other people to know bits of information without having to say anything. Someone with their arms crossed, eyes fading on a sofa at a party gives the signal that they are probably ready to go home for the night. Someone else on that sofa may be sitting on the edge of the seat, laughing loudly, signaling that they won't be going to bed soon. The signals help people around the beacon know things that they may not easily express with their bodies. Some are very good at picking up other people's signals, and some people struggle to understand those around them.

When it comes to persuading someone, there are some crucial signs a person will need to lead a conversation correctly.

Starting A Conversation

The next time you're sitting quietly in a room with another person, wait for the conversation to start to talk. It will allow you to study how they might start a conversation. Most people will give some sort of signal with their body that they are about to start speaking. They may clear their throats, turn their heads, adjust their shirts, or move to the seat. No matter how small it may be, there is usually something that a person does right before starting a conversation.

When it's your turn to start a conversation, notice what you do before you start talking. Don't start with an "um" or "uh." It lets the other person know right away that you aren't very sure what you will say. Try starting a conversation without doing anything. See if you can start talking without clearing your throat, moving your head, or doing anything else. Study how the other person reacts. They might be surprised or surprised that one of you has started talking.

Starting a conversation, especially one meant to persuade another person, is vital in laying your discussion foundation. Nobody will want to give their full attention to someone who is struggling to get started. If you are nervous and jump straight at the words, it will be much harder to keep up.

Lead the Conversation

Once the discussion has started, it can be challenging to maintain the right amount of back and forth. You don't want to be too pushy, but you also don't want to let them talk too much, not allowing yourself to make your points at any time. If you feel that the other person won't let you talk enough, there are apparent phrases you can use to express your opinion. You might try saying something like, "can I just say," "can I talk for a minute?" or "I'm listening, but can I say something fast?" These can be hard to say in some situations, and some people may even perceive you as rude if you make a big interjection. Your best choice may be to aid your body to redirect focus. Put your hands on your hips or tilt your head to let the other person know you have something to say. Try approaching to let him know that you want to take on the leader of your current conversation.

Leading the conversation can be tricky because no one wants to hear someone interrupt them. However, it is vital that you also have your turn to speak. There are ways you can practice conducting conversations to conduct it correctly when it comes time to have a critical persuasion. The later you want to say something, don't. Instead, let the other person keep talking and intervene later. Sometimes we are so eager to say our side that we distract ourselves from the real conversation, invalidating any discussion we have with the person we interrupted. An alternative way to practice leading the conversation is to talk the next time you want to say something. If you want to say but prefer to be silent, make an effort to say what you want. These two practice methods will give you two alternative perspectives for conducting a conversation that you may not otherwise obtain.

How Your Body Language Affects You

Believe it or not, the way you use your body can directly affect your functioning as well. Conclusion: there are ways to improve the way you think and your memory capacity by merely using your hands and arms. Not only are there physical differences in terms of how you use your body, but you will also be influenced by how others perceive you.

If you are closed continuously, always crossing your arms, there are probably many people who may not open up or talk to you because they assume you have no interest in the conversation. If you are always very open with your body, exercising confidence and holding yourself high, others may end up being intimidated by you. You may not intend to exclude others or to intimidate, but your body can demonstrate this in ways your mouth does.

It can be challenging to become aware of your body movements, but you can change what someone thinks about you once you do. Some people might have a robust conscious mind, but maybe they hate their bodies. So, they might shut others down by trying to hide their bodies, making others think they are judging. Sometimes, a person is just trying to cover their body and not themselves. You'd be surprised how much confidence you can feel just by changing the way you hold your body. People can still see what you look like, even if you keep your arms crossed. You may think you alter others' perceptions of you, but you are just closed in reality.

There are other ways your body language can affect you mentally.

Open Your Mind

Someone who starts to open their arms when they speak will begin to let others know that they are much more open-minded. If you stand with your arms outstretched or just relax by your side, let the people around you know that you are confident and willing to talk to them about different things. While having your arms outstretched is a signal to others, it is also a signal to your brain. Studies show that standing with open arms with crisscross verses can signal your brain to be more open. You will start thinking of new ideas that you would not have if you kept your arms crossed. The same goes for the rest of your body. The more open you are with your movements, the more you allow your brain to have different ideas.

Improve Your Memory

Those who speak with their hands also tend to have a better memory than those who do not speak. Using your hands can put physical reminders into your brain for ideas and thoughts you might be discussing. Suppose you imitate numbers or shapes when talking about different ideas, especially in a business context. In that case, you will not only remember what you are discussing better, but those around you will also find your story more memorable. Using your hands to talk while telling a story will also help you remember things you've been through. You're encouraging your brain to keep thinking and keeping your arms open, just like we alluded to in the last section, it will open your brain to new thoughts and feelings that you might not have if you talked with your arms folded and closed off.

Verbal Cues

While many things a person can say with their body, they can say many other things with their mouth. There is a seemingly limitless amount of languages out there, as each specific language has many sub-parts. Think about how many different accents there could be in New York City alone. As we continue to develop and blend different cultures and languages, we will only develop more. It's hard enough to keep up with what we already know, but there are ways to still grasp others' meaning without having to memorize every word in the dictionary.

Just because a person says, a specific word doesn't mean that they mean what they say. How many times have you told you were "fine" when you wanted to explode with thoughts in reality? We always say what we don't mean because it's not always easy to give words to our thoughts and feelings. Many people take their frustration or sadness out on others when they don't mean anything they say.

Knowing why people say they do can be one of the most complicated codes to try and crack. You don't always have to know what a person means to understand what they are trying to say. You can tell what a person's intention is by listening to how they speak and mixing it with their body language. It's crucial to read someone's mood, so you don't say the wrong thing or something that could potentially change the conversation's direction.

The next time you find something on TV in a language other than the one you can speak, try watching without subtitles. You will be surprised to see that you understand part of the plot. Don't look at what they say, but how they say it. Is there pain in their eyes? Do they look happy or sad? Sometimes, if you can't understand what a person is saying, perhaps because the room is noisy or talking in a low voice, try making eye contact. You may have a better gist of what they are saying than looking at the words their mouth is trying to put together.

There are some specific signals someone can give when they are trying to direct a conversation. When you're trying to persuade someone, you might want to try using different keywords to help lead the conversation.

Some people get too stuck on the words someone says when they try to hear the message they are conveying. It may seem challenging to try to decipher what someone else means, but it can be done. Think about your pets. You can tell if your dog is sad, sleepy, hungry, or in a playful mood, but you have no real conversations with him. Sometimes you can analyze what a person is saying best by finding out the noises they are making rather than dissecting every word they say.

Signs of Emphasis

When trying to persuade someone, you will want to have already prepared a good enough argument to build your case. You may want to include some cues of emphasis when speaking. It can be challenging to incorporate these phrases naturally, but it's good to practice so you can become a better persuader. "This is important," "you must know," "let me explain," are all phrases that catch the attention of the person you are talking to. You may begin to notice the emphasis of others better even after reading this section. You should listen to and use phrases in your speech that appear to emphasize an essential part of a conversation.

Sometimes, these emphasis cues aren't even real sentences. They could be verbal indications that something is essential, such as someone raising their voice when discussing an essential part of their argument. They may also repeat the word multiple times or pause for a break so the listener can understand what they just said. Emphasis cues are essential to understand better what may be necessary to an individual. If you listen to what they are stressing, you will also formulate your thoughts and arguments about the essential things.

Organizational Ideas

"First, second, third," "summarize," "the topic is," are all phrases that could be considered organizational ideas. These cues help a person indicate that they are trying to organize their thoughts, perhaps by emphasizing the most important things.

Organizational cues are vital for you to use in your arguments in persuasions to get people to your side. You want them to know that you are listening to what they have to say and that they should listen to you. You are trying to formulate a plan based on your thoughts and opinions, not just a specific individual's words. Organizational suggestions allow the speaker to emphasize what is essential while maintaining clear thinking and direct focus. Organizational signals may not be phrases either. It could just be someone clearing their throat, redirecting the conversation to a previous topic, or pausing so everyone can collect their thoughts.

Watch Your Presentation

The tone is an important key when trying to steer your conversation in their favor. Pitch is the level of your voice and the overall sound quality. Someone with a deep tone might have a more relaxing tone, while someone with a high-pitched voice might make their listeners more alert. Not everyone can help their natural tone of voice. Some people have extremely low voices that are hard to hear, and some people just have naturally high-pitched voices that seem to disturb everyone around them!

Even if your natural tone can't always be controlled, you can at least help direct that tone towards a more productive tone to keep your listeners engaged with what you have to say. Many of us let our tone get too loud and whiny when in professional settings, trying to keep our dictation sharp. If you feel that your voice is getting high and shrill, don't be afraid to stop, clear your throat and start over. People around you will likely be grateful that you are adjusting your tone for their listening pleasure.

Be careful not to raise the end of your voice when you speak. Many people, especially when talking on the phone, tend to let the end of their words come up as if they ask a question. This type of speech is also common among those who might be giving a speech. They will say a sentence very clearly with dictation, but they will also sharply end the sentence as if they ask a question. It should be avoided to keep the attention of your listeners.

It is crucial to find your optimal presentation. Some people have very soft voices, which can be challenging to hear. It is significant to practice speaking when necessary. Someone who tends to speak loudly should try to speak softly as often as possible to balance the tone. The best way to practice is on your own and if you record what you are saying. You don't want to thoroughly analyze how you talk too much, but practice always helps, especially for those who have difficulty pronouncing their voice. It's also essential to have a confident tone to let others know they should listen to you. Someone who always speaks shyly or asks questions will let others around them know that what they have to say is not impressive. If you are so unsure of what you are saying, why would anyone else listen to you? The best way to make sure others pay attention is to make sure you speak confidently.

Listen to Others

Talking about yourself can elicit the same good feelings that money and food do. Individuals appreciate talking about themselves more than they enjoy listening to other people talking about themselves for the most part. While it may sound selfish, indeed, most people would rather talk about themselves. It means that when conversing with other people, you should avoid talking too much about yourself.

You don't want to make the conversation about other people altogether, but no one will pay attention if the only thing you talk about is yourself. Giving advice can also be helpful, but people generally don't engage with those who offer too much advice as often, especially when it's not in demand.

Significant people can be difficult for some. They may have a hard time not letting their mind wander, especially if the other person is talking too much about themselves. Some people will find that they are usually forming their next thought while the other person is talking instead of listening to them. If you find your mind wandering when someone else is talking, redirect your thoughts to their words. Don't just listen to what they say. See how they say it. Listen to their voice and look them in the eye. People will notice if you are listening to them or not. Even if they are not experts in body language, they will still be able to sense at least that you may not be fully involved.

Don't just emphasize listening to others. Talk about them too. Ask questions about the person, trying to get to know them better. You will find that people usually like to answer questions about themselves. It is often a technique you will see in many sellers. They will ask you where you got the shirt or if you had a good day. It is to make the person think about themselves and usually open up a little more to the seller. People don't like being fair. While it can be hard to avoid, most people don't want to be interrupted by being told they're wrong. Most people will respect you a lot more if you let them talk instead of trying to prove them wrong. It is imperative to remember, especially when trying to persuade and analyze others.

Talk about "us," not "you." If you are looking to make suggestions, perhaps to a spouse or friend, about improving their lifestyle, use "us" instead. Don't say, "you should try to wake up early on weekends," say, "we should get up early on Sunday and go for a walk together!" People will respond much better to suggestions if you include yourself.

To Apologize

It can be challenging to apologize, especially for someone with a high level of pride, but it's vital to win the respect of the people around you. If you apologize for being late rather than giving all possible explanations, most will respond much better than if you tried to make yourself look better with an apology. They also like to see humility and that maybe you're not afraid to express yourself. If you can open up to someone and say, "I'm sorry I didn't respond to your message, I was just having a bad day," they will usually be very forgiving rather than if you would have just brushed them off.

However, don't apologize too much. It can cause others not to trust you. Sometimes we need to apologize for things that were out of our control to make us look better. We'll say, "I'm sorry the movie was so bad!" after going out for a movie night, even though we didn't have control over the production. It is nice now and then and certainly shows humility and vulnerability to those around you. But too much can also make you seem unreliable to others.

If you have to apologize after every little thing you say, why would anyone listen to you in the first place? The next time you get the need to apologize for something out of your control, try saying thank you. After having a long conversation with a friend, don't say, "Sorry, you had to hear me rant!" Instead, try something like, "Thank you for being such a great listener. I'm happy I have a companion like you!" People generally respond much more positively to a grateful person than someone who is always disabled. You'll find that you start treating yourself a lot better if you stick to this method of apology as well.

The Power of Your Body

Our bodies have so much power, and not just as much as we can lift or carry. Physical strength is essential, but even the weakest people can control a room with just body movements. It would help if you had a basic understanding of what a person's body language might mean by this point. We can't go into every specific detail of what someone's physical actions might try to convey, but the framework for analyzing those movements is there. Once you understand how someone else might use their body to persuade others, you can start working on your persuasion skills.

There are many ways someone can use their body to get others to do what they want, but it won't always work for everyone. Some people respond to sexual persuasion while the thought rejects others. Some people respond to a physical threat from those who seem healthier than they are, but others may be ready for the fight. There are many ways you can use your body to persuade others without being sexual or physically intimidating. Keeping your body open and visible is key to letting others know they can trust you. Try to remove physical barriers that could keep you separate from the person you are talking to. Move around a chair or table that prevents you from making a complete connection with the person you are trying to talk to.

It also shows that you are confident and interested in expressing your opinion while also listening to others. When you analyze other people's movements, you can also figure out what things you can do on your own to be more confident. Study some celebrities and see how they perform in various scenarios. Everyone has their movements, but imitating others can still help you find your position in having persuasive behavior overall.

Smiling Is Important

Our smiles are one of the most powerful tools we have been given. You can turn any situation from wrong to the right by merely raising the corners of your mouth. Some people feel like they don't have straight teeth or bright white smiles. They're worth nothing. Even those who don't have all their teeth can have much nicer smiles than someone who has spent thousands of dollars on dental work. A smile isn't just about the teeth you're showing.

It is a way to involve another person. Studies have shown that most people will smile if someone else smiles first. If they smile, they will end up having a better overall mood. It may sound strange, but merely smiling can lift someone's spirits. The next time you're feeling significantly down, smile. It sounds so silly, but it might work. Smile repeatedly, and while it may not change your mood, it will definitely help lift your spirits at least temporarily.

Subliminal Persuasion

The idea of subliminal persuasion involves convincing someone to do something below their conscious level. You won't openly persuade someone if you are subliminal about it. Instead, you would try to get to do what you want without even realizing what you are doing. The idea of subliminal persuasion is primarily thought of in advertising. Many companies will do everything possible to persuade us to buy something, even at the cost of partially brainwashing us.

The idea of subliminal persuasion doesn't have to be that insidious for those who wish to use these tactics to convince another person. There are many vital parts to subliminally persuading someone. First, make sure you do it for the right reasons. You don't want to become someone who brainwashes others. It's not about getting inside their head and getting them to think about something. Instead, you should look at what you know about them and use them in your persuasion plan.

It's Not About Manipulation

You certainly do not crave to make a person feel crazy. You don't want to make sneaky suggestions that lead them to question their sanity. Subliminal persuasion should only be used as an excellent way to tell someone how you feel when you might be too scared to tell the blatant truth. Some people have a more challenging time accepting the truth, persuasion, or reality than others. These types of people cannot be openly told what someone else wants. Sometimes, people like to disagree with others just for the sake of being controversial. There are ways you can ask someone something. Subliminal persuasion should never be about manipulation. You shouldn't "fool" someone into something that will only benefit you. You should use this method to try to prevent better being subliminally persuaded. It is also useful for stubborn, intimidating, or other people who cannot be conversed easily.

Trust Is the Key

The trick to subliminally persuading someone is to exude as much confidence as possible. Some people will see open trust as delusional, so you don't want to go too far. However, no one will be persuaded, no matter how subliminal you may get, by someone who can't even defend their thoughts and opinions. Trust is also vital to distract the person from realizing that you may be trying to persuade them of something. Imagine talking to your mom or dad, hoping to get a car loan again when you were a teenager. You would like to use some trust, but not so much that it makes them think you don't care about their permission. To subliminally convince them, you might raise the fact that no one else can safely take you to a party. Instead of asking brazenly and giving them a chance to say no, instead, you are more able to influence them how you think. It may therefore become their idea to get you to borrow your car for the weekend.

CHAPTER 8: WIN PEOPLE WITH SUBLIMINAL MANIPULATION

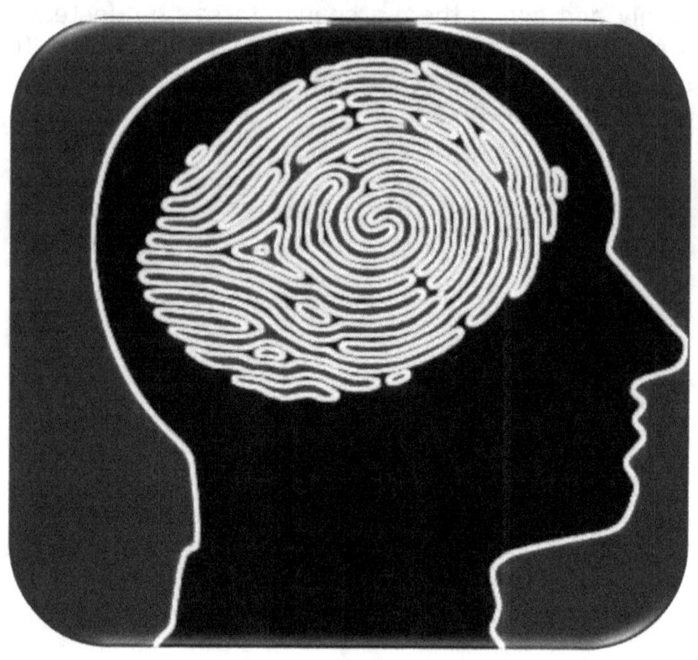

Subliminal psychology is just the tactic of influencing others using subliminal means. Subliminal means your follower isn't in the least conscious of what you're doing. They are doing not notice the pictures, sounds or other stimuli you employ to condition their mind. However, the subconscious is conscious of this stuff and strongly influenced by them. The subconscious will then direct the follower's thoughts, feelings and actions, creating an enduring and meaningful change in their life.

Subliminal psychology isn't as bad because it suggests. Subliminal psychology is just the technique of influencing someone secretly. You employ images, sounds and conditioning to urge someone to think a particular way or do something you would like. You do not need to influence anyone directly. You certainly never need to get caught. But that does not mean you've got to use subliminal psychology for evil. You can use subliminal psychology in a wide variety of contexts. When you use subliminal psychology, you can connect with anyone. You can improve your relationships and make people pay attention to you, even people who feel superior to you. It makes subliminal psychology excellent for relationships with loved ones, romantic relationships, seduction, and parenting. No one is too powerful to work on subliminal psychology.

This psychology can also save you if you are stuck in an abusive situation. It can help you soften and soften your attacker so you can escape the dire situation and protect yourself. Abusers like to control, so use subliminal psychology to give them the illusion of submitting to them and then flee when their guard is off.

Subliminal psychology is also something you can use on yourself. What if you have trouble losing weight and engaging in a healthier lifestyle or breaking down bad habits? What if you can't stop a habit, like gambling or compulsive lying? What if you have a terrible memory that you want to forget, or want to help yourself memorize lists and remind yourself to perform specific tasks? You have the most acceptable objectives in your heart, but you do not get what you want despite your best efforts. When you feel stuck in a version of yourself that you are not satisfied with, it's time to use subliminal psychology on yourself. You can reach the depths of your mind and train your subconscious to do what you want. Then you will notice genuine changes manifesting in yourself and your life. It works so well because the subconscious mind is the only part of your mind with real power. What happens in the subconscious mind will manifest in your conscious thoughts, feelings and behavior.

Subliminal psychology is not evil. This book will not teach you how to become an evil mind, plotting world domination in an underground lair while you rub your hands, giggling. Instead, it will teach you how to influence others for the better subtly. People hate being influenced, so you will benefit more if you can influence them in secret. Plus, the power of subliminal psychology is mind-boggling, so these methods are fail-proof. You will enjoy immense success with them. Just make sure you use these methods for good because they give you a lot of power to go wrong if you use them for evil. Learn to control your urge to dominate the world and simply use subliminal psychology to improve and promote the lives of the people you love, as well as yourself. Of course, if you use these methods for evil, it is at your own risk. You will enjoy success regardless of how you apply subliminal psychology to your life and the people you know.

Secrets of Subliminal Psychology

To employ subliminal psychology, you must first learn to understand it extremely well. The basic principle of subliminal psychology is mind-affecting or conditioning that passes below ordinary human perception limits. It means that a follower will neither notice nor realize that they are exposed to a subliminal stimulus. However, the stimulus is still present and still acting on his brain.

A person's senses are not necessarily reliable. The brain registers individual senses perceived when those senses fall within a specific range or spectrum. The brain may also register certain stimuli that are always present, but then choose to ignore them and prefer new stimuli. For example, you can see your nose 24/7. But your brain chooses not to process the image, as it's always there. So you are blind to your nose, even if your eyes perceive it a lot. You may be able to give someone a subliminal message using a constant, repetitive stimulus that the person comes to ignore. The brain still perceives it, however, and this allows the stimulus to act on the subconscious.

Something can pass below human perception if it is inaudible and falls above or below the human hearing range. Using a low tone can make a person feel depressed, even if that tone is too low for the person actually to hear. Using a high pitch can increase someone's anxiety, even though that pitch is inaudible.

It is believed that images in ultraviolet light or in other shades of the light spectrum that fall just below or above the reach of human sight can affect someone. Just because the eyes don't see the light doesn't mean they can't understand it at some level in the brain. The brain can perceive things far beyond the scope that our conscious mind perceives.

It is believed that we only use ten percent of our brains. So, imagine what the other ninety percent is capable of? You may be able to see colors or hear sounds far beyond human reach. You may be able to discern things that are not visible or audible to the naked eye or ear. It is the beauty of subliminal psychology: it penetrates the hidden side of our mind and activates responses that we don't even know we have. But the unknown aspect of subliminal psychology and how the subconscious works can make it a bit of a guessing game.

Perfume is a powerful way to condition someone, and the perfume evokes powerful feelings or memories. A person who has been abused might go crazy when he smells the cologne his attacker was wearing. A person can suddenly develop a craving for Chinese food after releasing the smell of takeout food into the room. Or he could get defensive after being exposed to the cologne scent his high school bully always carried. Perfume works so well because it instantly connects to the human brain and appeals to our primary ability to defend ourselves from ourselves by interpreting the world around us through perfume. We can't always see or hear things, but we can smell much better than we think. Our olfactory ability is incredibly strong, but most of the things we smell never become evident to our conscious brain. It is believed that a man can smell when a woman is ovulating, for example, but he won't immediately or consciously understand why he is so attracted to her.

Speed can make a stimulus subliminal. If a message or sound is fast enough, a person may not notice it. It is the technique behind subliminal advertising. The image of a Big Mac is shown on TV so quickly that people don't notice. However, part of their brains did, and now they crave McDonald's fast food.

You can use subliminal cues to unlock repressed memories in a person. These memories will then trigger a torrent of emotions and do their work on a person's behavior. A person who represses a memory has compelling reasons for doing so. The memory probably causes him considerable discomfort. Reminding him of the memory with a small hint or stimulus can throw him into a state of intense upset, terror, anger, or even confusion.

Use this information to monitor the person's behavior and perhaps even sabotage their reputation. You can also use it to help someone unlock and start healing painful repressed memories that won't go away. Remember that just because a memory is repressed doesn't mean it does not affect someone's behavior and feelings. A repressed memory can be responsible for anger, depression, drug use, and emotional feeding, even if they don't know it.

Subliminal signals or triggers are useful in hypnosis or hypnosis. When you hypnotize someone, you put them in a trance state where they are incredibly emotional. Then you can access his mind and train him to associate a trigger with a specific thought or action. For example, you could teach someone to punch a bell. When the person has returned to a conscious state, the association remains.

Then, when a trigger is presented, the person will act with the desired action. He can act with fear if he is reminded of a terrifying memory or acts with joy if he is reminded of a beautiful memory or a warm and happy memory from childhood. Her emotional response to memory can affect her mood and the decision she makes right now. It can help form associations for him even within his brain, making him harsh towards certain people or things and making him make decisions based on memories.

You can also use subliminal cues to influence your emotions without bringing out a memory. Memories are powerful emotional tools, but you can still inflict a mood on someone with no memory. Instead, flash an image or play a soft sound that is sure to affect someone's mood. A person who is terrified of spiders can become terrified for seemingly no reason if you flash a subliminal image of a spider around.

Use of Subliminal Psychology

Subliminal psychology is useful in a variety of skills. Primarily, it's used to train people to do what you want without their knowledge. It means that you can use it to persuade people to do what you want, especially if they don't initially want to.

Subliminal psychology is excellent for children. Children love to be stubborn. As a parent, you've probably learned that if you tell your child not to do something, he or she is obligated to do it. But subliminal psychology allows you to tell your child to do or not to do something, without actually saying it. He or she is less likely to resist if you step into his subconscious and plant an idea instead of telling him what to do or what not to do. She is beautiful.

It also works with other stubborn people in your life. It allows you to train family members, colleagues, roommates and partners to do what you want when you want it. Instead of asking and fighting for what you want, make it happen. It almost works like magic.

When you work under someone, you may feel that you have no power over him or her. You are not allowed to make requests or give orders to this person. He may feel this way with the bosses, the superiors in the military, or the individuals they control in your life. But with subliminal psychology, you can make them follow your orders without them even knowing that you ordered them to go around. It will feel like his or her idea so that they will be more open to it.

You may not have a lot of relationships with a stranger. Someone as a new customer is new to you and unfamiliar to you. Since he has no reason to trust you or like you, he may be reluctant to do what you want. It may resist buying your brand or doing you a favor. You can inspire confidence and make this person want to buy your product or do you a favor by using subliminal techniques. Create a relationship that is not there and make this person want to please you, without him or her knowing why. Subliminal cues can work great for advertising or sales. It can also work when meeting new people, and relating to strangers, gaining more connections and friends.

Subliminal methods can be employed in seduction. To make someone fall in love with you or want to sleep with you, you can plant the idea of romance in their brain. Inspire him to associate with romance. This association will make him want you. You can bypass the hard work of getting to know someone and charm someone and probably fail with subliminal seduction. Instantly become attractive to others by using just a few hidden psychological tricks.

You can hypnotize yourself to train your brain to think differently. It allows you to overcome evil thoughts and problems like addictions or bad habits. You can train yourself to become the person you want to be. Get rid of bad habits, intrusive thoughts, or problems like depression and anxiety.

You can see that subliminal psychology is beneficial in many areas of life. Knowing that it is a beneficial skill. You can make life easier by bypassing the power struggles and efforts required to make people like you and do what you want. People will bow to your will and won't know why. They will magically feel inspired to do something, and they will not realize that it is what you want. Benefits in many ways. The best part of all is that you can avoid many failures, and the word "no." Subliminal psychology works like magic.

How Subliminal Psychology Works

Subliminal psychology works by acting on the subconscious brain. The subconscious brain is the part of your mind that works in the background, just like code works on a computer. It is the part of your mind that controls complex algorithms, telling you how to behave and think without any conscious concentration or effort on your part. You save a lot of time when processes like breathing, how to deal with strangers, and how to talk are automated in the back of your mind, instead of being frontline things in your mind that you have to think about. Imagine how distracted and overwhelmed you would be if you had to think about every little thing you do, how to manage your organs and determine how to behave in each situation.

There are probably often situations where your behavior is automatic. Don't even think about it. You just have to do something and then wonder how you knew what to do. When this happens, your subconscious brain takes over and helps you make quick decisions. There is no need to think about why your subconscious brain is intervening.

The subconscious brain also handles a lot of memories and the way you think. It is why you may have intrusive thoughts or memories that surface randomly throughout the day. Nobody understands how or why the subconscious mind will bring out a thought or memory, but this is thought to result from conditioning. For years your mind has been trained to create an association between a stimulus and a thought or memory. So, when you are exposed to this stimulus, you think a certain way or remember something. A repressed memory can even come back, causing you considerable discomfort. You may not even be aware of what this stimulus is. It could be a perfume, an image or a sound. Anything from your environment can cause your subconscious to remember something, even if it doesn't make sense to you.

For years your mind has been trained and conditioned in ways you don't fully understand. You have learned things without realizing that you have learned them. For example, you may have experienced fourth-grade rejection that made you nervous with the opposite sex and now believes you are a loser when it comes to romance. Or you may have learned that blue-eyed people are terrible because someone with blue eyes has abused you, so now you don't automatically like certain people based on your eye color. The great thing about this is that it means that the subconscious mind can also be retrained. You can bypass the analytical and reflective part of your brain with no control over you and slip into the subconscious. You can perform a powerful workout that will change the way someone thinks and responds to the world. You can perform this workout on yourself or others.

The subconscious mind is incredibly susceptible to influence. It's just that the subconscious mind is buried beneath our conscious thoughts, so no one is aware of it or its processes. Many individuals had no idea when they were influenced or influenced by something. All they know is that they begin to think or feel a certain way, or they start doing things differently.

Who influences a topic? Well, anyone can, in the end. Even a stranger or an advertisement managed by a multimedia platform can have an intense and significant influence on any topic. But usually, a person who has a lot of contact with the follower has the most significant influence. A romantic partner or parent is the type of person who exerts the most influence. These people can actively train and influence the follower without the follower questioning it. Getting to know someone helps because you begin to understand how to connect with this person for training purposes. But repeated exposure to the follower is the main factor that helps you achieve training. You have to have repeated contact with the person to cement the training.

People may not realize they are training others, but when you try to correct a behavior or teach your follower new behaviors, training is precisely what you are doing. It is natural and even ethical to train those around you. Often these training methods fail because you are merely projecting them into the follower's conscious mind. The follower can think about it and choose to discard them. Alternatively, they may want to undergo training, but their subconscious is trained differently and has a different acting idea. For Instance, you may need your partner to stop drinking, and he too wants to stop to please you and put his life in order. However, he drinks to deal with the pain of personal ideas and hidden memories lurking in his subconscious. Therefore, telling him not to drink and pointing out why his drinking is wrong won't do much good. You have to get his subconscious to rely on different methods or heal his wounds to banish alcoholism.

Subliminal training works by getting into the subconscious mind and doing its job there. So, it works from memory. It is why military or torturers can alter someone's personality because they repeatedly perform individual training. To achieve subliminal training, you must first find a stimulus and perform discreet training to induce the subconscious to form a definite association between the stimulus and a thought or action. Therefore, it is necessary to repeat the exposure to this stimulus several times to make it adhere.

Is Subliminal Psychology Dark?

The unfortunate fact is that the worst people and dictatorships have used this type of psychology, giving subliminal psychology a very dark and negative connotation. When you hear "subliminal psychology," you probably think of the CIA conducting mind control experiments on people or McDonald's facing a class-action lawsuit regarding subliminal advertising.

In reality, subliminal psychology is not bad unless it is used for evil purposes. Subliminal psychology is what you make it be. You can use it for evil, of course. You can train people to hate themselves or to kill themselves or to kill others. But that's not why you should use it. Use it forever. Use it to improve your life and that of others. The power of subliminal psychology isn't a joke, so don't abuse it. Instead, turn to it as a last resort to make positive changes in your life. Influence yourself and others on a deep and intimate level that allows everyone to work together peacefully and do what's best.

Subliminal psychology could allow you to save a relationship while retraining your partner to abandon relationship-destructive behaviors. It can enable you to steer your business in the right direction and avoid business catastrophes by making your business partners rethink the harmful strategy they are determined on. It can allow you to train your children to love themselves and stay away from harmful people or bad decisions they will naturally want to make as children or teens. Finally, it can even allow you to save the world. Imagine yourself in a scenario where you meet a serial killer or a manic dictator. It may sound like a fantastic scenario, but it could very well happen in today's crazy world with its vast array of mentally unstable maniacs. If you can successfully retrain a psychopath's brain from not wanting to do the wrong, he set out to do, you can save many lives, including yourself.

The ethics of subliminal psychology is undoubtedly a subject of debate. Mainly individuals will agree that it's not okay to train someone's mind against their will and without their permission. Psychologists and psychiatrists will surely agree that mind control is never ethically acceptable; the American Psychological Association bans it. Experiments with mind control and subliminal psychology are severely limited due to the ethical problems they pose. But this ethical dilemma has a vast gray area. Is it so wrong to train someone if you are improving their life and situation? If you can positively influence someone through subliminal training, then what's wrong with it? Using it forever may not be ethical, according to most people. But that doesn't mean you shouldn't do it. It's not okay to violate others or harm others with subliminal psychology, but you should certainly use it in self-defense. In situations where subliminal psychology seems acceptable to you, be your moral judge and do so if you wish.

However, subliminal psychology is not generally accepted as an ethical means of treating others. Most people are vehemently opposed to having their brains rewired by others and want to control themselves. The fundamental problem is trust. Nobody trusts you to know what's best, so they oppose your redevelopment. It is why subliminal psychology should be kept as discreet and stealthy as possible. There is nothing erroneous or dishonorable about doing this workout yourself. Subliminal psychology about yourself implies your full consent and knowledge. But it's probably best to avoid telling others what you're doing, as people tend to misunderstand what subliminal psychology is. In reality, what you are trying to do is nobody's business. So, keep using this type of psychology under wraps and only bring it out when you need it. Don't go around telling people that you are using subliminal psychology on yourself, or people will think that you are trying to hurt yourself and that you are crazy.

How Effective Is Subliminal Psychology?

The short answer to the question "How effective is subliminal psychology?" is: very useful. The long answer is that subliminal psychology is incredibly powerful but only when done correctly. Unfortunately, it is not commonly understood how to properly perform this form of psychological training, as it is not well researched due to ethical complications with such research.

When you use the appropriate methods of subliminal psychology, you will achieve great results. Some similarities tie most people together. Therefore, you must understand how human being's work. What could motivate a person? What could scare a person? All people are driven by desire or fear. They will act to get a reward or avoid something that scares them. However, you also understand that all people are different, so what might scare one person may not scare another. You need to understand what rewards and threats push different people for subliminal psychology to work. Therefore, it may take some time and research, but you should also rely on your instincts. Look for clues about how a person operates and what matters to them based on what they say to you, their photos on their desk or the things they do in their free time.

You also need to understand that training can sometimes require several exposures. Just because a stimulus doesn't lead to an association with first exposure doesn't mean this form of psychology is crap. Some people are more resistant to training than others. Getting someone's full concentration and exposing them repeatedly to the stimulus can help form the association over time. A more violent and vivid stimulus may adhere better than a softer stimulus. Be patient, and keep working on it until it takes effect.

Finally, understand that some factors can get in the way of your subliminal mental training. A person with deep self-belief can be particularly resistant to your training because they hold on to their ideas more firmly. Meanwhile, distractions can interrupt your training, and rendering is less effective. Make sure your environment is peaceful. Try to develop trust with the person you are training. It will make training easier. Also, learn this person and their deep convictions. So, find ways to get around those ideas and replace them with better ideas. You may need to become very persistent with your training to stay, especially if other factors stand in the way. It's best to make sure no one else is working on this person and try to make your workout the most attractive and rewarding to get the person to choose to follow you if you have any competition in training.

How to Use Subliminal Psychology?

Subliminal psychology works by entering someone's subconscious mind and planting an idea or concept in it that can work in your favor. So, to use it, you want to give someone a series of undetectable signals or clues. These could be in the form of pictures, memories or a choice of words. How you talk to someone and how you touch them can also convey ideas and plant ideas in their minds. Subliminal psychology is a sleight of hand. You are using little tricks to make someone's thinking change without their awareness. So being prominent or energetic is not what subliminal psychology is about. You will use tricks like subliminal imagery and classic conditioning to train people. You will use words, hidden signals and physical touch. No verbal force or work is involved.

Control of Your Usage

Avoid using subliminal psychology for evil. Sure, you could use it for all kinds of bad intentions. It can certainly be used for obscure means. But do you want to be such a person? It is bad enough in the world. You can use subliminal psychology forever. Here are some tips on how to control how you use this kind of forbidden psychology to stay on the side of the light.

When you want to control or coerce someone, stop. It isn't excellent. You have no right to control another's mind. You can influence and persuade people, but don't try to control them or change who they are. Never try to get them to go against their morals and values.

When you want to use subliminal psychology to hurt someone emotionally or bring down their self-esteem, that's bad. Stop immediately. You have no right to make someone hate themselves. You can push someone to commit suicide by doing so, and then death will be in your hands.

When you want to use this psychology to get someone to do something horrible, like a crime, stop. It should never be used for crimes or illegal activities. You shouldn't get people to do evil through subliminal psychology, or you are just as guilty. You're not using it to train murderers or bank robbers to do your dirty work for you. You are merely using it to make your life easier, so leave out the legal complications.

To use it on yourself, you don't want to hurt yourself. Use self-hypnosis only forever. Don't use it to change yourself too much or to break your morals or to make you behave unnaturally. You can do a lot of harm if you start trying to change the very elements of who you are.

Leak Detection

The whole secret of this type of psychology is to avoid detection at all costs. You have to be discreet and stealthy. Use methods that help you escape detection by disassociating yourself from the source. Don't reveal you're the one showing subliminal images, for example, and don't pretend it was an unintentional accident. Always play like you're not doing this kind of psychology. When using subliminal methods, you shouldn't be detected anyway because word choice and other small gestures are hard for others to detect as it is. This type of psychology is already stealthy by nature.

Protect Yourself from Attacks

What if someone uses it on you? Now that you know its power, the idea of someone performing this type of psychology on you can be terrifying. You have every right to want to protect your mind from potential invasion and control by someone else. Also, you are wise. You'd be a fool to blab into thinking that people aren't already trying to tap into your mind. It always happens with advertising and manipulative individuals in your life. Protecting your mind is a beneficial skill to learn and develop. The first key to protecting your mind is to read people. When someone appears to have malicious intent, be very cautious. Don't let them show you the pictures and turn off the phone or TV around them. Preclude speaking to them for a long time.

Muting the TV during ads can help you avoid the subliminal effects of advertisers. You can also get up and do something instead of watching the commercial. Be aware that you are probably a subliminal psychology victim if you suddenly develop a craving for something. So, turn off the desire and don't force it. If you've prepared your mind about something and suddenly feel differently, you could be a victim of subliminal psychology as well. Stick to your visceral choice. Avoid talking to people about it. Notice how people make you feel. If you feel different than usual with a specific person, pay attention to that person. He or she can manipulate your emotions, probably subliminally. That person is toxic and not right for you.

Subliminal Psychology to Win People
Domination is a big deal at work. Everyone is fighting for power over each other. There is always a hierarchy at work, and sometimes that hierarchy doesn't obey titles. For example, if your boss is a weak leader, someone else who is not in the boss's position will likely take control and leadership and act as your superior. No matter what the hierarchy is, you probably have people you need to respond to. These people can block your way up the corporate hierarchy and can put an end to your bright and creative ideas or new policies.

Even if you're the boss, you probably have to deal with disobedient people and don't care what you want. It can often seem like everyone is working against you at work, and you are nobody to whom no one listens or cares. Subliminal psychology at work can offer you a position of subtle domination. Being dominant will allow you to get rid of the problem of control and allow you to gain power over everyone, even your superiors. The best part? Nobody will realize that you are dominant or have power over them, and nobody will be able to resist your control. You will rule the office, and no one will know why. No one can tell you no, harass you, or make you do what you don't want to do.

The Chair Tricks

Where and how you sit, you can portray a lot without anyone noticing. Why do you think bosses like to sit in tall chairs behind desks, while others have to sit across from them in shorter chairs? Why do you think bosses like to sit at the head of the table or choose reclining swivel chairs that allow them to rest their feet on their desks? There is a reason for this. And that reason is control. To gain dominance over people, you need to position yourself powerfully. The way you sit down can convey your power and dominance subliminally. When someone walks into your workspace, ask them to sit down. Give them a lower chair than yours, so that they look down on them. You can stand or sit on a higher chair. This height gives you an immediate advantage because it makes you look more imposing and dominant.

Add Height to Your Stature

Being taller than others and looking down on them as you speak helps get people upset. They feel immediate and natural submission and submission when you look taller. Your imposing height may not feel natural, so wear high heels or shoes that increase your height at work. And remember the chair trick described above to add height to your appearance too.

Wasting People's Time

One way to subliminally enter someone's mind and gain dominance is to dominate that person's time. Calling pointless meetings, bombarding people with small talk, and sending constant messages may not earn you much favor with your colleagues. But guess what? It continually puts you on your head and gives you a monopoly on your time. Micromanaging also makes it possible to achieve this result. By always being there, you make others think of you and assert dominance that can help you immensely in the workplace. People will look at you more when you are dominant.

Excessive Planning

When you plan too much, you subliminally send the message that you are actually in control. The moment you start meddling with plans and injecting your ideas, you tell others you are taking over. You can gain a lot of control at work by actually taking control. Regularly plan and assert your domain in all situations. Join planning committees and become one hundred percent involved in business lunches, happy hours, meetings, office parties, and work trips.

First Session

It can be rude if you sit down first in a meeting or interview. But that's just because you say you're the boss. When you sit down first, you send the message that you are in control. You are not postponing for somebody to give you directions or to sit first. Choose your seat and take it without any doubt.

Posture

Have you ever wondered why your boss likes to sit in his seat, legs on the desk? This posture of power sends the subconscious message that his time is his to spend. You can adopt this position yourself. Having an overly casual and dominant power posture at work, whether sitting or standing, makes people seem to like you're in control. You are not troubled by the stress because you are totally in control of the situation. Being overly casual and confident in how you talk, walk, and sit at your desk causes others to subconsciously associate you with being the boss, even if you're not in the boss position.

Deepen Your Voice

A more resonant, more masculine voice lends you an incredible dose of dominance, even as a woman. People will think twice before challenging you or disobeying you when you go with Barry White. Doing this can give you a lot of credibility and respect, even with your superiors. People may not notice that you have deepened your voice, but you know your little secret. Put it to work and see what happens.

The Firm Handshake and Eye Contact

Send a clear meaning that you are not afraid of anyone by maintaining clear and constant eye contact and offering a firm handshake. Offer your hand first and overwhelm the other person with your grip. People will subconsciously associate you with trust, power, and security when you do this. The handshake and eye contact are not something to sneeze at. There is a reason why it is so emphasized in the business and professional world.

Be Quiet

Silence can make you seem like you're holding back a lot of thoughts. You watch everyone calmly, making them nervous and making them a little nervous about what you think. When you hold back your judgment and sit quietly or create uncomfortable pauses, you are subliminally sending the message to others that they are doing something wrong. They will take a moment and wonder what they are doing wrong, which gives you effortless control over their thoughts and actions. You can also talk when you choose, which adds dominance to your stance. People will be surprised when you talk and listen more. They will give more importance to your words since you are so thrifty with them. Be very careful with silence, though, because if you come across as a rat, no one will pay attention to you. You want to insert dominance in your posture when you use stillness as a subliminal weapon.

Establish Dominance and Submission

All relationships have some sort of unspoken balance between domination and submission. A partner is increasingly dominant and always makes decisions. When you establish dominance and submission, you end the need to fight because of one person delegates all decisions to the other. However, the problem in most relationships is that there is no division of power, and both partners want dominance, so they fight. You can eliminate this problem by assuming dominance using subliminal techniques. In this way, you are the leader, and your way is the law. Your partner obeys you and doesn't fight with you. Your partner is more likely to sacrifice things for you, and you don't have to anymore.

Take control of the relationship and put an end to all conflicts and power struggles. Does it seem like something your partner will never put up with? All right. Because your partner won't even guess what's going on, he or she will feel the sudden, inexplicable desire to submit to you and let you have your way. He or she won't even ask questions or put a strain on you. From one day to the following, the whole dynamic of your relationship will change in your favor. If you are a loving person, it means that they too change in favor of your partner as you gain control, because now you can take better care of your partner and provide more love.

The subliminal secret to gaining dominance is to make a power move that floods your partner's subconscious mind with respect and awe. The method to do this is to use guidance and rhythm. So, when you go out with someone, you already have some relationship. You already have a natural reflex that connects you like people in a relationship. But to strengthen your bond and set your driving mode and pace, you should start practicing mirroring regularly. Then you can start making a few small movements to see if your partner mirrors that. For example, after imitating the other person's gestures for a few minutes or even hours, flip your right hand over.

Ideally, the other person will also turn their right hand. Once someone from your partner starts following your lead, you know you've gained some control. Now you can start driving. You can guide them to do what you want just because they want to follow you. #You trained your partner. He starts using this control to start planting ideas in others' minds and guide them to new ways of thinking. They will be inclined to follow you as they already know they are following your subtle movements.

Using truly emotional language, start walking by stimulating some emotional response you desire in your partner. Playing on his hopes, doubts, fears, likes and dislikes will increase his emotions as you wish. Summon the things that will make him think positively or negatively about something; then, you come up with another idea, and he'll associate it with his bad mood and won't want to, or he'll start thinking darker thoughts. Or vice versa to make him feel happy and more receptive to an idea.

Remember that people form strong memories and associations with their emotions. It means that while you are talking about a person, you can get someone to form a negative association by mentioning their fears concerning the person you are discussing. So you could raise your mother, an overbearing mother-in-law, to your partner to sadden him before asking him to make a decision. In his negative frame of mind, he will decide to help him avoid his mother-in-law. Bingo, you just influenced his thinking. The pace allows you to set the pace for what someone does while driving, which means that you lead someone to do what you want. Combine the two to get superpower over someone's mind.

Create A Good Vibe

The atmosphere you give off is probably the first thing people perceive when they meet you. If you show off a bad vibe, people automatically shut down and want to avoid you. It gives off a good vibe, and people will feel more attracted to you and appreciate your company. But how do you control the atmosphere you convey?

Nobody understands what makes up the vibrations that people perceive in others. Social scientists have studied it well and concluded that vibrations are likely a combination of body language, facial expression, appearance, and the associations they create between you and other people they know. But you can help the way you present yourself to others. Essentially, you want to make a great first impression and give off vibes that you are a warm and welcoming person that others can comfortably talk to.

The initial way to do this is to smile. Smile as if your life depended on it. Smile until your cheeks hurt, and you're tired of smiling. Be the first to look at someone and smile. A smile increases the good vibes you transmit to other people. Smiling and making eye contact make others think that you are the right person. They feel you like them; why else would you smile and keep eye contact? Expressing positivity with your facial expression is great for attracting others. A smile is a massive part of the good vibes you're trying to put off.

Another way to give off good vibes is to look your best. Being well-groomed, well dressed and comfortable with your appearance increases the impression you make. People will have good vibes if you are pretty. They will feel more relaxed talking to you and appreciating you if it seems to you that you care about your appearance and that you have your stuff together. So, put in a little effort to look good and boost your confidence. Others will understand this very quickly. The more elegant or cute you are, the more confidence and warmth you will exude just because you feel good.

To increase your sense of well-being, you can try wearing charming underwear. Of course, other people may never see that underwear. But you know you're wearing them. You feel that you look great under your clothes and that gives you a nice little confidence boost. As a result, you naturally project more good vibes and safety vibes than yourself. A subliminal trick is to wear red lipstick like a woman. The red lips make you more seductive. It gives the idea that you are a warm and positive person. Find a shade that suits your skin tone and wear it when you go out to meet new people. As a man or woman who doesn't like lipstick, you could try a red tie, a red hat, or a red scarf. The splash of red can make others associate you with warmth, power, and even sex. The result will be good automatic vibrations.

Another subliminal trick for giving off good vibes is to warm your hands. When you offer your hand for a squeeze, a cold hand can make a wrong impression. A sweaty hand is also unpleasant. Then rub your hands into the pockets to create dry heat, so that when you shake someone's hand, you give them a warm and lasting impression. A trick to up the ante? Offer the person you meet a hot drink to give the idea that you are a loving person. When people hold hot drinks in their hands, they tend to associate you with that heat. Offering someone cold your coat is a courteous gesture that can charm people and give those good vibes you aim for.

Finally, you want to be positive. It could mean you have to pretend. But when you talk to someone, you don't want to sound down. You may complain a lot to new people you meet without even realizing it. When your first words to someone are, "This weather is hot, huh?" or "I'm so tired," you are projecting negativity. It creates a hostile atmosphere, and people may feel sorry and may not make any positive association with you. Communication will most likely be reduced quickly. So, you want to minimize complaints and talk about good things instead. Offer positive comments or compliments. He looks optimistic and happy, even if you aren't. Try to say positive things to people and find ways to uplift them.

Also, you want to create similarities. People bond with similarities. You may subconsciously reject people with negativity when you say things like, "Oh, you watch films? I hate films. Not for me!" See how saying things that make you different from others can give off a bad vibe? You want to create a positive vibe by finding a similarity instead. So, going back to the previous example, maybe someone loves to watch films, and you hate it. Then say something like, "It's great that you enjoy films. I went to the theater and saw a great film." Alternatively, ask them questions to find out what else they like so that maybe you can find something you too share in common and talk about. Stop rejecting people with unconscious negativity and attract them with positivity instead.

CONCLUSION

The use of psychological principles of influence and manipulation to undermine or limit the freedom and power of the person, although it may benefit the perpetrator. From now on, we call "dark psychologists" those who employ tools of influence and persuasion that harm the recipient. Dark psychology is a tool for dark psychologists, manipulators, cheaters, or outright criminals and harassers. Of course, sometimes, the line between an ordinary person and a dark psychologist can be blurred. You can also manipulate others to exact revenge or to create personal defenses. However, let's not get lost in the sea of relativism. Let's be realistic. Some are "darker" than others; others are much more manipulative than others, and vice versa. Some people have more important values and ethics, and you can more reliably expect them to be honest and fair.

Most of us have a desire to satisfy our needs and desires, and when these ideas are realized, the person can be analyzed better. The way a person was raised and how they grew up is significant in determining what makes a person unique. When analyzing another person, you start by looking at their body language. Do they hold high, or do they hide behind their bodies? How people use their eyes, face, and arms is essential to determining what they really might be like. You can understand that their anxiety could actually debilitate someone who seems confident if you start to notice the way they hold themselves.

You may also find that someone you thought you could trust is deceiving you. It can be challenging to pinpoint what it is about a person that separates them from others and why they might behave that way. You will never have a complete understanding of another person, but you will at least be able to begin to understand why they might act that way. Once you have been able to analyze someone, you can start persuading them. It is essential in some cases to get what you want or, at the very least, what you deserve. Just like we discussed in the first book, you can read it repeatedly, but unless you take action, nothing will change. It can be stimulating to become aware of yourself, but it is vital to becoming aware of those around you. Once you can analyze yourself and others, you will persuade and convince them better. When you do, you will realize all the power you have over your own life.

COPYRIGHT

distribution of parts of this text, in electronic or written form, is not permitted.

The recording of this document is strictly prohibited. Any retention of this text is only with the written permission of the publisher and all liberties authorized.

The information provided here is correct and reliable, as any lack of attention or other means resulting from the misuse or use of the procedures or instructions contained therein is the total and absolute obligation of the user addressed.

The author is not obliged, directly or indirectly, to assume civil liability for any restoration, damage, or loss resulting from the data collected here. The respective authors retain all copyrights not kept by the publisher.

The information contained herein is solely and universally available for information purposes. The data is presented without a warranty or promise of any kind.

The trademarks used are without approval, and the patent is issued without the trademark owner's permission or protection.

The logos and labels in this book are the property of the owners themselves and are not associated with this text.

BRAIN TRAINING AND MEMORY IMPROVEMENT

Train Your Brain Improving your Learning-Capabilities - Declutter Your Mind to Boost Your IQ! Accelerated Learning to Discover Your Unlimited Memory Potential!

BY

TED ROBBINS

TABLE OF CONTENTS

COPYRIGHTS

misuse or use of the procedures or instructions contained therein is the total and absolute obligation of the user addressed.

The author is not obliged, directly or indirectly, to assume civil liability for any restoration, damage, or loss resulting from the data collected here. The respective authors retain all copyrights not kept by the publisher.

The information contained herein is solely and universally available for information purposes. The data is presented without a warranty or promise of any kind.

The trademarks used are without approval, and the patent is issued without the trademark owner's permission or protection.

The logos and labels in this book are the property of the owners themselves and are not associated with this text.

CHAPTER 1: INTRODUCTION TO MEMORY & MEMORY TRAINING

WHAT DOES MEMORY MEAN?

Memory is a crucial element of your intelligence. Everything you learn in life is organized and stored in some way. The efficiency in accessing this information defines the memory error. Scientists spend a lot of time looking for locations in the Brain where memories are stored and identifying the hippocampus and cerebral cortex as possible locations. Oppose to what we all think, and modern studies suggest that memory cannot be confined to a single part of the Brain. It is a mistake to think of storage as a storage device that fills everything. We have learned so far and looked into when we want to get information. Memories are activities and experiences, not places. When I remember something, I build it out of the details that I think it is most beneficial. Your Brain is explainable and can select, and the mechanisms that distribute throughout the Brain. Two people who have experienced the same event can get a completely different report. So, think about what the event means to you, not the exact details.

CAN YOU INCREASE YOUR MEMORY?

Absolutely! You can train, improve, and promote your memory. The information in your memory is affected by the meaning you give it. For example, remember that these are personal experiences and emotions. You can improve your memory skills by providing the information you need for more critical meanings and associations. Memories work by making something unforgettable, storing this personal information, and call it up at any time.

MEMORY CONCEPT

The things we have heard about it is our memory decreases with age. It is wrong, and if the Brain stimulates regularly, it can improve with age. People in the 80s and 90s can have the same memory as people in the six months. Brain cells do not die as we get older. Psychologist Tony Busan reminds us that the essential memories do not necessarily belong to young people but to those who continue to improve their cognitive skills throughout their lives. Older people who are mentally stressed, learn new skills, and continue training may be mentally healthier than younger adults. Brain training offers good cognitive training. Here is a way to train your Brain and strengthen your memory. Come back to learn killer techniques.

HOW DOES MEMORY WORK?

Before we present the tips, let's look at the three types of storage that you need to receive and track.

SENSORY MEMORY

It receives information from senses such as seeing and hearing, processes it by holding it down for 1-2 seconds, and decides what you want to do. What you ignore quickly disappears and cannot do so often that the sound melts. Think about how you would see a sentence or echo from someone you know if you are not careful.

SHORT-TERM MEMORY

If you pay attention to something, the details transferred to the short-term memory can only save up to 7 data at a time. For example, you can only save your internet bank account number or your PIN code in this memory if you have to enter the key. As soon as short-term memory is "filled," no new neuronal mechanisms (meaning and associations) are created, and later information (i.e., data for removing old information) becomes available. Some scientists believe that evolution shaped this memory to have a limited capacity. Can you imagine keeping all the visual information you get in one day? What if you remember all the strangers you've passed and all the signs you've read? Well, your Brain will eventually experience data overload. The advantage of limited memory is that you can set priorities to focus on the task at hand.

LONG-TERM MEMORY

What does information transfer into long-term memory? All information can insert into this memory through the process of the rehearsal and the meaningful assignment. The processed data can be accessed weeks, months, or even years later. To do this effectively, you need to create as many links as possible to increase the number of starting points to save space, coordinate, review, and analyze information to make connections. Associations are mainly dependent on visual memory. It is an effective way to get a list of different items. One of the things we know about memory is that it is remembered rather than associated with personal experiences and emotions. If you are not sure, think about your birthday. What do you remember for 10, 15, 18, or 21 days? Probably 18 or 21 days because of its importance.

Everyone wants their brains to work optimally. It doesn't matter if you wish to keep up with your child or be at the top of the workplace. What is exciting is that science is now providing evidence of what works and what doesn't. So, training your Brain doesn't have to be an attempt to try one thing, determine that it doesn't work, and try something else. People who use the Brain more efficiently tend to have better jobs, better relationships, and a happy and more fulfilling life. And it's exciting. You can change your mind and thus your situation. You may have said that you were in your Brain a long time ago, but scientific research has shown that it is not! The plasticity of the Brain, the incredible ability of the Brain to adapt and change, is an exciting and growing field. And it's great that you can change your mind to make it work more effectively. Brain training doesn't have to involve a radical overhaul of your life. Here are some simple tips. Take a small blueberry on the way to the door. Play brain games on the move. Spend a few minutes every day. Find the best exercise to rejuvenate your Brain and enjoy the benefits of green tea. And discover the power of sleep in your heart.

NO MOTIVATION

Friendship not only increases motivation but also improves brain function! Just 10 minutes of social networking gives your Brain the same benefits as a crossword puzzle.

BRAIN TRAINING

I've heard of the left and right Brain. A heart is consisting of left and right hemispheres with different left and suitable functions. However, it is not entirely true that some people are "left brain" and others "right-brain." For example, language skills are in the left hemisphere, and everyone is using this part of the Brain! You do not have to hide behind the excuse that you are a right-brain to make your name unforgettable. Both halves of the Brain can achieve optimal values. There are key players in the world of brain training. Let's talk about how you can get attention. Most notably, different parts of the Brain do not work in isolation. They come together like a team. The training part of the Brain benefits the rest. You all must work together.

MEMORY TYPES

Long history Long-term memory consists of different types of memory.

AUTOBIOGRAPHICAL MEMORY

For example, childhood memories and meaningful events refer to as autobiographical memories. These types of memory are extreme, and their loss is an excellent early indicator of dementia and Alzheimer's. You can do a lot to keep these memories fresh.

MEANINGFUL MEMORY

Knowing the facts and random information called semantic memory can be handy when converting a new pointer from short-term to long-term memory.

PROCEDURAL MEMORY

Procedural memory is a mechanical skill that you do not even have to think. Driving or writing a name. You can find ways to automate new things to make your Brain work more efficiently. Short stories Short-term memory use to store linguistic, visual, and spatial information. If you do not "move" to a place in long-term memory, people usually do not remember anything in short-term memory for a very long time. The following are the ways to use short-term memory.

VERBAL

Do you remember what you said during the conversation? Do you remember how you stood on the stairs and why you went there? These are common phenomena and are not a sign of severe memory loss. However, if you want to keep your head shape, you can find ways to improve your language skills. Regardless of whether you want to keep an eye on your user list or age your memory, brain support can help you overcome the signs of Alzheimer's disease.

VISUALLY

Why are some people used to remembering their names but having difficulty remembering their names? An example of visual memory at work. Improve your Brain by using tricks to recognize your face and other types of visual information.

SPATIALLY

Are you always having trouble learning direction? Spatial memory is the key to achieving the right goal, not the wrong region. One of the tricks is a bird's eye view when you are in a new location. An active lifestyle leads to more efficient brain people, who react better, remember information, and can watch out for stress. What you eat, what exercises you do, how much sleep you get, and how much caffeine you drink, everything affects your Brain. It is essential to understand how daily decisions in these areas affect how the Brain works. So, before you drink another sandwich or wine, you should find one that suits your heart. Here is an overview of the tips and strategies you will find in this book.

EAT FOR YOUR BRAIN

Chocolate: It makes your Brain healthy. The Juice helps your memory. Steaks benefit your attention. Eating the right brain food doesn't mean eating salads or non-flavored foods. On the contrary, lots of delicious and beautiful foods filled with the proper nutrients for your Brain.

GET HELP FROM STIMULANTS

Caffeine, alcohol, drugs - these are all double-edged swords. In some cases, stimulants can help your Brain work better. However, many of these stimulants are expensive. Not all stimuli are the same. And you can do harm instead of your heart.

The Brain only weighs 3 pounds, but the whole body is still smooth. With 100 billion cells, your mind is like the CEO of a huge company. If you are wondering whether such small things have a great responsibility, you have come to the right place. This chapter contains some necessary information about how your Brain works. This understanding provides the basis for knowing how best to train your Brain.

DISCOVER THE FUNCTION OF THE BRAIN

Understanding the Brain has come a long way since the concept of four-touch humor (black bile, yellow bile, sputum, blood). According to the ancient Greeks and Romans, an imbalance in one of these moods causes illness and affects both mental and physical health. This general view persisted until the advent of modern medical research in the 19th century. Scientists are studying how the Brain works and making exciting discoveries every day. According to our current understanding, the Brain comprises of four parts.

BRAIN PARTS

FRONTAL LOBE

As the name suggests, the frontal lobe is in the front of the Brain and takes up most of the heart. One of the main functions of the frontal lobe is to plan and organize incoming information. When planning a party, drawing up a guest list, and managing the catering, the frontal lobe is crucial for carrying out all of these activities. The frontal lobe also helps regulate behavior and emotions. The Frontal lobe is associates with a chemical called dopamine. Dopamine is known as an area of brain pleasure because it is associated with reward and enjoyment. The frontal lobe does not appear until the age of 20. It can explain why it is difficult for a child to convince them not to experience a tantrum or why it is difficult for young people to consider the long-term consequences of their decision. In each of these scenarios, use the frontal lobe to plan the behavior, review the results, and change the action as needed.

PARIETAL LOBE

It is essential for the integration of information from various sources such as sensory and visual communication. The parietal lobe is divided into right and left hemispheres.

TEMPORAL LOBE

The temporal lobe is the home of language processing. The realm of humor lies in this part of the Brain. Part of the temporal lobe is responsible for visual information and object recognition. The temporal lobe is also home to another important player, the hippocampus.

OCCIPITAL LOBE

The occipital lobe is the smallest of the four lobes and lies in the back of the Brain. The visual cortex is responsible for visual processing information, motion detection, and color difference detection. This book doesn't touch that part of the mind very much. Elements of the mind are isolated and do not work. They work together as members of an orchestra. However, not all parts work together. In some cases, one element's performance may decrease while another element's performance may improve. This example shows the attention Deficit Hyperactivity Disorder.

BOTH SIDES OF THE BRAIN

The Brain composed of the left and right hemispheres connected by a "bridge" called the corpus callosum. But do you know that both sides of the Brain have different functions?

SAY HELLO ON THE LEFT SIDE OF THE BRAIN

Language is the most common characteristic of the left hemisphere. Grammar, vocabulary, and reading all relate to the left hemisphere. The left hemisphere is associated with language skills. Brain imaging studies show that general readers use the left occipital, temporal region, known as the word-formation region, to pronounce words as they read. Does the dyslexic Brain show the same pattern? A recent study looked at a 20-year-old group diagnosed with dyslexia in kindergarten. Brain imaging studies show little activation of the left temple area. Instead, 20-year-olds had higher activation of the right temple area. Some psychologists recommend people with dyslexia to bypass the left-brain mental pathways associated with phonological awareness skills and instead support reading in a more visually.

DO YOU KNOW THE RIGHT SIDE?

The right hemisphere controls the movement of the left side of the body. Responsible for spatial skills, facial recognition, and other visual processing. The right hemisphere also has thinking ability. Damaging this area can make inference more difficult, cause attention problems, and reduce the memory of graphical images.

The researchers used the split-brain experiment to understand better how the right and left hemispheres work together. The brain part corpus callosum (the bridge between the two hemispheres) surgery recommendation is offered by Doctors to treat epilepsy. It prevents the information from crossing between the two hemispheres. The general experimental mechanism is as follows. The image is processed by the speech-sensitive left hemisphere so that the patient can easily recognize the image and call it a dog. However, if the image flashes on the left side of the computer (processed by the right hemisphere), the patient says that he cannot see anything! If the corpus callosum for linking information between the two hemispheres is not intact, the Right Brain cannot say what the left hemisphere sees, and thus a person translates what they see into language.

DOES YOUR BRAIN SHRINK WITH AGE?

The answer is yes! Like you think. If you grow 2% every ten years, brain training can make a difference. This contraction begins early in adulthood but only becomes noticeable at the age of 60. Higher brain contraction leads to dementia. So, some brain contraction is normal, but too much is a clear sign of problems like Alzheimer's and dementia.

TIPS TO AVOID

Keep the following tips in mind to avoid or at least delay principal brain contractions.

GIVE ALCOHOL

Studies have confirmed that alcohol is not suitable for your Brain. In addition to all the harmful effects, the heart will be smaller. Even light drinkers (and "light" means 1 to 7 alcoholic drinks a week) are affected by these alcohols in the Brain. Studies in humans in the 1960s have shown that even drinkers have less brain mass than those who do not. With more than 14 drinkers a week, heavy drinkers were the most affected by brain mass. Be especially careful with women. The female brain volume is more affected by alcohol than the male one. In other words, the effects of light drinking can be more pronounced in women than in men. Why does alcohol affect brain volume? Alcohol empties your tissues, and if this happens all the time, your most sensitive tissue and your Brain will slow down.

RELAX

Stress can also affect the Brain. It is especially true for repetitive stress, such as illness and work difficulties. The prefrontal cortex, which is associated with decision-making and attention, and the hippocampus, which is related to long-term memory, are most affected by stress. Stress makes it difficult for people to concentrate on the task at hand or to absorb new information. When people are under pressure, they lose the ability to be mentally flexible. So, when you face an immediate problem, it is difficult to solve it in a new and creative way.

The brain contraction was normal. However, this contraction does not have to affect the work of the Brain. Research shows that people in the 1960s and 1990s could "mitigate" the effects of brain contraction. Keep your mind active by learning new things. People who spend time discovering and learning something they do not know strengthen their Brain's protection from dementia and memory loss. By continuing your intellectual activity, you train your Brain mentally to keep it healthy in old age.

TIPS FOR IMPROVING BRAIN FUNCTION IN CHILDREN

TURN OFF COMPUTER GAMES

Some schools use certain computer games for this purpose. The game may be fun, but do you have any clues to improve learning? One study compared the benefits of certain computer games to playing Scrabble in elementary school. In your opinion, which group was the best memory test? It wasn't a computer game group; it was a group that played scrabble and word puzzles. So, if you want to power your kids up, the best thing to do is turn off your computer and buy Scrabble games instead.

THEY ARE NOT JUST MEMORY NUMBERS

Does remembering phone numbers improve your Brain? Some programmed brain training uses this approach. Students are trained for several weeks to learn random sequences daily or to place associations. Unfortunately, some students can achieve a higher working memory after training, but they do not improve immediately after exercise. Why? For the simple reason that these brain training programmers train to test - if the child remembers the number for weeks, the number test is of course better. These improvements are called exercise effects.

TRY IT IN THE JUNGLE

In my study, I wanted to confirm the metastatic effect of brain training. Does your child's brain training improve your learning outcomes? I saw a programmer named Jungle Memory, who trains working memory along with important learning activities like reading and math. I took a group of challenging students and randomly assigned them to one of two groups. Half of the students received brain training with jungle memory (training group), and the remaining students received targeted learning support at school (control group). Before starting the exercise, the students measured IQ, working memory, and learning outcomes. At the start of the research, both groups performed similar results on all of these cognitive tests. The fact is important. It means that the improvement that a child receives after training is the result of the activity and not the child that starts on another level. After training, the results were dramatic. The control group had no different results. In contrast, training groups using jungle memory significantly improved IQ, working memory, and, above all, learning outcomes.

CHAPTER 2: POTENTIAL OF BRAIN

HOW MUCH DO YOU LEARN FROM WATCHING?

According to a survey, about 76% of learning is visual. Take your baby, for example. They are curious and discover behavioral traits by watching what the people around them do. It processes and interprets facial expressions and body gestures. The baby can see briefly whether the mother is happy or angry. It doesn't always change. Imagine the two of them going out on their first date. How much attention do they have in conversation, and how much attention do they have when reading each other's body language? It is natural to get a lot of information from visual material since about 40% of the Brain takes on the function of displaying and processing graphic material. As a rough estimate, most people know the names of around 10,000 objects and cognize by their shape.

VISUAL

Your vision is the key to interacting with the world around you. The estimation shows that most children promise to remember the names of a fifth of the objects they know in their lives when they are six years old. Studies have shown that visual stimuli are most useful for brain development and more advanced types of learning, both during growth and in adulthood. People have different options for collecting information from more abstract graphic types such as spreadsheets, diagrams, the Internet, maps, and illustrations. By interpreting information from such sources, you can find meaning, reorganize, and group similar things, and compare and analyze different information. Your learning is arguably the most useful and widely used in education.

GET THE STEPS

The great thing about the visual part of the Brain is that when you look at it in a certain way, it tries to develop your memory. For example, when someone looks at someone else's performance to learn a dance sequence, the Brain attempts to collect, process, and remember visual information. You can then use memory to practice and develop your skills. Inspire your vision to learn new things.

VISUAL INSTRUCTIONS

The puzzles and exercises throughout the book contain essential visual elements. This principle shows that brain training programs enable specific interactions between words and images. This synergistic effect allows optimal training of the cognitive muscles. Some sources say that people who communicate with visual presentation tools are 43% more successful than those who do not.

SEEING MEANS BELIEVING

Of course, it is a maple leaf with the Canadian flag as a motif. By learning to respond in any situation, you can understand feelings that are difficult to describe in words. It gives your insight into your own deeper motives and can educate you about personal fears and frailty that you may not have noticed before. To access these emotions, create or search for a fictional story or fable. However, there are some similarities to the actual situation we are facing. Ideally, you can read it (or paint freely). You do not have to be a good draftsman or writer if you want to do it yourself (bar graphs and amateur analysis are enough). You do not have to see or read your work, but it is usually more productive if you get someone else's views and reactions. You can feel free to be creative as the stories and pictures do not describe the actual situation. You can do whatever you want. You can present things in any way just because you feel right. You can write down what you need to feel comfortable with. Be careful and scared. By inserting something into this frame, you can explain your concerns to others and, of course, increase the number of metaphors and images that you can use when talking to others. If some areas of history evoke strong negative emotions, it could indicate that you need to find a positive way to deal with similar feelings in real situations. If you think someone in the story is critical or harmful, you may need to develop ways to look at those people more compassionately. Over time, you will become aware of cultural assumptions and expectations - what you should and shouldn't do (but may not be the custom of others).

WHY DO YOU IMPROVE YOUR MEMORY?

RECOGNIZE THE POSSIBILITY OF MEMORY

Your memory train, just like any other human teacher. With the right techniques, you can teach memory precisely what you want. You can improve yourself through training and practice, just like playing an instrument or speaking a foreign language. Memory training techniques only work by developing the Brain's natural capabilities.

Starting pointless memory training is like a goalless journey. Identify areas of life that would benefit from a stronger memory. When you focus on them, you get incentives to learn.

BUILD UP TRUST

A lack of trust in your memory paralyzes it and blocks the information it contains. Training ensures that you can access information quickly and accurately. Improvements are generated by yourself. The more memory you use, the better the performance. The higher the storage performance, the higher the utilization. You will find that this improves not only your self-confidence but also your social skills. You can remember your name and the date of your life accurately and efficiently.

IMPROVE RESEARCH SKILLS

Memory training doesn't help you understand new information better, but you can save it and retrieve it correctly. It increases your chances of getting data from your exam quickly and accurately. Instead of finding trouble, you can test your skills, enjoy the exam, and get better results.

WORK MORE EFFICIENTLY

Improving memory improves work efficiency. For example, you can spend less time looking for facts and checking appointments. With complete and accurate information, you can speed problem-solving and decision-making, memorize the names of colleagues, and customers, and improve relationships between work and customers.

SOME TIPS TO SUPPORT YOUR MEMORY

Memory plays a vital role in the Brain and parts of the body. So, if you want to maximize your memory potential, you need to take some simple support measures to keep your body healthy.

LAY THE FOUNDATION STONE

Most people assume that their memory works very quickly with unprecedented accuracy and at any time and in any situation. This laissez-faire attitude leads to inconsistent memory performance. As with other parts of the body, memory must be kept constant over long periods to maximize its potential. The first step in building a solid foundation for memory training techniques is to understand the importance of conscious efforts to maintain awareness.

EAT WELL

Do not underestimate the power of eating as a good memory enhancer. The neurotransmitters that control the ability to exchange information between neurons must be maintained appropriately. The Brain is susceptible to oxidation, so antioxidants are needed. These include foods that are rich in vitamin C, vitamin E, carotenoids, and selenium. Other brain enhancers are fatty acids, especially omega-3 fatty acids: b vitamins and certain minerals. To increase your intake of these nutrients, eat as much fresh food as possible, and avoid cooking. Ginkgo balboa, as a supplement, is believed to improve blood flow to the Brain.

TRAIN YOUR BODY AND MIND

Your physical health plays a vital role in your mental performance. The Brain consumes 20% of the oxygen intake, but only 3% of the total body weight. Improving blood flow through cardiovascular training provides essential oxygen that directly affects brain performance. The exercise should be of moderate intensity. So, do not hold your breath. Aim at least 20 minutes three times a week.

REDUCE STRESS FACTORS

Training your memory improves both your efficiency and your skills, but it's essential to avoid exaggeration. Do not try to do many tasks at the same time. Take control of your life and learn time management techniques to control it. If you tend to exaggerate naturally, know to say no to people. Relax at home or work with stress-relieving techniques such as simple relaxation exercises and meditation. If you are out of the world and have fun, you should have a little time for yourself every day. Spend relaxing days with family and friends every day and plan regular vacations.

PAY ATTENTION TO THE RHYTHM OF LIFE

The energy level relates to temperature. So, if you monitor the weather, you can see the biorhythm and thus the storage capacity. High-temperature stories usually reflect high energy levels. Check the temperature 3 hours a day and plot the results in a graph. Do this for a week and usually record when the optimal time has come.

SLEEP WELL

Sleep is generally essential for good health, and lack of sleep can lead to mental disorders. Rest plays a vital role in memory consolidation. The same area of new tasks performed during the growing season continues to process information while you sleep. Sleep enables the Brain to store additional information in memory for future use. Therefore, a good night's sleep is essential for a healthy life.

CHAPTER 3: HOW TO KEEP YOUR MEMORY SHARP?

You can remember some of this information for years. For example, an unforgettable birthday, but no other memories last longer than a week. Think of your long-term memory as a library full of books. Some books read more than others, which makes it easier to remember the book you submitted. Some experiences can never forget more than others because they think more in long-term memory. Chapter 5 describes short-term memory. Library check-out table. There are several books in front of you, but you may not be able to remember this information for a long time.

DISCOVER THE IMPORTANCE OF CHILDHOOD MEMORIES

Retrieving reminders before the age of three is often tricky due to poor language skills. If not, how do you talk about what you did that day? And if you can't figure out what you did, how can you add it to a long-term library shelf? Another difficult reason to remember our childhood memories is that our Brain is not yet fully developed at this point. Let's talk about Kaaba. This area plays a vital role in the synthesis of memory and does not develop until the age of two. It is challenging for young children to combine their experiences and transfer them to a long-term memory library.

Take a stroll along memories road to remember your childhood memories. Flick through your photo album to trigger Happy Holidays and read old birthday cards and letters that you exchanged with loved ones. Sometimes it is important to remember how happy you were. Do not keep photo albums in hard-to-reach places such as the attic. Instead, keep the album in a prominent location. Place it for regular access to the bookshelf. Not all memories are reliable. As the name suggests, bad memory is the memory of an event that has never occurred or the decoration of an event that happens. This outbreak is most common in childhood memories. You may remember an unprecedented event like a rabbit when you were young. You can also have a memory that lists the event that occurred. For example, if you had a dog as a pet, you could remember that you and your dog chased a rabbit in a nearby field. But your parents can point out that you lived in a busy city with no nearby areas.

USE THE POWER OF HAPPY MEMORIES

Emotions play an essential role in memory. We may remember that as a child, we spent all the time and spent the summer in the local pool. Other memories that preserve because of a vivid snapshot to create the instance. It may be a surprisingly happy event, but it can also be shocking. Do you remember when you first heard about Diana's death? What did you do when the September 11 bombing reported? Most people, though familiar, recognize these memories in minute detail. Why? Flashlight memories are emotional memories. As a result, trivial events suddenly become more meaningful, and we remember the unimportant information. However, placing an event does not mean that all the details you remember are correct.

SOME TIPS TO IMPROVE YOUR MEMORY

Here are some tips on how to focus on beautiful memories:

THINK HAPPY

Positive thinking can make a difference in your life. In my childhood memories, I seduce the event as I get older instead of looking at it from a positive perspective. It can be the result of subsequent life experiences such as stressful events. But do not let it happen. Think about how an event made you stronger and better instead of letting yourself down. You can also think about why people did what they did.

SCRAPBOOKING IS NOT A DIFFICULT TASK

It is easy to forget a great vacation. Over time, I have to take care of my daily work. Some people keep tickets for events they have visited, brochures, and postcards from places they have seen, or coral and flower stumps from their favorite parks and walks. You can add all these souvenirs to your scrapbook. If you are a little creative, you can buy fantastic books and resources.

HAVE A SNACK

Remember a relaxing sunny day where you can spend the day in the park without going to school. Eating is an excellent trigger for happy childhood memories, as taste and aroma remind you of certain events. If you do not have enough family or childhood friendship, you may get angry at what you ate earlier.

LEARNING PROCESS

Learning something new is a three-step process:

1. Encoding refers to how information is in memory.

2. Memory is a way to monitor messages.

3. If necessary, you can access the data via the entry.

CODING TIPS

IMAGINE

If you need to remember a list of new words, create a visual image in your head instead of repeating the words in your head. When attending a party, do not just think of the person's name. Think about what people are wearing and remember where they were when you met them. All of these visual cues trigger memory when you later need to remember the person's name.

DEEPEN

It's easier to remember something new when you look at what a word looks like or what it sounds like when you look at something superficial or flat. Try to remember as best you can. But this method doesn't help at all. Instead, think about what you mean and rhyme with it. It will be unforgettable to show people more meaningful information.

TO ORGANIZE

"I've said it a lot, why do not you remember it?" Everyone knows this feeling. But you can change that. Create a framework for organizing new information. When reading, think of the framework, and attach what you have read to the framework. It will help you remember what you have read many times.

CREATE A CONNECTION

Link new information with what you already know. Do not only think carefully about what details you learn but also how and how you can link them. As you learn new historical facts, think about what you are used to and connect new recognized historical facts. This process, known as semantic linking, helps you to retrieve the information later.

TIPS FOR LONG-LASTING MEMORIES

Use the tips below to remind you where you left the information. This way, your memory will not be lost.

CONTEXTUALIZATION

When you listen to information, you can release your memory. If you can't remember anything, hear the statement first or return to where you read it. At work, return to the room you were in and re-create the scenario to trigger your memory. If your friend gives you essential information, go back to the cafe or restaurant you spoke.

REMEMBER YOUR CONDITION

You can also quickly identify information based on how you feel about it. If you feel good when you first hear about a new project you've involved in, think about it.

TO TRAVEL

Traveling is the combination of new information and mental images of familiar ones, is a trick that some storage professionals use. Example: Suppose you just woke up and see the John Travolta poster in the closet. You loved Grease in the movie. When entering the bathroom, there is an unfinished school project (model of the Eiffel Tower) in the middle of the floor. You sleep in the living room and watch your brother spill pasta sauce on the sofa.

PROCEDURAL MEMORY

Procedural memory refers to skills that are acquired automatically. You no longer have to think about writing a letter or tying a tie. Your Brain remembers what to do without taking any steps. As a result, it is often difficult to list every step. The problem is how to learn new things. It's a procedural note, and you do not have to think twice? For example, you can discover a new language or complete a dish. The next section contains tips on how to transfer this detail into long-term memory.

PRACTICE FOR PERFECTION

I heard someone say, "Practice has to be perfect." The statement contains a lot of truth. When you do something repeatedly, you train both your Brain and your muscles to learn. Athletes use this muscle memory to "remember" things like cycling and skating and automatically perform actions. Applicable statements are important because if you do not learn the right thing first, the body must first understand the wrong way before it can learn a new and better way to do something. Think about how you hold a pencil. I remember that my teacher was very strict with all the students. If you only have one pen, you have a problem. I am particularly concerned with how to hold a pencil, and I feel strange how to keep a pencil. It also applies to many other activities.

For example, if you enjoy skiing and choosing a lesson, you may be surprised by poor posture and body shape even after skiing for years. Teachers should try to change their form rather than teaching beginners. It is because the muscles do not have to store a specific ski method and must learn the correct shape. The next time you know something new, make sure it's the right way for the first time. So, you do not have to learn twice.

The power of reward in improving memory is known as the law of effectiveness. This law is simple. If you learn something new, you are more likely to repeat the action that triggered your learning. As a child, these rewards can be great results for gold stickers or exams. For adults, this can be praise from relatives or even work promotion. The validity law has another dimension. If you learn something new and get negative things like criticism or disappointment, you are less likely to repeat this action.

Reward yourself! Gold stars and colorful stickers found in the classroom. If you want to learn something new, set up a reward system. Divide the information into smaller parts and give yourself a "sticker" each time you know the role successfully. When you have completed the task, use the rewards that you have set (new clothes, short breaks). A treat doesn't have to cost money. It could be a special day with friends. The goal is to train the Brain, absorb information, and create incentives that connect positive emotions with the learning process. This method not only makes learning more enjoyable, but it also helps you to remember information much longer.

When you look at the rewards and photos of the event, you can remember the information you received as an extra. Many famous athletes do little routines of what they do before the game. Maybe you tie the threads in a certain way or sleep in a uniform the night before the big game. One of the major league ice hockey players put a hockey stick in the toilet before the game. Such superstitions are not uncommon for athletes. While these routines rarely help establish a lasting connection in memory, some people find that repeating regular exercises helps reduce anxiety about actual results or activities.

TRAINING IN YOUR SLEEP

Sleep is a great booster when you learn. When you rest after learning, the information known is amplifying. Do you remember your school days? Do you remember these multiple-choice tests? They look straight-forward but can be very confusing if multiple-choice seems the right answer. Many everyday situations can confuse people. For example, you can forget whether you switched off the stove on the way to the door. Sleep not only improves memory, but it also reduces mistakes when working on tasks. When you sleep, your Brain uses this time to load real and information and separate it from false information. As a result, it is not only updated but also less confusing and forgotten whether the stove was on or not. When musicians try to learn music, they do not just play songs repeatedly. When every musician plays music frequently, the muscles learn to move, but the distraction in the middle of a piece makes it difficult to record and continue playing. Some people have to start over because they can't play at random points in the music.

You do not have to be an excellent musician to use musical techniques. I get nervous when I must learn something new or do something. At a presentation at work. Focus your attention on what you need to do and involve the Brain. First, remove the distractions. You can keep the display on your head instead of repeating it out loud. Consider the various questions that your employees may ask. Finally, consider the answers to these questions in the middle of your presentation. Then continue where you left off and continue production.

TIPS TO IMPROVE YOUR SHORT-TERM MEMORY

There are several ways to improve short-term verbal memory for a better brain:

TIME IS ESSENTIAL

Hearing information affects how well you remember it. Suppose you remember the story at the top of the list instead of the word in the middle of the list, you can try more. It is known as the primacy effect. If someone gives you a long list of tasks, break them up into many plans, and avoid the "slump" in the middle of the list.

REDUCE DISTRACTIONS

Irrelevant thoughts are the disability or another distraction in the region. If they ignore the content of short-term memory, they quickly deteriorate and are lost forever. Minimizing the distraction is essential for the effective use of working memory. Background noise also affects the amount of material you can store. The silence makes it easier to remember the right short-term words. If you are trying to remember important information, reducing music can be helpful.

CONCENTRATE ON ONE THING

Activities that need to draw attention from one thing to another can speed up the process of forgetting. Switching and multitasking can be overwhelming and even forget the simple things. If you are up the stairs: "What have you done here?" If you do many things at the same time, you cannot do one thing well. To reduce this, do one task at a time. It makes it easier for you to remember things at work and home.

KNOW YOUR LIMITS

Think of bite-sized blocks of information to avoid memory overload. It is more important to remember the information you need to remember than to keep an eye on the latest news and prove to be your next memory champion. Repeating the information, you need to remember will help you remember what you need. However, there are two things to consider:

LENGTH CALCULATION

he length of a word makes a big difference in how easy it is to remember. Check out these words: fridge, hippo, Mississippi, aluminum. It is easier to forget than words that are easy to repeat, such as baths, clocks, spoons, and fish. The longer it takes to duplicate or rehearse, the more difficult it is to learn. It is called the word length effect. Long names are hard to remember. To improve your memory in the long term, ask more than just listening to the list.

SOUND IS IMPORTANT

Remembers a list of clearly distinguishable words (bass, clock, spoon, fish, mouse, etc.) and not a list of frequently heard words (rhythmic words such as people, cats, cards, mats, cans, hats). It's painless. If things sound the same, you are more likely to get confused and forget what you need. Therefore, when trying to get a shopping list, do not group the items by category (dairy, meat, bread) and not alphabetically.

CHAPTER 4: READING AND REMEMBERING

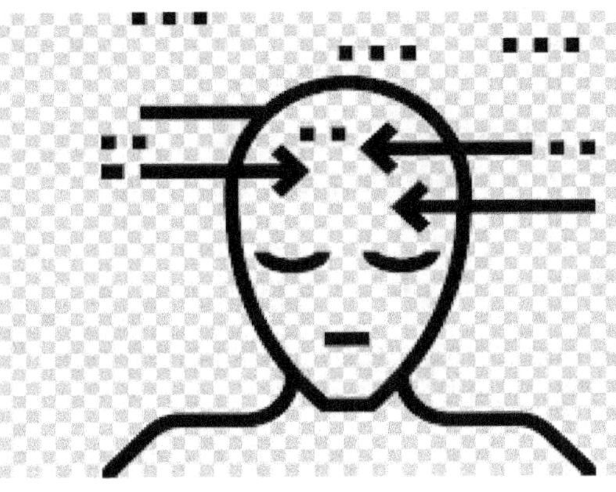

Whatever you do when you survey the area, you will not only learn to read but also remember what you read whenever you need it. Being able to remember without checking details is an excellent benefit for all students. Universities can place very high demands on reading a single course. So, when you have most of the information you need, make your textbooks more efficient and your exams and routine tasks more efficient. Think about what you can prepare. For the first time! This chapter briefly describes how to do this.

Think about the difference between writing and presenting in a newspaper or textbook. The newspaper edited and designed so that it is easy to read. Most newspaper articles organized according to the "pyramid" approach. The first paragraph (above the pyramid) will be the main point of the story, and in the next section, we will add more details and create related topics to fill the pyramid. Read all the headlines and the first few paragraphs to understand the news of the day better. If you are interested in the details, read on.

TO SUMMARIZE THE SKIMMING PROCESS:

1. If you have a title or heading, rewrite it as a question. That is the purpose of your reading.

2. Check all subheadings, images, and graphics. These help to identify important topics in the text.

3. Read the introductory section, overview, and questions at the end of this chapter carefully.

4. Read the first sentence of each paragraph. You will always find important ideas here.

5. Evaluate what you got from this process. Can you answer the questions at the end of this chapter? Can I intelligently participate in class discussions on class materials?

6. Write a summary of what you learned while skimming.

7. Use this assessment to determine if you need a full reading.

READ QUICKLY WITHOUT READING SPEED

The author's headings, subheadings, first sentence, and other tips can help you quickly understand the content of the chapter. However, a few words in this chapter focus on what is essential and what is not. Some things can help you ignore them. Knowing when to accelerate, slow down, skip, and focus can help you read faster and more efficiently. Mathematics, economics, and science texts require a slightly different treatment. You need to follow the steps outlined, but with some significant additions. Do not proceed to the next section unless you fully understand the concepts contained in the various charts and graphs and master the previous quarter. If you have a sample problem, make sure you understand the concepts given by solving issues related to the extent you are reading. If you still do not understand an important idea or equation, start over. However, do not continue. It just wastes time. "Trial and error" are a recognized method of scientific research. However, it is essential to try it out and provide the information. In other words, clearly state where you are going and what you learn from each mistake. Trial and error are appropriate, but much more critical than merely applying the same analysis (solution, conclusion) to a slightly different problem and requiring a real understanding.

MEMORY TRAINING TECHNIQUES

Memory training techniques take full advantage of the natural characteristics of memory. You can order information in various ways using the methods described here. You can use them alone or in combination, depending on what you learn.

INFORMATION ORGANIZATION

Minimize losses and increase efficiency. It is essential to organize the information you receive. Splitting or arranging information into simple patterns is an easy first step in data collection. Simply put, if the Brain is somehow actively involved in processing the data, it is more likely to remember it correctly. Motivate your mind to work more efficiently; the data must be focused on using visions and other sensations and converted into more memorable forms.

IMPROVED CONCENTRATION

Focusing is an essential practice when using storage technology. Compare the memory of a TV show that you saw when you did something at the same time with the memory of a program that was entirely focused. The first case is more accurate and less detailed than the second case. Imagine being asked to learn to concentrate more later. Listen to the radio and answer your friends' questions. This process of checking information after first learning is also essential for improving memory.

USE THE SENSES

Seeing and listening are sensations that commonly used in learning. Develops, seeing, and hearing to make it sharper. Artists are more used to seeing things in more detail and from different perspectives, so they can "see" 30% more than the average. Make a conscious effort to notice the small parts to improve your senses. For example, spend a day observing the color, nose, and ear types of your neighbors. Listen carefully to their voices - do they have the accents and phrases that they like?

LOCATION USE

Think about how you can mentally go back in time when trying to lose something and remember where you came. It is what your Brain does naturally and is the key to the essential skills of memory training. The "travel" technique uses routes that pass through a known number of locations.

IMAGE CREATION

The basis of all memory training is to create mental images from the learned information. The most memorable thing is that it is rare. Decorate your photos according to the principles of image creation to make them unique and unforgettable. The more you pay attention to the details, the brighter the picture becomes.

USE OF THE ASSOCIATION

Your Brain loves building a repertoire of related information and making connections between data. When the Brain receives new information, it looks for similar things in long-term memory so that it can "understand" what it is. It happens quickly and is not a conscious process. Creating associations improves your memory. By actively creating personalized links for the Brain to connect, you can do some work in your memory and restore it later.

INFORMATION STORAGE

Organizations are the key to properly managing information in many areas of life. The library is a good example. Without a sorting and coding system for organizing books, the library would not work at all. Most offices have efficient filing systems, and all the information you need later is stored in folders in the filing cabinet. The storage technology also takes this into account when receiving new information. For example, create a framework for patterns, locations, etc., and save the data in future storage. It enables the memory to process and store information so that it can recall as efficiently as possible.

CHAPTER 5: SOME MEMORY TECHNIQUES

IMPROVE DAILY MEMORY

The ability to regularly remember what you need is invaluable. Having this critical information at hand not only increases your confidence and efficiency but also saves time.

SAVE YOUR PIN AND PASSWORD

If possible, use an available date such as your relative's birthday to store your PIN. When you use your password and PIN together, you use words and numbers that you already remember. A friend's house number or zip code. Or use the numbering system image and another image associated with the password. In both cases, create a story that links the image to something that you need to access (e.g., an ATM).

MEMORIES OF EVERYDAY WORK

Mental notes help you remember the tasks of the day. To plan 4-5 days, use travel techniques to plan 4-5 trips. Use the principles of imaging to create a mental picture of each task and insert it into your day trip. For example, if you need dry cleaning, imagine clothes that dance with music and songs. If you need to complete the task at a specific time, add a digital image using any numerical system. Fill out the notes in a few days and save them. If new jobs arise, add them at the end of your trip. You should review your project regularly. Move your head three times a day to make sure nothing is behind you.

MAINTAIN A MENTAL PLANNER

Most people rely on entirely written or computerized planners to organize their monthly hours. Neither system is perfect. Keeping the planner on your head can be very convenient and time-efficient. The learning planner helps you make quick decisions when you make appointments and other arrangements. The basis of the mental planner is travel technology. Initialization can take some time, but once the system set up, it is relatively easy to perform updates.

CREATE A PLANNER

If you are a three-month planner, you need to create three trips (one for each month) and one stage for each day of the month. Take certain breaks at level 10 and level 20 to determine the individual days for each trip. Use three rides in rotation. Create a picture for each planner entry and insert it in the appropriate place. For example, with an 18-day appointment at the dentist, your vision is for the dentist to hit the entire chair. Paste the image on line 18. If you need to add more time, add the corresponding image from the numerical system.

TECHNOLOGY EXPANSION

If it is easy to work on three trips, you can expand the planner to create more trips. Six months or one year is probably enough. You can keep the same imaginary route every year. Start each month with an essential photo of the month. If it is more convenient to use it for three months, you can write down the dates that are older than three months and add them to your trip later.

SPEAK IN PUBLIC

Public speaking is a challenging perspective for many people. You can do this naturally and engagingly by learning to remember some crucial points in your speech, presentation, or play.

PLAN WHAT YOU WANT TO CONVEY

One of the best ways to create a speech or presentation is to map it. Write down the keywords first, and then add the related items that you want to create. This method makes the transmission more natural instead of writing every word. However, if you are going to write your speech entirely or at least linearly, add headings so you can choose keywords.

A MEMORY OF THE LANGUAGE

Remember your speeches and presentations using travel techniques. It is also useful for the timely delivery. For example, if you are planning a 20-minute speech without notes, search for 20 keywords, and take 20 steps. Take one keyword at a time, create a picture, and add one at each stage. If you want to add more information, use Statistics, images of the required numerical system and add them to the appropriate level. Practice your speech to make sure you meet your timing goals. Your language will be a little different every time you grab it, so it sounds fresh.

LEARNING LINE AND QUOTE

If you need to learn theatre lines or read poems or quotes, you can learn the keywords in a fixed order, just like you can in that language. But since we must complete the words, we have to go one step further. We use travel technology to rehearse the line and continue to deliver critical points. Next, you must go through the names to fix minor heart problems. If there are areas that are difficult to remember, take a photo that is easy to remember.

SKILL IMPROVEMENTS

You can apply memory training techniques to a variety of skills that you use in your daily life, from recording information about sports and games to learning languages. Also, the learning experience is fun.

IMPROVE READING

Reading is what we all do - for work, joy, or learning. But most of us cannot read as efficiently or effectively as possible. As a result, we do not remember what we wanted. One way to speed up reading and make the material more memorable is to turn books and articles into mind maps. You must do this from the start, read analytically, and question the order and hierarchy of the information. Organize the story and add it to your mind map.

MEMORY OF FACTS

Fact files and diagrams:

If you can remember facts and maps, improve your general knowledge. Very useful if you want to take part in quizzes and competitions. Create images from every piece of information and link them with associative techniques. For example, if you are going to remember that Michael Douglas won the Oscar in 1987, take a picture from 1987 and attach it to Michael Douglas, who owns the Oscar statuette. The most important thing is to create a fantastic image and save relevant information.

LEARN SPORT

Time and attention are increasingly devoting to both the mental and physical aspects of athletic performance. Memory is a great way to speed up learning as it helps you build good habits from the start. When learning new techniques such as tennis shots and golf swings, the technical aspects divided into essential points. Create a simple, vivid picture for each of these points. For example, if you need to keep your head motionless on tennis serve, imagine wearing a ruff to keep your head steady. Create a trip (probably at the gym) in which essential points saved one after the other. When you start the game, the image of each point crosses your head.

PLAY CHESS

Chess is a technical and strategic game. Opening and closing movements can be learned and used, with previous games remembered as a precedent for future games. To learn chess movements, you must first understand the standard chess notation. Learn these movements with travel techniques, phonetic letter techniques, and your preferred number system. Create a mental picture for each activity, design a trip, and paste the picture on every stage. The full opening may require a journey of 50 steps. To remember whether your hand is black or white, mentally color the image black or white.

IMPROVE CARD SKILLS

If you can remember the card, you have an advantage in the game. Especially if you need to remember what has already played, use the numbering system to create pictures with numbers from 1 to 10. Each picture card has its vision. Create a composite image of the two components for each card. That is, the three clubs could be handcuffs that swing the golf club. To remember the pecking order, create a trip in 52 steps and place the cards in the order in which they come out.

LEARN A LANGUAGE

You can learn vocabulary as the name storing techniques. You can use this technique for words in any language. The most important thing is to listen to the story and then make the association. Create a picture from a foreign language sound and attach the image to the word in your mother tongue. The German language for newspapers is, for example, the newspaper. To remember, you could imagine someone you know reading a newspaper, dropping his tongue and calling it Simon (Si). Visualize this scene in the newspaper section to improve the picture.

SUCCESSFUL EXAM

The memory plays a vital role in academic performance. Improving your memory not only increases your chances of success in the exam but also helps your Brain develop good habits. The more effectively you learn, the more efficiently your memory works.

USE OF MEMORY AIDS

There are several ways you can approach your study to improve your memory of information. 30% of people hear learners - they prefer to hear rather than read. If you want to learn by listening, record some information on tape or minidisc. Play for yourself at different times of the day, for example, during a car ride or before bedtime, just before bedtime. Another technique is the use of flashcards. Write the question on one side and answer it on the other. You can give the card to someone else to help you learn or change the order in which you use the menu to understand information. It will help you remember the exam if you can ask the questions in any order.

STORAGE OF LARGE AMOUNTS OF INFORMATION

The key to learning large amounts of information is to reduce it to a manageable amount. Mind mapping uses keywords for this. It also provides a way to organize the information logically and comprehensively so that the links and related information are specific. Only the mind map keywords need to save. Then the mind map automatically leads you to the relevant area.

THE REMAINDER OF THE FACTS

You can use travel techniques for several facts, including several historical events and the structure of flowers in biology. For example, if you get to know nine planets in the solar system, you first create an image of each world. In other words, Mercury is a thermometer, and Earth is a bargain of Earth. Create a nine-step journey, a stage for every planet. The travel location must be thematic and preferably in a familiar place. In this case, you may be in a fictional spaceship. The next step is to insert the picture into the trip.

STORAGE AND RETENTION OF CALLBACKS

Up to 80% of all information learned lost within 24 hours. Reviewing data is essential for high retention and good recall. Doing this at the right time will reduce the total number of reviews required.

CONFIRMATION OF INFORMATION

For better learning, new information needs to check before the level of memory gets too low. In the first 24 hours, the Brain plays with further information and is bound to exist data. In other words, this time, it is relatively easy to remember. Once this process is complete, the recall level drops quickly. To prevent this, you should check the information regularly. In this way, the Brain can continue to access new information, evaluate it, and remember it in detail.

PLAN

Written planning can integrate learning by regularly requesting information. It is particularly essential for studying, but necessary for information that you want to keep for a long time. The best time to check the information is 1 hour after the first learning. Then you have to check it every one day, one week, three months, and finally every six months after your first degree. Mark this data in the planner and make it part of your action plan.

SET NEW GOALS

Maintaining a high memory strengthens your confidence in your memory and encourages you to continue your learning path. When storage technology becomes part of your life, you can spend quiet time looking at information or remembering new information. It will be a habit, not a chore. If you spend more time reflecting and remembering, you want to try new challenges. Setting these high goals can update your action plan.

USE A STORAGE AID

In addition to transferring information to memory, you may also need to share it with others. Then another storage aid is installed. These are particularly useful when used in combination with storage technology.

WRITE A LIST

Lists are part of everyday life for many. They can be used to remember some important things or to organize work or leisure activities a day, a week or a month ago. Not only does it help you feel that you are in control of your life, but the process of writing the list itself helps your memory. In many cases, it is enough to remember and write something down.

LIST REUSE

Some lists can use several times a year. A good example is a vacation list that lists everything you need to bring. Save time and fear in desperate times before departure and avoid irritation if you forget to use insect repellants on your way to your destination. Keep the list for reuse in a safe place. For example, save your vacation list in a notebook and the names and addresses you need when writing a postcard. All types of plans that are maintained or written might lose their value if they did not keep up to date. Regularly review the list of items as needed and add or remove items as necessary to make a list available.

RECORD THINGS ON PAPER

A household address book is a great way to keep and maintain critical information when other members of your household need access. Planners and individual organizers can combine the functions of address books and notebooks. It is a great way to monitor birthdays, anniversaries, meetings, and dental appointments.

ORGANIZATIONAL INFORMATION

It is a sensible way to keep an eye on yourself at home in an efficient filing system. It is combined with a planner or personal Organizer; it can remind you of quarterly bills, car maintenance, and more. The logical structure of a filing system is likely to be alphabetical, by date or subject, and probably essential. Some people use separate boxes for household accounts, cars, etc. If you have "pending" files, check them regularly.

EXCHANGE OF INFORMATION

When more than one person needs to access the information, it's usually best to write it down somehow. In the office, a wall-mounted mop is a precious way to remind your team of schedules and tasks. In addition to tracking progress, the board serves as a central point for building relationships between groups. At home, the fridge and bulletin board notes can help keep your family organized. Coordinating time together as a family is comfortable with a family calendar in which the entire family participates in family social and extracurricular activities. It also teaches young members to take responsibility for their lives.

LEAVE A RECORD

It is easy to forget what I said at the meeting. It may take a few minutes, but please note if you do not have an official record. The memo is displayed so that you can read it later. Some people find a small tape recorder or dictation machine useful but must ask for permission before it can use.

USE DIGITAL STORAGE

The computer software that stores names, addresses, meeting reminders, and more are common and can include for free on some operating systems. Many programs can set to warn future appointments. An electronic screen display that is compatible with "sticky notes" made of paper is practical. They have the advantage that they do not get stuck and lose valuable lists and memories.

USE AN ELECTRONIC ORGANIZER

Most of us have computers at work or home. These are great ways to save lists, calendars, and other storage aids. Handheld devices, often referred to as PDAs (Personal Digital Assistants), use storage aid functions.

In addition to transferring information to memory, you may also need to share it with others. Then another storage aid is installed. These are particularly useful when used in combination with storage technology.

WRITE A LIST

Lists are part of everyday life for many. They can be used to remember some important things or to organize work or leisure activities a day, a week or a month ago.

KEEP MEMORY ACTIVE

If you train your Brain and keep your memory active, your memory will grow stronger with age. You can do things you have never thought of, e.g., language and musical instruments.

PLAY CROSSWORD PUZZLES AND WORD GAMES

Exercises that keep your memory and Brain active require some mental effort. Crossword puzzles and word games are great because they remind you of words that you may not use regularly. It promotes more use and makes it more transparent. You can also improve mentally by buying books and newspapers in a familiar foreign language. As you read, think of words you do not understand.

USE OF MENTAL ASTHMA

If you can, train yourself to do simple calculations in your head. For example, you can sum up the cost of items in a shopping cart before checking out, or split a restaurant check into several people in your head. You can check the result on the calculator at any time, but you can increase the efficiency of your chair with a simple calculation. So, we learn to rely on estimates rather than calculators.

STAY INTERESTED

Apply the developed memory to your interests. For example, if you want to learn chess, join a local club. Increase the amount of material you learn by keeping the technology under development up to date. The Internet, in particular, can open up a whole new world of information. Continuous learning keeps your memory active and more information provided to absorb it. Reading is an integral part of this process. Read as often as possible. Change the type of book or magazine you read to cover as much material as possible. You are always more likely to remember more exciting information than a dull, uninteresting story. Still, it is common to read something in new areas to expand your memory and interest.

CHAPTER 6: REMEMBER THROUGH NAMES AND FACES

If you have trouble remembering names or faces, do not think you are unique. The 14 storage tasks keep people busy, from placing important data to reading and learning, regardless of where you put it or whether you did it. Four of them relate to identity. The next technique is to avoid that embarrassing cocktail party guff's. It is supposed to prevent the properties of stories and photo series.

LOOK CLOSELY

When you meet someone, look at their face and pay special attention to some great features. Does this person have a big nose? A huge earlobe? Dimple? Big and beautiful blue eyes? Cracking chin? Mole? How do you play card comb? It doesn't have to be incredibly ugly or beautiful. It only differentiates people from the rest of the room. As soon as you unlock it, stop staring. Use your imagination. Let's decorate and highlight it. Make the big nose as big as the toucan's beak on the head. The dimple must be the same size as the crater. A large earlobe should hang on a person's shoulder. Do not assume that everyone you see needs to use this technique. It's easier to jog memories with specific clues. Can you know the person's spouse at the party? Do you remember his name? Voila! Suddenly you remember her name. What if you recognize someone and do not know why? Think about where you know him instead of focusing on one person or face. We remember people in certain situations, and meeting them outside of this situation can lead to difficult problems. Perhaps the same guy had a full tank of fuel once a week for several months, but suddenly a baseball game confused him. If you remember working for a gas station, you could probably recognize his name.

MAKE SURE YOU HAVE IT

Remember introducing your friend Tony to the first three who arrived at your house for dinner. A minute later, he went to the kitchen to fix the drinks for everyone, and Tony was next to him. "What's the name of the brunette in the mini skirt?" He asked quietly. "Monique," he said. "A bald man?" Asked Tony. "This is Joe," Tony asked, feeling very embarrassed at the end. "What about the other woman?".

The first thing he taught him was to repeat his name. Tony is a handsome guy and doesn't pretend to be the main character in the being their remake. He says his name as part of the greeting - friendly to meet you, Monique. "Joe, hello. It would be better if he heard it." Not only do you know the person's name, the use of such techniques, but you can also check that the name is correct. When you are thinking about links, think of some links that exaggerate between names and functions.

YOU SAY TOO MERELY

Something is more convenient. Do not overlook the obvious before taking an unforgettable photo in the distance. Some names are impressive, and you do not have to work hard. Try "Boomer" Elias's son ("Um, maybe you need to work on Elias"). Your organization can use your knowledge. When Klein speaks German, she works with her favorite little athletes, films, stars, and writers who are associated with job-specific terms. The list of possible partnerships is endless. If such a link is still unthinkable, you can always rhyme. The wallet weighs 1 ton for the wallet, George Spouge, Bert Chad, Freaky Frank, and Ron.

Once you've found these similar sounds and photos, you can link them to an image made up of the person's main facial features. For example, when I approach a man named Vince Dolce (pronounced Dorsey), I found some black bears under his eyes. In my mind, the circle is more significant than the raccoon because I'm used to the technique above. When I heard that his name was Dolce, I immediately thought of it as a "boring sheep" and imagined a sheep that was tired and sleepy and was grazing in a more massive ring under Vince's eyes. Of course, the sheep bothered him, which made him stupid (for Vince). It's about turning a room full of strangers into good and bad people who will never forget!

REMEMBER THE NAME

Many people find it difficult to remember their names. I try all kinds of memories with varying degrees of success, but I'm confident that I do not have to do anything else, especially with the name learning method.

USE ASSOCIATION TECHNIQUES

I feel special when I remember the name of the person I met. In business situations, it is advantageous to be able to name customers or to work with them. In the first minutes after completing a new person, you can use this name to build a close relationship. There is an easy way to improve the memory of words. The key is to use your imagination. The technique of remembering names over time is called an association technique. It has two steps. Create a picture and attach it to a person.

CREATE A PHOTO FROM YOUR NAME

When you hear a person's name for the first time, an associated picture immediately created. First, listen to the associations that come to your mind and learn to use them. These are the associations I remember. For example, the name Julie could promote the image of jewelry, but the words are similar because Bill reminds me of dollar bills. You see a picture of a phone booth in the last name booth and remember the microphone Shin sang. Look at a person's face and attach it to their head to look for unique features.

ATTACHMENT

After meeting the person, we use the principle of image creation to describe the photo taken for the name in detail and attach it to the person. Her picture was Julie's jewel. You can see her wearing a piece of jewelry. Enhance your image by imagining bright and shining eyes. Hear the flickering of her gold chains as she leaves. When you meet the person again and look at their face, you will ask to remind them of the photo that triggers their name.

USE OF SNAIL TECHNOLOGY

The letters represent the introductory slowdown, hear words, use names, and confirm terms. When introducing someone, you usually have little time to implement association techniques effectively. The SLUG technique is a simple 4-step process. When most people forget you, they are briefly named and remembered.

LISTEN, USE, CHECK

You may not be able to come for pick up later unless you ask for the other person's name. Therefore, concentrate on the moment of the first name and consciously record it. Then it is essential to use the new name. If possible, use it three times during the first meeting, immediately after the introduction, during the conversation, and when you say goodbye. A short introduction can identify you by your name. After all, you must remember your name shortly after leaving the company and the next day. About 80% of the new information can forget within 1-2 days without confirmation.

COMBINATION TECHNOLOGY

Both association and SLUG techniques help you remember names. However, you can use both methods together to increase the likelihood that you will remember your name when you meet a new person. Use the SLUG technique while referenced to someone else and use the related methods to assign words to that person during or after a conversation. This way, both the person and name are stored in your memory and can be easily retrieved when you need to use the next meeting or word.

REMEMBER THE WORDS AND LETTERS

Store strings like names, phrases, or lists using one of two simple techniques. The acronym creates a memory trigger while the audio procedure applies an image to a character.

CREATE AN ACRONYM

Acronyms are the old way of storing lists. To create an acronym, take the first letter of each element and put it in a word. For example, the Great Lakes are Huron, Michigan, Superior, Ontario, and Erie. Sort by Huron, Ontario, Michigan, Erie, Superior. The first letter creates the acronym HOMES.

USE EXTENDED ABBREVIATIONS

Extended acronyms take the first letter of a word and use it as the first letter of a sentence word. Useful when you need to view articles in a specific order. A popular acronym for rainbow colors in the right order (red, orange, yellow, green, blue, indigo, purple) is, for example, Richard von York Gabe Battle in Vine.

WITH LANGUAGE TECHNOLOGY

From passwords to license plates, one or more characters displayed in different places. Most letter patterns are not suitable for photography. Therefore, it needs to convert into something that can connect to memory. The Furigana lettering technique uses the Furigana alphabet. It is the international system of English-speaking countries that assigns words to every letter. This term uses to create an image.

IMAGE PERSONALIZATION

The next step is to create an image for each word. For example, the photo is a scale (kg) for K kilos and a whiskey bottle for W whiskey. It is essential to create images that are easy to remember. Please think of the picture. Words and letters returned. To reproduce the text, make the story in the correct order for the photos.

REMEMBER THE LIST

Travel technology is a very versatile and surprisingly powerful way to learn the wrist. You can learn a lot from weekly planner entries to important past exam days.

UNDERSTAND TECHNOLOGY

This technique is probably the oldest known storage aid. It works on the principle of storing information that you need to remember mentally. So, you can take it with you wherever you need it. This technique also uses images and associations to use all of the brain's natural memory tools used to maximize the effect.

TRAVEL DESIGN

Organize the list of items to learn. The route must follow a logical path from start to finish so that you can remember it more easily. The number of travel levels should match the number of elements that need to learn. The vacation list contains six parts, so the move requires six steps. Get a pen and paper to practice your trip once you've decided on a route, place objects at all stages of your journey.

ASSUMPTIONS ABOUT OBJECTS IN THESE PLACES

After inserting each item in the list at its assigned position on the trip, the next step is to use imaging principles to create a stupid scenario for each room. The more bizarre the scenes, the easier it will be to remember. Objects on the vacation list have no particular order and can be placed anywhere in the house. The charge is not mandatory here, but it can be vital if you learn, for example, what to do in a speech. The illustration shows four objects on a vacation list and four fictitious scenarios for four rooms on an example trip.

CHECK YOUR PROGRESS

After pasting the images in these places, let's go back and have fun. If you are satisfied, write the list on another piece of paper and test it. Why did you think for the second time that both the number of recalled items and the recalled speed has improved dramatically? Your self-confidence is more important because you are confident in things. The guesswork is gone. You will find that the information you have learned is correct and complete.

REMEMBER NEW LIST

If you know a list of information that you only need to visit once or twice, you can reuse the trips created for it. Use the new list of trips about a month after the trip ends. However, if you want to learn a plan that you want to keep for a long time, you need to think about a new journey, especially for this one project. Creating a recent trip is not that difficult. As with any mental ability, the more you do it, the easier it will be.

REMEMBER THE NUMBERS

A series of numbers from a credit card PIN to a telephone number is part of everyday life. It's easy to learn how to store numbers. Using numbers to improve your skills develops all aspects of mental performance.

TRY A DIFFERENT SYSTEM

There are two central systems with which numbers can memorize. Number Rhyme and Number Shape System. It's fun and easy to use. It is the base on the rule of combining numbers and photos and creating stories from them. Try both systems to find out which is better. If you choose one, leave it alone. Do not use both methods at the same time and do not exchange between systems.

LEARN THE NUMBER SYSTEM

The Number Lime System is particularly suitable for auditory thinkers who can think, listen, and naturally explain ideas. The first step is to change the numbers 1 through 9 into an image that rhymes with that number. Here's one of the lists, but if you think of words that rhyme yourself, you can learn photos more efficiently.

REMEMBER THE NUMBERS

The next step is to attach an image to the information. There are two different methods. One is a number, and the other is multiple numbers. Suppose a friend recently moved in and needs to remember a new home number to explain the one-digit method. For example, if the number is 3, imagine it in front of a tree. Here the photo is selected as number 3. Imagine building a wooden house to emphasize that it is a house number.

THE MEMORY OF SEVERAL DIGITS

The multi-digit number storage method requires you to create a short story and link the images for each number. Of course, the photos must display in the correct order. Imagine the theft alarm code is 4583. Imagine a story that includes doors (4 views), honeycombs (5), gates (8), and trees (3). To link an image to a robbery alarm, you can look at the scene and imagine a robber with a mask on his face.

NUMBER SHAPE SYSTEM LEARNING

Those who think visually usually think a formal numerical system is appropriate. The visual thinker looks at the photo in his head and notices what the object looks like. The number format system works the same way as the number rhyme system, but the images you create have a similar shape to numbers instead of rhyming with numbers. Here is a list of recommended photos.

FORM NUMBER

Next, you need to add an image to the number you want to learn. Take a picture of each number and link it in the correct order with the other users in the story. Suppose you take flight 267 and meet someone at the airport. With the suggested picture, you can imagine a swan (2) (7) with an elephant's trunk (6) playing the saxophone. If you do this in the cockpit of an aircraft, you can remember the number and link it to the flight.

THE MEMORY OF LONG NUMBERS

Most numbers used daily, exceed four digits. By combining your chosen numbering system with travel technology, you can further develop the corresponding numbering system. Numbers with more than four digits are divided into smaller numbers and put on a mini trip. Divide numbers with more than eight digits into at least three sections. Phone numbers are usually the most massive numbers that need to be processed. Suppose your new doctor's number is (414) 555-1678. Use a numbering system of your choice to create and place three stories in the clinic, one for each part of the number. The excursion has a parking lot, a waiting room, and an examination room. When traveling, the images should be used in chronological order so that they can display in the correct order.

CHAPTER 7: NUMERICAL REASONING & VISUAL REASONING AND SPATIAL AWARENESS

NUMERICAL SUITABILITY

Numbers are everywhere! But please indicate that due to math, many of us are afraid. It can be surprising since even babies and animals can register rudimentary counting mechanisms. Everyone has a natural number of talents. It built into our being. We always deal with numbers and use them for mental exercises. Think about it. When we wake up, it is usually because the alarm clock turns off at the set time (time to read and interpret the number). When you buy something, you use numbers to quantify its value. Use the numbers to get the right ratio when preparing your favorite dish according to the recipes in the book. Numerical thinking forms the basis for logic, rationality, reasoning, and proof. When asked if they are good at math, they tend to give negative answers because they fill the memory of the struggle between formulas and fractions, geometry, and trigonometry.

NUMEROPHOBIA

Some people find it challenging to deal with the number of young people. They cannot respond, be it due to fear of school or mental illness. To overcome anxiety, you need to learn, recognize, and continue to overcome. You will be amazed at how quickly your brain reacts to new responses that are aware of persistent fear.

VISUALIZE THE MATH

The visualization of mathematical concepts makes numerical thinking easier. Einstein once claimed that his thinking process triggered by visualization, but he rarely thought. Brain scans must show that the activity to be calculated is not limited to the left hemisphere, but is also present in the visual, auditory, and motor cortex of the brain. Due to the nature of the geometry and the diagrams, graphical skills must also use to understand complex numerical data. Complex numerical data immediately encompass the area of the right temporal lobe. What we do know is that when a math problem observed, it becomes more transparent and accessible, and the brain can later remember that knowledge.

IMPROVE ARITHMETIC

Constant practice is the key to improving your numerical skills. If you are serious about strengthening general mental arithmetic, do not rely on calculators for now. Of course, a calculator is a convenient and necessary tool. The problem is that most of these parts are somewhat lazy on both sides of the brain. Therefore, if you want to improve your arithmetic skills, do not use the calculator for all the arithmetic calculations required. Another thing to remember is that improving your math skills can give you a significant psychological reward. You feel wise when you get it. The mathematics that goes beyond the necessary calculations, such as Geometry, has powerful visualization capabilities because the mind's eyes use them to solve. The more you practice, the more you concentrate. You will be more focused; it is an essential part of success in life.

VISUAL MATH TRAINING

When you start creating math graphics, different parts of your brain become active, which leads to more extensive brain training. You will also learn to understand the language of mathematics by finding ways to visualize its logical meaning. The truth is that when people presented with large numbers and esoteric symbols, they are distracted by numerical problems. No wonder that adding visual components to your math learning is appealing from the start.

LOGIC FLIES OUT OF THE WINDOW

RULE OF THUMB

Most of us apply heuristic knowledge based on intelligent reasoning rather than the logic known in psychology. It is the natural answer to incomplete information and complex problems. Our brain encoded with these generally efficient rules that can learn or inherited to fill gaps. It leads us to well-founded assumptions and intuitive decisions. In other words, we use common sense. There is only one minor mistake. Most of the time, our brain can give the right answer, but it can confuse us if we do not stop and step back and use logic. But it's easier than you think. The problem is that although we are wrong and biased, we believe that we are right. It is a recipe for trouble. For this reason, psychologists are very interested in the use and effectiveness of heuristics.

NUMERICAL PUZZLE SOLVING

Puzzles are like logic errors but ultimately use the wrong logic. Puzzles are usually vague expressions in a pictorial or allegorical language. They designed to trip you up. So, you need to think carefully to find the right solution. The best puzzles allow your brain to fill missing gaps without correct reasoning and to confuse you with all possible methods. The secret of mathematics is abstract, so it is essential to pay special attention to information that is not important the first time you read it. Some of the "important" information you get may be there so that you won't notice the problem yourself!

ROOM DETECTION

Of course, visual and spatial thinking is critical in memory. Think of a taxi driver navigating a tangle of city streets. But it is also an essential skill in many other professions—visual thinking required for intricate design and layout work areas such as architecture and urban planning. People who work in these areas rely on the ability to represent ideas graphically. If you are planning a day outdoors and need to fill your picnic basket, how do you fit your groceries, dishes, and utensils in a confined space before you start loading?

SEEING IS LEARNING

Unlike other types of thinking (like numerical and verbal thinking), visual thinking is not something that most education systems deal with directly. A separation such as linguistic thinking (language) or numerical thinking (mathematics) is probably not sensible, as already used in various subjects such as art, sports, mathematics, and music. There seems to be almost none. Nourish this unique mental ability. As a result, most people do not learn how to make the most of their visual thinking skills. Some psychologists also suggest that classifying an educational system as defective is an error in the educational system. Visual thinking is a proven way to organize ideas and find consistent solutions to problems. Optical thinking techniques improve memory, focus, organization, critical thinking, and problem-solving.

IMPROVE SPATIAL INTELLIGENCE

Spatial reasoning skills are always required but are usually the result of repetitive tasks such as moving a shopping cart through a supermarket aisle or parallel parking on a familiar driveway. Work with the autopilot. In this way, they do not stimulate spatial intelligence but rely on spatial memory to work on new spaces, shapes, forms, and dimensions. A simple and efficient way to improve spatial intelligence is to do a mechanical 3D puzzle-like Rubik's Cube. Research has also shown that playing video games has a significant impact on general spatial perception. If you are not good at shooting maps or simulating racing cars, there are other easy ways to improve spatial compatibility.

CHAPTER 8: BRAIN CREATIVITY AND DEVELOP A POSITIVE MINDSET

ENHANCE CREATIVITY

From music to drawing, there are many ways to be creative. The benefits of creative brain work include the ability to think across borders, find unique solutions to problems, and even enjoy certain activities. Have fun with regular training. Your working life also benefits from your creative activities.

INCREASE YOUR STRENGTH WITH CREATIVE EFFORTS

Training your brain is not difficult! Creative thinking - where you can find solutions to problems - is a great way to encourage your mind to include information from different sources. It means finding an alternative perspective (abnormal or unique) instead of giving up when the problem seems complicated. Not everyone can be the next Beethoven or Da Vinci, but here are some suggestions on how to develop your creative side.

GET READY

"Chance only supports the prepared mind." A quote by the renowned scientist Lewis Pasteur summarizes what scientists know today by examining brain patterns. Shortly before the problem occurs, different parts of the brain show activation. In other words, the mind is ready and gathers information from other functions to find a solution. When problems arise, solutions rarely come from the air. The answer is often the result of hours and hours of preparation. The next time you have issues, do your homework, and be well prepared. Creative solutions will follow shortly.

OKAY, I WON'T TALK ANYMORE

Talking too much about a problem can ruin the creative process. Studies show that the creative process works best if the plan not spoken continuously. In many ways, innovative solutions are automated processes. Some say that creativity has an unconscious element. You do not have to be creative. The next time you try to be creative, do not talk about it, and let the brain do the work.

LOOK AWAY

Focusing too much on a problem can affect creativity. Scientists have found evidence that if the problem concentrated over a long period, the brain generates excessive amounts of gamma waves with extreme attention. This increase in gamma waves causes mental disorders, but of course, it does not help to solve the problem. So, if you lose your creative atmosphere, it's time to get up and get away from the situation. Do something else unless the activity relates to the issue you want to solve. After a short pause, your brain will recharge when you return.

TIPS TO INCREASE YOUR INTEREST IN MUSIC

Here are some tips to promote the musical side:

SING ALONG

Young children react to the pitch and rhythm of the language. The term mother refers to a loud and humble voice from her. Talk to your baby often. Studies show that babies pick up these pitch patterns and return in the same way. Early communication characterized by imitation of the pace and rhythm of the language. When a mother is tired of a method, so does her baby.

PLAY AND PAY ATTENTION TO MUSIC

Music lessons help students understand the lessons better. Studies have shown that playing musical instruments frees young people from the significant distractions of school and enables them to focus more on the teacher's voice. Playing the tool not only teaches the brain to increase the volume of all sounds but also helps the brain effectively differentiate sounds from related information. When someone learns a musical instrument, they train the mind to extract relevant melodic patterns such as harmonies and rhythms. The brain can use the same functions to filter and record speech and other sounds in the classroom or on the playground.

LISTEN TO MUSIC

Listening to music activates various parts of the brain that are involved in processing attention, memory, information, and emotions. Music can also heal the hearts of adults. Studies have shown that listening to music can speed up cognitive recovery in stroke patients. The patient's verbal memory and attention improve faster than those who only listen to the audiobook. As a bonus, listening to music while your stroke is recovering helps avoid negative moods like depression.

IMPROVE YOUR MEMORY

Studies have shown that adding words to music can significantly improve the memory of people with Alzheimer's disease. The part of the brain associated with memory works more slowly in the amount of the mind with Alzheimer's disease. However, inserting words that you need to remember into your music creates a more robust memory connection than repeating the comments themselves. So, if you know that people with Alzheimer's have trouble remembering their daily chores, add them a list of tasks in the music and sing.

KEEP YOUR BRAIN AT THE PERFECT PITCH

Scientific evidence shows that music training improves memory. Despite educational background and age, musicians tend to remember more information than non-musicians. In other words, playing an instrument activates a part of the brain (cerebral cortex) and improves access to information. Musical education is suitable for scientists. When children exposed to music lessons with complex rhythms and tones, they usually understand reading better than children of the same age who do not take music lessons. But improvement is not the only problem. Psychologists have found that math skills and spatial thinking are also suitable for students taking music lessons. What music helps children use their heads at school? When people listen to music, various systems activated throughout the brain. In addition to working memory, the brain processes musical information about both the left and right brain.

DRAW AND UNLOCK THE CREATIVE SIDE

Drawing a picture increases your imagination. It is essential to find a creative solution to your problem. If you feel sloppy, you can draw something more complicated than a wavy line. Here are some ideas to attract and unlock the creative side.

MAKE A MAZE

Start with a clue. It doesn't have to be profound. In simple cases, it can also be an object. Write your thoughts on paper. Next, let's think about another idea. How can I combine two pictures? Continue until your paper looks like a labyrinth of thoughts and ideas. The maze may not make sense at first. However, if you try a few times, the process will be more straightforward. And you will find that your brain can make more connections between different events that can blow up your creative process.

MAKE CARDS

The next time you need to buy a birthday card, create one. From drawing to drawing to restoring the precious memories you've shared with old photos. You have unlimited options. It is not just a more meaningful way to share your thoughts. You can also be creative by creating cards. Making scrap cards is not what you want. Consider scrapbooking. With all the photos around, you can finally do something. It's a great way to keep memories. If most of your photos are digital, you can do virtual scrapbooking on many online sites and share your pages with family and friends.

DRAW A CARTOON

Comic and graphic novels are a great way to capture your thoughts. Why not draw instead of looking for the right words to describe your feelings today? You may also be surprised! If you dare, you can publish your comic on your blog online and get feedback from your friends. You can also create your manga. Whatever you choose, making this type of diary is a fun way to express your thoughts and be more creative!

MAINTAIN A POSITIVE ATTITUDE

Sometimes "suddenly loses life" or "throws a curveball at you." Crises and problems can suddenly occur at unexpected times. However, you can determine how the issue affects you. Overwhelming issues can lead to stress and anxiety and impair brain function. If you choose to overcome the problem, you will experience superior benefits in your brain.

SMILE THE WAY TO A BETTER BRAIN

"A smile will find someone to smile at you," I remember growing up in that little tolerance, something on the map that my school friend gave me. When I was younger, I liked the idea that a different face made me smile. But a smile makes you feel better, and you may be wondering if it's perfect for your brain. Studies have shown that positive emotions, such as happiness and joy, are closely linked to physical and mental health. In contrast, negative emotions such as worry and sadness can worsen your health. Positive emotions promote health in countries where people cannot meet their basic needs, for example, where they live and what foods they eat. There are other reasons to look at the right side of life! When life is stressful, significant life events can cause stress, but this also enables the accumulation of everyday responsibilities that can be overwhelming. The more you have to take into account, the more pressure you feel. However, the right approach cannot be overwhelmed but can change potentially stressful situations in a variety of ways. Here are some ideas:

ASK QUESTIONS

Instead of saying, "I can't do this" or "It's too difficult for me," try to paraphrase it as a question. Ask yourself, "What can I do?" Or by asking a problem instead of leaving a negative comment, "What can I do?" Instead of recognizing the hurdle, you can change your thinking about the opportunity. For example, when asked to complete a challenging project at work, do not let potential customers know what they need to accomplish. Instead, tasks break down into smaller, achievable goals that are guided by questions. What should I do first? How can I do this first step? And so on.

CHANGE MINUS TO PLUS

It is never too early to think of a harmful situation. You may not have this action at work, but you may have found something useful. Can you spend time with your family or start a project you always wanted but didn't have time? Concentrating on the silver lining in unexpected situations may not always be easy, but it may be difficult.

HAVE A HERO

Imagine someone who inspires others to overcome difficult situations and win. For example, Lance Armstrong diagnosed with cancer, but he didn't stop it. He won the Tour de France for several years in a row. He was the only one to set a record and win seven times. Inspirational stories like Lance Armstrong are great because they can motivate people to create their own success stories that can share with others.

THINK POSITIVE

What you read can have a more significant impact on your brain than you think. Studies show that reading laughter is enough to change behavior. Even if you try to control what you feel, happy feelings permeate. If you have questions about why you can't skip the steps, read the documentation. It may be time to replace the Whippy Story with a brighter one. Try the following techniques to benefit from positive thinking and optimism.

DO NOT GIVE UP

Even if it doesn't start or the project doesn't work as expected, everyone stumbles on the way. What you do after you fail is essential. Do you feel sorry for yourself and avoid trying again? Or do you sit down and try again? Imagine a story like the Walt Disney story. Remember that life is not the golden path to success. It's an uneven, bumpy road and whether to get up and keep going.

GOODBYE STRESS

Positive thinkers are less stressed than those with negative thoughts. People who receive positive reviews believe in themselves and in what they can achieve. However, if something goes wrong, they will find a way to turn the situation into a good one and quickly find a way to overcome the setback.

CHANGE PERSPECTIVE

You know that feeling. Since something is wrong, I can't stop thinking about it. Rumination is a term used by psychologists to describe the process of trying to solve things in the mind.

Psychologists identify two types of ruminants:

REFLECTION
Reflection is a positive reaction to a problem and leads to finding a solution. Now is the time to identify the problem and develop an action plan to solve it.

BREEDING
Breeding is more harmful and involves strong emotions, such as worries and fears. Breeding means repeating something in your head or playing something with an ambitious (or not ambitious!) listener. Such behavior

usually causes stress. Because it only focuses on the negative side of the situation (the "dummy" syndrome), not on what you were thinking about before, for example, on what you want right now. Then plan a proactive solution to your problem. If you repeatedly play a scene or event in your head or are self-critical, you can simply feel dark. So, do not do it. Sometimes you can be your worst critic. A regular criticism of yourself can affect your mental health and lead to self-fulfilling prophecies. Start believing what you think of yourself (e.g., failure). The next time you want to criticize yourself, stop, and think about what's right in your situation. List all positive answers.

Compulsive regret for something not only takes time but can also lead to more serious mental health problems. If you are always worried, do the following to avoid negative trends.

KEEP AN EYE ON YOUR GOALS

The goal is to solve the problem. Do not upset your heart, and do not get discouraged when you say things like "it doesn't work for me." These ideas are useless and do not help me find a solution. Write down the problem. Then we list two or three things you can do to solve the problem. A written review of the problem (and possible solutions) can make a big difference and prevent dark thoughts from accidentally whirling around in your head. Please be strict.

FIND THE MIDDLE

Sometimes you may need to lower your expectations. It can be impossible to get the perfect answer. Please do not hang around. Find the solution that suits you best. Remember that a healthy brain is a dark, laid-back brain. So, do not waste your spiritual energy and hope to change the past. Finding a workable solution can change the future.

TAKE SOME TIME

Sometimes you must take a break from the problem. Be mental for a while. You can meet your friends and have fun together and not to mention your time problems.

CALL FRIENDS

Seeking help is not a sign of weakness. Do not bear the mental burden of the problem yourself. If you cannot create an action plan to solve the problem, ask a friend for help.

DEALING WITH STRESS AND FEAR

Stress plays a vital role in the development of several severe mental disorders, including depression. One of the interesting questions is why some people are more stressed than others. The answer may link to combat or flight mechanics. If someone gets into a stressful situation, does he avoid it (escape), or does he adapt and try to deal with it (fight/deal)?

Answering this question seems to indicate whether stress can overwhelm you. Studies in mice have shown that those who avoid stressful situations with large, aggressive mice are more likely to suffer from anxiety. In contrast, a person that had found a way to adapt and deal with the case had a healthier brain. Therefore, flight options are not always optimal. Sometimes figuring out how to coordinate and deal with it is less stressful, and in the long run, it is better for your mental health.

UNDERSTAND WHY STRESS KILLS BRAIN CELLS?

Which parts of the brain are most affected by stress? Scientists have found that the hippocampus associated with long-term knowledge and spatial memory suffers the most. It could explain why depression also affects memory. Depressed people may have difficulty receiving new information (this is the responsibility of the hippocampus).

Stress can also cause the brain to contract physically. Studies have shown that high levels of stress can reduce the amount of hippocampus and anterior cingulate cortex associated with stress hormone control. Stress kill - that's what people say, but is this statement correct? Well, some strains are suitable for your brain; others are not. Here are the main reasons why you should avoid stress if you want to keep your brain in top shape:

AVOID SABOTAGE

Know when your actions can disappoint you. Some people can deal with stressful situations in a way that makes the situation worse. Offensive behavior is an example. Quietly expressing emotions about the situation without shouting or stressing is better than being aggressive. Assertiveness means making your claim without harassing or manipulating others. You calm down and clarify your intentions. Another example of self-annoyance is overeating or overeating rather than finding a healthy way to deal with the situation.

LOWER BLOOD PRESSURE

Stress leads to high blood pressure. Scientists have found that in a group of almost 1,000 adults over the age of 65, people with high blood pressure are at increased risk of mild cognitive impairment. It means that these adults have had difficulty concentrating, having difficulty performing simple mental activities, and forgetting things more often.

SLIDE DOWN A SLOPE

If you think something you forget can live with you, think again. Slight cognitive impairment can lead to dementia and Alzheimer's. 15% of people with mild cognitive impairments then fight dementia and Alzheimer's. Studies show that mild cognitive impairment is the strongest predictor of memory loss. In other words, the level of education, e.g., Where you live, male or female, is less critical. It is all the more important to avoid stress on the roof—another reason to spend a weekend relaxing and not being able to work.

CHAPTER 9: GETTING PHYSICAL: BRAIN-FRIENDLY DIET & LIFESTYLE

Eating has tremendous strength in the brain, from memories of happy childhood memories to relaxation of blunt nerves. But most people probably consider food to be purely functional. It's something you must do to keep moving. Eating is something you can do without much worry. Occasionally with friends in a new fashionable restaurant, sometimes even watching TV. However, this chapter emphasizes how food can transform the brain from childhood to adult life. It is always a good idea to get advice from a suitably qualified doctor before making significant changes to your diet.

FOOD FOR LIFE: UTERINE NUTRITION

Lifestyle changes during pregnancy are usually the last thing a woman has in mind. The only difference a pregnant woman wants to make is to raise her leg and enjoy the relatively quiet final months before the baby arrives. However, choosing the right food can bring significant benefits to both you and your baby's brain. If healthy choices mean a change to you, do it - the minds of you and your baby will thank you.

DESIRE FOR MALT

You may have heard of a woman waking her partner up in the middle of the night, wild goose hunting, and sending an elusive food combination like chocolate dip cucumbers or the store's special nut bread jam. They loved their vacation. The list goes on. Most of the time, these weird demands are just food cravings, but with some food cravings, the brain tells you that you are missing something, like calcium and protein, in your daily food intake. We do not intend to provide a list of essential nutrients needed during pregnancy. Instead, I'm trying to develop the three best brain boosters that can only live when you are pregnant.

MILK - MORE THAN JUST CHILDREN

If you've never had milk, unless you've drunk a few drops of tea or coffee, pregnancy is a time of change. In addition to the apparent benefits of calcium, which strengthens the baby's bones and teeth and improves muscle and nerve function, milk also has other advantages. Pregnant women who drink milk during pregnancy can reduce the risk of Multiple Sclerosis (MS) in their children. Symptoms of MS include fatigue, weakness, and acute or chronic pain. But do you know that MS also affects the brain? Cognitive deficits, such as depression and language problems also occur in MS patients. Pregnant women who drink less than one milk a week are more likely to have a higher risk of developing MS in children. The benefits of milk lead to vitamin D. The next time you are thirsty, drink a carbonated drink and reach for milk (or vitamin D supplements instead - ask your doctor).

IRON IS NOT JUST FOR MUSCULAR PEOPLE

Iron is essential for the baby's brain development and has severe cognitive consequences if the mother does not get enough iron. For example, iron deficiency in a baby growing in the womb causes learning and memory problems later in the baby's life. These negative consequences are often irreversible. So, the takeaway message is to give your baby the best starting point and get enough iron. Most pregnant women get folic acid and iron supplements from their doctors. But you can also get iron from food sources. Red meat is the best source and the largest source of iron. If you are looking for a vegetarian sauce, you can get iron from cereals and legumes. You get the same amount of iron in just a quarter cup of bran.

EAT 1, 2, AND OMEGA 3

Omega 3 is a polyunsaturated fatty acid found in fish and various seeds. Fats are not popular, but polyunsaturated fats are one of the four types of fats that your body gets mainly from what you eat. And your baby needs it to develop his brain. You may be familiar with common omega-3 food sources such as fatty fish (salmon and mackerel) and olive oil. But do you know that you can probably get omega-three from the spices in your kitchen? Some of them are cloves, basil, sage, oregano, and mustard seeds. If your baby does not get enough omega-3 fatty acids from what you eat, he will take them out of his business, which may result in you losing up to 3% of your brain cells.

The news is simple, but 15-20% of women smoke during pregnancy. As I heard, this message is so important that I must repeat it. Smoking during pregnancy carries severe risks for you and your baby:

1. Smoking mothers can give birth to immature, underweight babies.

2. Smoking has consequences in children.

If the baby of a mother who smokes during pregnancy grows, the mental health of her child can have serious consequences. Mothers who smoke during pregnancy are at increased risk of developing psychotic symptoms such as hallucinations and delusions in their teenage years. In the womb, tobacco can affect the brain by influencing impulsiveness, alertness, and even mental development.

RESIST A SWEET IMPULSE

If your area is a food lover, you may think that pregnancy is the time to buy all of your favorite foods, regardless of calories or fat. But before you pay attention to the wind, you should remember the effects on you and your baby.

DO YOU LIKE FOOD?

Pregnant mothers who eat high-fat sweet foods affect the development of the baby's brain. The baby's brain pleasure center became increasingly unresponsive. That means they have trouble saying no. As a result, these children develop the habit of overeating, are prone to obesity, and can show habitual behavior in adulthood. Babies born to their mothers on a high-fat diet during pregnancy are more susceptible to high-sugar foods than mothers who are pregnant on a standard diet.

HIGH SUGAR

Gestational diabetes occurs in up to 10% of pregnancies and is characterized by hyperglycemic women during pregnancy. If a pregnant mother has high blood sugar, her child may be less sensitive to insulin, a risk factor for type 2 diabetes.

FOOD FOR LIFE: CHILD NUTRITION

The good news is that a healthy and nutritious home environment can give a child the first step in life. Many successful epidemics claim that children have the magical combination of nutritional values they need to succeed. Avoid taking supplements unless an official agency approves them (e.g., the British Food Standards Agency or the United States Food and Drug Administration). Many supplements on the market claim to be "vitamins" and not approved by government agencies. Do not get stuck in advertising for these supplements. After all, not only do we harm, we also follow the advice below that is based on scientific research and not on current food trends.

FISHING FOR YOUR BRAIN

If you need to convince your child of the benefits of providing fish, this study can change your thinking. Scientists examined teenagers who ate fish more than once a week and found that their IQ was much higher than that of their classmates who ate fish only once a week. How do omega-3 fatty acids help your child's brain? Docosahexaenoic acid (DHA) and eicosatetraenoic acid (EPA) are polyunsaturated fatty acids in the omega-3 family. Your body cannot make these essential nutrients, so you need to get them from the food you eat. DHA is a crucial element of the brain and nervous system. The lack of omega-3 fatty acids causes various cognitive problems in childhood, including learning difficulties, poor memory, and low concentration. Scientists are discussing whether fish oil supplements can offer the same benefits. Some studies show that children who take fish oil as a dietary supplement have higher brain activity in attention-related areas than children who take a placebo. Be careful with supplements and only buy from trusted sources. If you do not want to use supplements, try serving oily fish once a week to see the benefits.

Here are some fish-like delicacies that are perfect for your child:

SALMON
Salmon is high on the list of the best fish for your brain. But it's not just salmon that does the trick. Wild salmon is much better than farmed salmon. Wild salmon is not only a good source of omega-3 fatty acids, but it is also low in mercury. Fish caught in the wild can grow, which means that their muscles and tissues are stronger.

SARDINES
Another fish is an excellent source of omega-3 fatty acids. Like salmon, sardines have low mercury content. However, be aware that canned sardines can have high cholesterol levels.

TUNA
Eating tuna has many health benefits, including canned tuna. For example, tuna is an excellent source of omega-3 fatty acids and is associated with a reduced risk of Alzheimer's. Keep in mind that this section contains tuna, but it should remember. Canned tuna is rich in mercury and can be dangerous for pregnant women. Mercury is a toxin that can damage the baby's

brain during pregnancy, and some doctors recommend pregnant women to avoid tuna altogether.

TREAT PEOPLE YOU LIKE AND PEOPLE YOU DO NOT LIKE

Inspirational children are known, especially when it comes to food. My three-year-old is no exception. Therefore, we always follow three rules when introducing new foods.

COOK WITH AN EXCITING STORY

If your boy loves to talk about pirates and dinosaurs. When we made salmon-based fish pies for the first time, we had a fantastic pirate adventure story during a meal. It worked, and now he's enjoying his explanation so much that he has a positive relationship with eating salmon. If you do not want to tell the story, go to your local library and get a book where your children can read the instructions and relate them to a new food. For example, when Sousse gave gifts to children with spinach and eggs, the mother spoke of reading classic green eggs and ham. Give your children another activity that they can enjoy when introducing new foods. If your child likes to dye, get him a new coloring book when you give him a sardine meal. When a child thinks of a fresh meal, he combines it with activities that he enjoys. So, the idea is positive.

BECOME A MODEL

If a child sees you are enjoying a fish, it is also more likely to eat it. Serve new food while eating with your family. When a child sees another person enjoying food, they are more interested in trying it. Think about how much food you want.

WAIT UNTIL YOU ARE HUNGRY

Do not give snacks or drinks (enough water) just before eating. This way, the child is more likely to enjoy every meal and try new foods. Snacks for a better brain Researchers suggest that child nutrition is the culprit of behavioral problems. A lot of research has done in this area, but most importantly, the wrong food does not cause Attention Deficit Hyperactivity Disorder (ADHD). If you are a parent and are concerned about your child's behavior at home or school, this section provides advice on how to control your child's behavior through diet.

DO NOT ADD ANY ADDITIVES

Additives are food colors and preservatives that usually found in highly processed sugar-rich foods. As you read the food label, you may see items like FD & C Yellow (E number) have the proposes to increase.

SKIP CANDY

On average, children consume about two pounds of sugar a week. The next time you go shopping, look at the size of the sugar pack. It is a tremendous amount of sugar that goes far beyond what children need. Too much sugar can lead to hyperactivity and impulsivity. Given these behaviors, we can imagine the pictures of children bouncing off the wall. But it can be much worse. A high sugar intake not only leads to destructive and aggressive behavior such as throwing and kicking but can even damage them. Younger children are most affected by the dreaded "sugar high." That's why we often eat snacks, but we leave sweets as they are. It is a snack and not a typical meal for children.

EAT GOOD FAT

Omega 3 is also ideal for children. However, your body is unable to produce these types of fatty acids. So, you have to remove them from the food. Studies show that children with low omega-3 levels are more likely to have behavioral problems like hyperactivity. Another side effect of the lack of fatty acids is an increased risk of eczema, allergies, and asthma. All of this can alleviate by boosting your child's fatty acid intake. The "Brain Fishing" section in this chapter provides tips on how to include fatty acids in your child's diet.

KNOWLEDGE IS POWER

Studies show that parent groups with little information about ADHD and the effects of diet on children are less likely to seek support and treatment. Do not wait until it's too late to give your child the help they need. As a parent, you can get the best start by making sure that your child's diet is healthy, nutritious, and does not process sugary foods.

Both fructose and glucose are the sugars your body needs. It is a form of carbohydrates that your body converts to energy. Your body uses this energy not only for physical activity but also for mental work. Low sugar levels can affect decision making and thinking. Where do you get sugar from if you need to avoid it from processed foods like candy bars? Fructose and glucose are different fructose found in some vegetables like fruits, juices, and tomatoes. Most carbohydrates (including rice, pasta, potatoes) contain glucose. At the beginning of the day, we recommend eating foods that are high in glucose. There the body can transform itself into the body and brain energy. When you eat foods that are high in glucose, your body ultimately stores them as fat instead of converting them into energy.

DEVELOPMENT OF EATING HABITS

In life, most people are probably on a diet at some point in their lives. Most people are concerned about the challenges of calorie counting, whether it's a good-looking event or a health issue. However, counting calories and switching from one diet plan to another is not the right way to live. You know that the diet plan that is likely part of your lifestyle is much more effective. This section lists foods that show that research is a critical element of every lifestyle. Do not worry. You do not have to eat like a rabbit.

HEAVY

Juice bars are everywhere these days, and nowadays it is not difficult to find even a small airport. What is so great about juice? And how can they benefit your brain? For starters, the liquid is full of vitamins. If you use juice, you can throw it together. You can try all kinds of combinations like celery and apples, cabbage and mango, broccoli and raspberries. The list is endless. You do not even need cooking skills! The following is a list of fruits that should be at the top of the juice list.

POMEGRANATE

Pomegranate juice has become popular recently. Pomegranate juice is great fun to drink, and studies confirm that unlike most food-borne illnesses, this does the hype justice. First, pomegranate is a "superfood." However, pomegranate is rich in antioxidants and more common than other fruits. Pomegranate juice characterized by pregnancy to adulthood. At the end of life, pregnant women who drink this juice can help the baby's brain to resist brain damage from hypoxia. At the other end, research has confirmed that pomegranate juice helps prevent Alzheimer's disease and maintain the health of older people.

TRIM

When pomegranate is a "trendy" fruit, people often think that plums are out of date. Most people associate plums with relief from constipation and other related bladder disorders. But do you know that plum is suitable for your brain? Plums contain vitamin A. Vitamin A not only strengthens the body's defense system but also helps the brain cells to repair themselves quickly. You can make plum juice by soaking 1 cup of plum in 5 cups of water for 4 hours. Remove the seeds, make a puree, and enjoy.

BE "ELEGANT"

Grape juice is rich in flavonoids. It lowers blood pressure and increases cholesterol. Studies have shown that grape juice can improve memory and coordination. If you already like grape juice, try drinking red or purple grape juice. These grapes packaged with excellent brain-promoting properties. A study found that grape juice is better for the heart than cranberry or orange juice.

BLUEBERRIES

Blueberries are another superfood and are rich in vitamin C and potassium (which help the bones). Clinical studies have shown that 2 cups a day is enough to improve learning and brain strength. Frozen blueberries have the same effect on the brain so that you can enjoy them all year round. You may have heard of the Atkins diet. It means that you must cut out all of the sugar (including fruit), but you can get plenty of protein and fat like steak and bacon. We do not recommend the Atkins diet (or any other diet!), But a high protein diet has advantages. When you eat protein, your brain produces a variety of chemicals, gives you energy, and stays alert, but not used much. Protein-rich foods make up only 10-15% of daily calories. Chicken and lean meat offer the best sauce. Vegetarians can fix proteins in dairy products, legumes, and nuts. As with most good things, you pay for a high protein diet. Red meat is high in cholesterol and can affect health and the brain. Scientific studies have shown that people who are rich in saturated fats and cholesterol are more likely to suffer from memory loss. Their working memory (ability to remember and manipulate information) is insufficient. How does such a diet affect your brain? This type of malnutrition causes inflammation of the brain. This inflammation affects not only memory but also physical functions such as seeing and hearing. The key is to use the right amount and limit red meat to once a week.

CHAPTER: 10 VERBAL REASONING & MIND-BODY CONNECTION

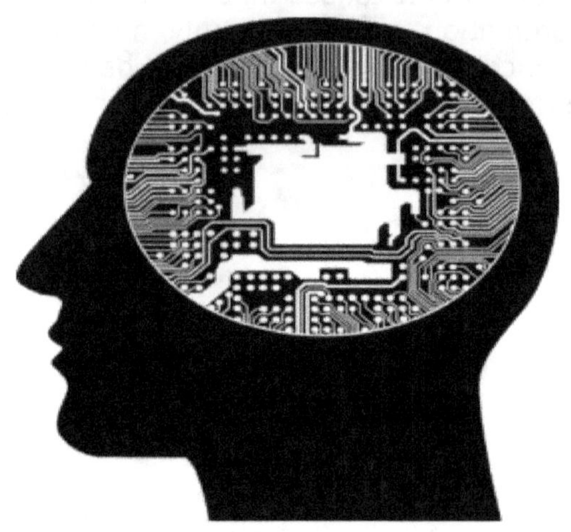

SHOW THE WAY TO SUCCESS

There is a direct connection between vocal talent and success in life. Not only do they complete crossword puzzles, unravel anagrams and understand antonyms, but all of these activities are also great for verbal use. Talk generally about the ability to use words, manipulate language, and communicate ideas, thoughts, opinions, and emotions well. Maybe politicians and lawyers make the most of this ability, as do rap artists and talk show organizers. All of them are good at attracting a broad audience with the power of words and influencing the mindset of the audience. In short, the higher your verbal intelligence, the more confident you are at enforcing your needs and desires. They are better understood and can build closer relationships. Whichever way you go, improving oral fitness can have a significant impact on social progress and prosperity.

LANGUAGE AND VISION

At the age of five, scientists believe that the vocabulary already contains about 2,000 to 3,000 words, but they do not know the exact meaning of these words. For example, a child watching a ball might say something else, but it could say "ball," which points to a balloon, chocolate egg, or pebbles. It suggests that seeing at an intuitive level has a profound impact on language development. For example, consider the first alphabetical book a child sees. Images used to decorate the letters of the alphabet and give them meaning. Not surprisingly, infants use the same words in similar shapes until the vocabulary grows, such as Apple's "A" and Bear's "B." And while you might think that this "visual" dependency increases with school attendance (a vocabulary of around 50,000 words has accumulated), analogies, metaphors, and synonyms. Consider using visual concepts affect language throughout your life. For example, speakers and powers know that using words to tell a story that reminds you of the "big picture" increases the likelihood that you will stay involved. Words may evaporate, but when you use them to convey a picture, the ideas behind them become more unforgettable. Great speakers always relied on "visual" for their fashion speech. Consider Martin Luther King's famous national address. The sentence "I have a dream ..." immediately opens a window to his vision of the future.

LANGUAGE AND INTELLIGENCE

Fluid intelligence and crystallization intelligence are common elements of intelligence. Fluid intelligence is the ability to make sense of chaos and solve new problems. Crystallized intelligence is the knowledge and skills accumulated over a lifetime and is used to perform familiar tasks. How does the language fit? Well, as a child, you will learn to use your fluid intelligence to understand your parents' language and then communicate with them. All nuances of grammar, syntax, and other languages take shape during puberty. At this point, the main areas of the brain that body new information and skills are smaller. Therefore, learning a language is much more comfortable at a young age.

DEVELOP A BILINGUAL BRAIN

Learning a new language in adulthood is not impossible. I recommend this as it is one of the best ways to activate neurons, keep your brain active, and record instruments. These activities are psychologically demanding because they force the brain to process new information and make new connections. Learning a foreign language also protects the brain from age damage. Studies show that bilingual people have fewer mental disorders due to aging than people who only speak one language.

FLOWING WORDS

Improving your vocabulary will quickly improve your intelligence. The average person speaks about 1,000 words, and more than 3 million names can give to the brain. So, there is a lot of room for improvement. The wider the vocabulary, the more it stimulates the brain by interacting with cells when speaking, reading, and writing. Public speaking can be beneficial in schools, business, and social situations. You can think more carefully about more complicated things. Verbal language skills offer the double advantage of thinking faster under pressure and speaking more calmly under pressure.

READING COMPREHENSION

Reading is an integral part of language development. The ability to understand and manipulate text can move the brain in various ways to improve perception, reason, problem-solving, and other cognitive skills. It is an essential skill that you can learn as a child, grow as a student, and apply to your career and daily life. A typical reading usually answers some questions related to a passage of text. Exercises test your ability to derive logical thinking from simple life situations.

READ EYES

Understanding requires adequate reading comprehension, depending on your ability to recognize words quickly and easily. The eye plays an important role here because it conveys information about the visual pathways. The average reading speed for Roman is 200 to 220 words/minute. Nothing interferes with your ability to decipher the meaning since you put more effort into reading individual words and sentences than trying to understand the idea expressed.

WORDS AND PICTURES

Historians follow a method of storytelling through a series of photographs of the earliest civilizations of humanity. Since then, however, art forms that combine words and images have developed. For example, until the advent of American comic book formats in the early 20th century, there were devices such as speech bubbles, flashing lightbulb symbols above the word head, bright idea symbols, and certain typographic symbols. They introduced to represent curses. The first comic book was a newspaper anthology with a humorous story about the adventures of Buck Rogers, Tarzan, Phantom, and Tinton. The late cartoonist Will Eisner called it "sequential art" rather than "comic." Over the years, many educational institutions have used comic book stories to develop oral thinking and understanding skills. We will respond more proactively to the combination of words and images. In a world where there is too much visual material, comics offer a fun and effective way to improve reading and writing. For fun exercises, you can cut the cartoon into individual cells, mix them, and put them back together. You can also combine sections to find another way to create an entirely different story.

BUILD A STORY

Storytelling is an ancient verbal art that shows the power of words to express thoughts, ideas, and emotions. We used it to spread the news, convey wisdom, and learn about the history of others and our culture. Storytelling is a widely used tool to connect people of all ages and races. It is also a powerful tool for developing and improving skills in language areas such as semantics (word meaning), syntax (word formation), and phonology (speech sounds). Storytelling uses language artistically to develop all the essential components of the communication process. Storytelling improves hearing, improves verbal expression, improves understanding, creates mental images, and stimulates oral thinking. It is the most comprehensive way to improve your oral fitness.

THE CONNECTION BETWEEN BODY AND MIND

HEALTHY BODY, STRONG MIND

Physical exercise is required to maintain the shape of the body. Nobody agrees. But how does the brain work in all of these areas? Well, the famous Latin word in ancient Roman times is "Sano Manzana of the human body," which means "healthy mind of a healthy body." It seems that the Romans were interested in something here. Sport has long known to maintain overall health and well-being.

Further research shows that activity is one of the best ways to protect your brain. If previous scientific studies did not show this, it would be surprising if it did not. Physical activity increases your heart rate, and jogging for 5 minutes at the beginning of each day also increases blood flow to your entire body, including the brain. People in their fifties who exercise regularly have better memory and concentration than people who live sedentary lives. People who continue physical activity up to the age of 60 are less likely to suffer from mental decline as some age-related cognitive impairments are due to physical inactivity and lack of mental stimulation.

WHAT ARE AEROBICS?

Physical activities such as walking, jogging, and dancing raise your heart rate to 60-80% of your maximum capacity in 15 minutes. It allows the lungs to draw more oxygen than the heart pumps through the vascular system. You should be able to speak while doing aerobic exercise. If you haven't exercised for a while, it is a good idea to have a medical exam before starting an exercise program.

PHYSICAL CHARGING

Maintaining energy levels throughout the day is difficult. At some point, you may feel tired or feel that your brain is no longer able to think clearly. When many people are sick, they drink coffee or take a bar of chocolate and use caffeine and sugar spikes to restore energy levels. However, this is an unhealthy and short-term solution. Another way to increase energy is to move the body for a few minutes. It improves blood circulation and immediately increases attention.

STRESSOR

Stress arises when a person feels overwhelmed by the pressure of life and cannot handle it. The keyword here is "feel." Stress weakens creativity, and memory because priorities are recognizing mental demands that affect physical well-being. Focus is not necessarily a bad thing. You need to reach a moderate level to stay focused and stimulated. However, if the stress is too high and out of control, the effects are counterproductive and can affect health. A chemical called glutamate gets into the brain and can be harmful. People are fed up with too many demands, lose confidence, and are ultimately frustrated. It can lead to forgetfulness, misplaced things, misunderstandings in conversation, snapshots with others, etc. Excessive stress makes both the brain and the body inefficient.

BUSTER FOR PHYSICAL EXERCISE

If you find that most reviews are in the very tense fields, you need to find a way to adjust your stress level. Many people use a common technique called Progressive

Muscle Relaxation (PMR). PMR is about exaggerating tensions to promote calm and body. Tense every muscle group in your body until it hurts (about 20 seconds) and then release it. Blood flows into this area, creates warm feelings, relieves tension, and soothes. PMRs also act as sleeping pills.

GO EAST

For thousands of years, people in the Orient have been using various techniques to seek harmony between mind, body, and soul. Western medicine is traditionally skeptical of oriental therapies such as Zen, Tai Chi, and Yoga. However, increasing evidence, especially from scientific studies using brain scanning techniques, has shown that ancient Eastern Buddhists lower blood pressure and breathe. It shows that you know how to slow down, release muscle tension, and organize your mind. In today's fast-paced world, people are under more significant pressure. The body responds typically by releasing stress response hormones like cortisol. It circulates the system and incorrectly blocks the formation of new neurons in the hippocampus. We now know that all types of meditation exercises help the body regulate stress hormone levels.

ZAZEN

Zen meditation is a practice that is at the center of Zen's belief. The goal is to focus your mind, sometimes with mantras, sounds, or breathing, to promote a completely calm state. The meditator sits quietly, pays attention to simple songs, and sorts out all the antiques in his head, such as negative thoughts, and feelings. This state of mind often referred to as "mindfulness." In the West, about 10 million people practice meditation every day. There are different techniques, but the primary purpose is to recognize the flow of thoughts, generate ideas, and die without interruption. Empirical data suggests that Zen meditation relieves depression symptoms and improves sleep quality.

MEDITATE

Whether you are sitting or standing, it is essential that you keep your back straight and in the right position. The goal is to get rid of all distractions and achieve a "heartless" state. To achieve this, you need to pay attention to the sensory experience, not your sense of it. For example, if you suddenly hear the noise, do not think about it, just listen. When entering meditation, the EEG pattern should shift from the right frontal cortex to the gentle left frontal cortex. It reduces the adverse effects of stress, mild depression, and anxiety.

ACUPUNCTURE AND BRAIN

Acupuncture is an ancient Chinese cure for many diseases, in which practitioners insert thin needles into defined points on the patient's body from which the life energy "Ki" flows. There are more than 1,500 "points" on the whole body. Acupuncture works by inactivating or "calming" critical areas of the brain and is used to relieve acute mood disorders, pain, and food cravings. The science behind it is not yet understood, and clinical studies on acupuncture are still inconclusive. However, several studies in volunteers monitored with fMRI brain scans have shown that within a few seconds of receiving acupuncture, blood flow in some regions of the brain reduced. Other studies have found that acupuncture helps treat depression, eating disorders, addiction, and pain. However, critics believe that positive results are likely the result of a placebo effect. There is general agreement that acupuncture is safe when administered by a qualified doctor using sterile needles. However, many doctors generally reject the treatment because the idea of "Qi" and its various pathways is incompatible with modern biomedical knowledge.

YOGA

Yoga is an ancient custom that started in India and has existed for over 5,000 years. Like Thai Chi, it combines breathing exercises with postures and meditation. Although tai chi is classified as a gentle martial art and requires energy to focus on the elegance of the workout, yoga is similar to traditional body training. It is maintaining a particular posture and control of breathing. Yoga is said to calm the nervous system and balance body and mind. Some practitioners claim that yoga can keep specific energy paths open and give life energy to prevent certain illnesses. Yoga is becoming increasingly popular around the world. Yoga has been used to lower blood pressure, relieve stress, improve coordination, flexibility, focus, sleep, and digestion. In one study, regular yoga exercises increased Gamma-Aminobutyric Acid (GABA) levels in the brain. This amino acid plays a crucial role in regulating neuronal excitability throughout the nervous system. It is advisable to look for yoga as a possible treatment for depression and anxiety disorders associated with low GABA levels.

SLEEP AND BRAIN

Nothing is refreshing enough to sleep soundly. We feel ready to get up and face the challenges of the day. It is because the growth hormone is released during sleep and heals damaged tissue, including brain tissue. Sleep also helps lubricate the gears of the cognitive system and transfer information to long-term memory by "reviewing and remembering" the day's experience. Sleep regulates a body clock known as the "circadian rhythm." The body clock is, of course, recorded by the eye in sync with the daily cycle of light and dark. For this reason, jet lag occurs after a long flight, and it takes a while for the body clock to reset.

HOW MUCH SLEEP?

The amount of sleep you need depends on the person. Some people spend 5 hours a night, while others take 9 hours. It is essential to know what your "magic number" is and to stick to that number. Otherwise, you risk losing productivity and being less able to remember and process information. Lack of sleep puts a massive strain on the brain. Studies have shown that sleepless minds lose efficiency. Other parts of the brain must support areas that are usually active during specific tasks. It is like driving a vehicle with flat tires, which results in significantly reduced performance. Deprivation of sleep also increases the level of stress hormones and reduces the production of nerve cells (neurogenesis) in the adult brain.

PHASES OF SLEEP

Sleep is divided into separate brain stages. There are theta waves that occasionally squeak with sudden movements. Next, there is a triangular wave activity. In the meantime, you completely lose your sense of direction when you wake up. While sleeping, these two EEG patterns alternate in a 90-minute cycle. Then go to REM sleep, where the eyelids appear to be on alert.

CHAPTER 11: SOME HABITS TO TRAIN YOUR BRAIN

NEW HABITS TO TRAIN THE BRAIN

You can quickly enter the rut and repeat the same thing every day. Well, today is the day to make changes. The idea that learning something new is a great way to keep your brain sharp has scientific reasons. The hippocampus guarantees that new neurons created every day to support learning and memory. When you learn something new, these neurons can stay alive and slow your cognitive decline. This chapter presents some ideas you can use to start keeping your brain healthy and sharp.

TRY LINE DANCE

If you think line dance reserved for a dusty bar full of smoke swirls and cowboy boots, think again. Line dancing not only keeps you healthy, but it also increases your serotonin level and makes your brain more comfortable. As the name suggests, line dance is a place where a series of steps take place in a room. Line dance is not as easy as it looks, but it is fun. And you can choose from many different routines and steps. Keeping the brain active is difficult when you learn new steps. Grab a partner and go to the next salon! Optional cowboy boots.

Here are some dance tips to get you started:

DO NOT LOOK AT YOUR FEET

Line dance is useful when you look up to the teacher or the DVD. If you look up, you can gather information about body and leg movements. A look down can distract you if your legs do not move as expected. Raise your eyes and move your legs!

LEARN THE PROCEDURE

Remembering is a great way to train your brain. It encourages the brain to learn new things and dedicate them to long-term memory. If you do not have to worry about the next level of the dance routine, you can enjoy the experience even more.

THINK AHEAD

Predict the next step in the routine. Close your eyes and think about what your feet should do next. In this way, the brain trained not only to keep track of what others were doing but also to remember a series of dance sequences.

PUZZLE

Puzzles are not just for children. Creating puzzles is a great way to improve collaboration and spatial thinking. If you haven't done a puzzle in a while and you feel like you can't start, choose a mystery to get started. Do not try the 1,000-piece landscape puzzle. Let's start with the secret of your favorite animal. It can be a favorite animal or a well-known painting. This way, you can use the knowledge of the image in your head to solve the puzzle.

BEFORE YOU START THE PUZZLE, DO THE FOLLOWING:

1. Before you begin the puzzle, you must first make sure that all the pieces are facing up. It may take a little longer, but the puzzle time becomes much quieter and, therefore, fun. And if you have a good time, you are more likely to continue the puzzle. You can also stack them in batches with the pieces facing up or create different piles with puzzle corners and edges.

2. Go to the border. The next step is to build the wall. It's relatively easy, but "miracle" gets a lot easier. If you can't find all the edge pieces, make sure they're not too long. It circulates in an open room.

3. Then start working on the mountain. Start with the simplest. Some people find it best to start with a large object in the puzzle. Others think that color classification is a good starting point because they are so diverse and easy to combine. Do not be frustrated. Do not forget to start with a simple puzzle. You do not want to face such a difficult challenge that you can't even solve the first puzzle.

LEARN A LANGUAGE

There are many cheap airlines out there, so it was not easy to take a short weekend trip. And is there no better excuse to learn the language than ordering Italian ice cream on a hot day or looking for the essentials in an exotic place in the market? Not only are you happy to feel like a local during your vacation, learning a language can bring considerable benefits to your brain. Brain scans show that some bilingual people in mind have dark gray matter associated with their visual-spatial abilities (parietal cortex).

Language learning has become even more convenient, with so many digital resources. You can learn in less than 10 minutes a day, from a range of for Dummies titles (using the iPhone app for language learning) to free online sound clips with common phrases in different languages of interest. Recommended new words and sentences.
It helps you know that you can use new skills. So, think of the language you want to switch to immediately. If you'd like to stay here instead, here are some suggestions on how to practice your language skills at home.

FIND FRIENDS

Develop friendships with other language learners and native speakers. Then speak and plan only in that language. It may be difficult to talk at first, but learning the language itself is much faster. Choose a place like a cafe or a restaurant so you can practice writing before you meet.

READ A BOOK

Most local libraries have books in the language that came with the CD. If you do not want to invest in a language programmer, we recommend a local library. A great way to practice your language is to look for children's books written in the language you are learning.

SING A SONG

Songs are a fun and catchy way to learn new sentences. With rhythm, lyrics, and buzz, you can quickly learn new things. Increase the volume. Who knows, maybe you'll discover a sentence or two to make your vacation more romantic.

GO TO NEW PARK

Changing the scene can make a big difference in mental health. No significant changes required, e.g., Moving to a new city. But small changes can make a big difference. For example, if you bring a dog that runs in the same place every day, change the route today! You may not notice it, but seeing the same trees and flowers every day can be distracting. It is easy to find new places to enjoy. You will be amazed at how energetic you are when you can look into your new surroundings. Refresh your mood when you return from vacation. My eyes are bright, my worries are gone, and everything in the world is right and wonderful. You can restore the experience a bit by changing the physical environment. If you are usually on foot or by bike, change the route frequently. If you can stop working early in the morning, you will be back on a more extended, picturesque road home. Enjoy the chirping of the birds and the blooming of the flowers. Think about the beautiful things you will see on your trip.

EAT NEW FOOD

Sharing experiences with friends is always more fun. So, if you do not try a new meal yourself, invite friends. Encourage your friends to try something new. In this way, you can strengthen your brain and enjoy the benefits of foods that enjoy each other's company. The entire menu does not have to consist of new food. Try a new one once a month.

JOIN THE BOOK CLUB

The Book Club is a great way to regenerate your mental muscles. Reading is a great activity, but it's even better to share what you are reading with a group of friends. Book clubs are a great way to share ideas and discover new things. If you do not have a book club near you, get started. Here are some tips to get you started.

FIND THE TIME

The first thing to do is to choose the best time for you and your friends. For example, if you need to take your child to school to meet. Or if you are in a hurry to work, nights are probably the best time. It is essential that you do not view the book club as a chore or additional activity, but rather that you can relax part of your schedule.

THINK OF NIBBLES

Everything seems to have improved with snacks! When you host a book club, you do not have to be a slave in the kitchen for hours. Simple things like vegetables or dips are fine. You can rotate them and bring them one after the other. It not only relieves your pressure but also ensures that everyone can bite something while you are discussing the book.

SELECT A BOOK

The most important part of the book club is, of course books! Please choose a different genre for each month. You can start with a detective story for a month and then switch to another genre the next month. It can be a popular science book. You can also choose the fiction bestseller first. Often the bestsellers are included in the film, so you can think about your plans before you start reading the book.

WRITE A FILM REVIEW

Think about what you like and what you do not like in this film and write about 100 words to explain your thoughts. Think carefully about why you focused on an aspect of the film. You must come up with one or two ideas. Movies are more comfortable to speak.

SAVE THE SCREAM

Doing what is logical in reviews is more beneficial to you than being emotional. Do not shout at reviews. Instead, carefully review the discussion for a review. If possible, do not generalize the view. Discuss this in as much detail as possible. Focus on one scene and use it as an example of what you like or dislike in a movie.

BECOME AN ENTHUSIASTIC FILM FAN

Explain how a film improves or deteriorates by comparing it to another movie. Anchors help develop ideas. By comparing the two, the brain can combine different images. As a result, you will find that you can improve your daily conversation.

LET US PUBLISH!

Spend 5 minutes every morning. Mental health is essential for brain function. So, make sure your problem doesn't overwhelm you. Calm down, meditate, and find the moment every morning to prepare for the day. You may need to wake up a little earlier so you can escape the morning madness in your home. But it's worth it. Perhaps you have a cup of coffee or tea ready for the day. Or maybe you just want to sit and enjoy the silence.

CHAPTER 12: GAMES FOR BRAIN TRAINING

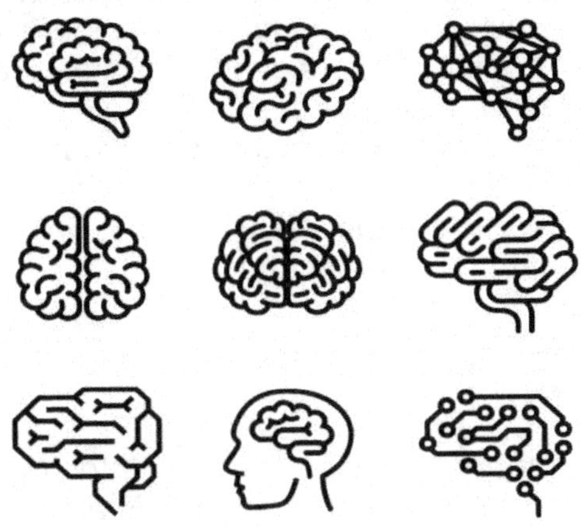

CUSTOMIZE THIS FACE

The next time you are looking for a recognizable face in a newspaper or magazine, list three things you can remember about that person. A person can be a politician, actor, or singer. No matter who he is, try to find out what facts you know about him. You can also do it with your friends. Check out the school yearbook and old photo albums. It's a great time to move your brain and remember not only a person's name but also the facts about that person. It could be something like sitting next to him in chemistry class or changing a joke in music class. Above all, practice these connections, prevent weakening, and keep your brain active.

FIND AN OBJECT

This game is perfect for visiting new places. If you are waiting in the clinic or café, try this game. Look around the room for 1 minute. Close your eyes and think of 10 things you saw in the room. It takes 10 seconds to create these objects. Please note down as much as you can remember. For example, if you have a magazine on the table, do not just of magazine. Think of a magazine title. What was on the cover, are there any main keywords? How about the plants? Did you see it in the room? Think as detailed as possible. Would you like to try more? Try this. Give only 10 seconds to remember 20 in the place. Here too, you name not only the object but also remember its function.

TOP GAMES

Please choose a category. Let's say its food. Set a time limit. 1 minute? Name as many foods as you can in a minute. How was it? Most people can list about 30 foods. Push yourself to hit that number. Buy 60 items. Here is another way to make this difficult. Choose a category and a time limit. Then select the letter. Say the letter D. Within 30 seconds after the letter D, name as many foods as possible. You can exchange "race" words with your friends to see who can name more food. Remember to pay attention to the timer. An essential part of this training game is to find as many objects as possible in a short time. It trains your brain to think faster.

NUMBERS GAME

Start with a high number like 100 and countback with 2. That count is 100, 98, 96, 94, and so on. It will be easy. Count down 3 or 4 and challenge. If you want to challenge yourself, set a time limit. Or try another method to make it even more difficult.

MEMORY GAME

This game is called the N-Back task, and you must save it in the order you saw it. Psychologists have found that people who have been trained in these activities three times a week for 20 weeks have improved IQ and memory. It is your job. Ask a friend to read the next letter. Every time you look at the bold letters, you will ask if you heard the same name three letters before.

X C E B S E I X OS X P O W E Q W X K H K (etc.)

For example, the answer to E is yes. For the letter S, the answer is no. You can also do this activity with shapes and photos. Is it too easy? Try the same action. Do it now while singing your favorite song. It's too easy to try the same activity but look at the same letter (or figure or photo), three letters (or model or image) to see if you sang your favorite song. Can you help your friends? Would you like to try this game by car on the street? Think about the color of the vehicle. Then ask yourself: "Are there two red cars?" It is more complicated than we expected!

PLEASE TELL ME THE STORY

If you get bored and wait at the train station or airport, this is the perfect game. Find someone who looks interesting. Now think about the story for that person. Why is he there? What is the reason for his trip? The goal of this activity is to be creative. Imagine that you are a novelist, and that person is the character in your story. Create his motive, the reason for his actions. Think about what will happen next in the story. Be as creative as you want. After all, this is your story. Read Chapter 8 for more information on the benefits of the creative mind.

DRUMS FOR YOUR BRAIN

I need a friend to help me with this, but it's a great activity while I'm waiting. Ask a friend to sing a song in his head. But he can't tell you what the subject is. Next, ask about the rhythm of the music you play at the table. Listen carefully and tap the rhythm once your friends complete. Try to remember the rhythm. Make the beat as accurate as possible—rhythm memory, which is closely related to speech memory. You will also improve your language skills by training how well you can master a certain rhythm.

READ A CHALLENGING BOOK

It doesn't just read the usual newspapers and magazines that make you happy. Would you like to try something new? Usually, when reading fiction, you choose a historical novel instead. Reading new things is a great way to broaden your horizons and think about your brain in new ways.

FUN TO SHOOT

If you can't let go of the daily newspaper, you'll find newspaper and magazine activities here. Hold down the stylus and set the clock for this activity. Proceed as follows:

1. Set a time limit. Start from 10 seconds.

2. Select a word.

3. Within 10 seconds, take the pen and round off the dozens on the side.

The game is perfect for visual training, learning how to find visual clues quickly, and training the speed of your brain.

HURRY-UP

Choose from crossword puzzles, word puzzles, logic games, and Sudoku for simple, complicated, or dangerous options. Chapters have something for everyone and make your brain work.

SCRAMBLE WORD

Some people love crossword puzzles, logical puzzles, word searches, word encryption, and other word playable puzzles. They seem to have the trick to solve them. Others are talentless and do not recognize it when they hit their foreheads. How do you get the hang of it? What if you wanted to say, "Do not wake me up tonight!" From the front of the puzzle (other than having the answer at hand)? Many start puzzles at school and teachers hire students to solve puzzles and improve spelling, reading, science, or other lessons. You may have known the structure of most of these puzzles for a long time and have probably experienced them at least.

But that doesn't mean we're satisfied. You can be very nervous today when you play crossword puzzles. What is a better way to test the amount of knowledge that we have collected and stored over the years? And what could be nicer than staring at a hint and feeling more like a full dipstick? And maybe you are ready to overcome fear. It's still fun after overcoming fear and frustration.

Word scramble puzzles can play in different ways. Look at a group of letters arranged in a random order, use all the letters, and rearrange them into words. Sorted words are only 5-8 characters long. To solve this puzzle, for example, decipher the capital letters. Where the sauce gets darker: _ _ _ _ _ _ _ By the way, the answer to this puzzle is the kitchen. Decoding words of this length is usually not very difficult. The difficulty increases with the increasing number of letters and words. Try to solve this, for example: Where is the best place to meet the headmaster? _ _ _ _ _ _ _ _ _ The answer is the classroom. The strategy against word encryption is simple.

• If you are dealing with a series of swear words, check them one by one to ensure that they do not pop out. You will be amazed at how quickly some problems can be solved. The mind seems to have made it for this kind of work.

• If you do not see the answer, write the letters in a different order. Do not worry if you write a sentence right away. Merely rearranging the letters in a new order can cause the moment you watch.

• It is still confusing but tries to group the characters logically. Consider the number of vowels. If there are twice as many consonants as vowels, the word can start with a consonant. Sort the letters until you find what you are looking for. You can also randomly arrange the letters in a circle to change the appearance of the letters. Eventually, you will come across a brilliant combination.

For example, when you write down a player, you must write down the game, the rays, and the levels. You can write salaries, years, etc., but most importantly, carefully arrange your words in the long-term order you create. These are the easiest ways.

CONCLUSION

I hope the information provided in this book will help with your Brain Training. It will help you in learning and will make you perform co-curricular activities more effectively. It will improve your memory. Different methods and experiences will help in your Brain Training. We want to keep the body active, but why not keep an eye on the same amount of care? Everyone is told to go to the gym and exercise to stay healthy, but somehow the same need for our brain health isn't given. We may think that just reading or studying here is enough, but research shows that changes in our mental activity are key to long-term success.

Intelligence is not just a fixed function with which you were born. Here at Neuro-Nation, we strive to keep our brains busy, so we can maximize our potential. Whether you want to improve your memory, be more intelligent, or have a better attention span - we're here to help you. Try it out and start training today.

COPYRIGHTS

This document aims to provide precise and reliable details on this subject and the problem under discussion.

The product is marketed on the assumption that no officially approved bookkeeping or publishing house provides other available funds.

Where a legal or qualified guide is required, a person must have the right to participate in the field.

A statement of principle, which is a subcommittee of the American Bar Association, a committee of publishers, and is approved. A copy, reproduction, or distribution of parts of this text, in electronic or written form, is not permitted.

The recording of this document is strictly prohibited. Any retention of this text is only with the written permission of the publisher and all liberties authorized.

The information provided here is correct and reliable, as any lack of attention or other means resulting from the misuse or use of the procedures or instructions contained therein is the total and absolute obligation of the user addressed.

The author is not obliged, directly or indirectly, to assume civil liability for any restoration, damage, or loss resulting from the data collected here. The respective authors retain all copyrights not kept by the publisher.

The information contained herein is solely and universally available for information purposes. The data is presented without a warranty or promise of any kind.

The trademarks used are without approval, and the patent is issued without the trademark owner's permission or protection.

The logos and labels in this book are the property of the owners themselves and are not associated with this text.